Heterosexual Plots
and Lesbian Narratives

THE CUTTING EDGE
Lesbian Life and Literature

THE CUTTING EDGE
Lesbian Life and Literature

Series Editor: Karla Jay
Professor of English and Women's Studies
PACE UNIVERSITY

EDITORIAL BOARD

Jane Marcus
English and Women's Studies
CITY COLLEGE AND CITY
UNIVERSITY OF NEW YORK
GRADUATE CENTER

Elizabeth Wood
Musicologist and Writer
Committee on Theory and Culture
NEW YORK UNIVERSITY

Bonnie Zimmerman
Women's Studies
SAN DIEGO STATE UNIVERSITY

The Cutting Edge
Lesbian Life and Literature

Series Editor: Karla Jay

The Cook and the Carpenter: A Novel by the Carpenter
By June Arnold
With an Introduction by Bonnie Zimmerman

Ladies Almanack
By Djuna Barnes
With an Introduction by Susan Sniader Lanser

Adventures of the Mind: The Memoirs of Natalie Clifford Barney
Translated by John Spalding Gatton
With an Introduction by Karla Jay

Sophia Parnok: The Life and Work of Russia's Sappho
By Diana Burgin

Paint It Today
By H.D. (Hilda Doolittle)
Edited and with an Introduction by
Cassandra Laity

The Angel and the Perverts
By Lucie Delarue-Mardrus
Translated and with an Introduction by Anna Livia

Heterosexual Plots and Lesbian Narratives
By Marilyn R. Farwell

Diana: A Strange Autobiography
By Diana Frederics
With an Introduction by Julie L. Abraham

Lover
By Bertha Harris

Elizabeth Bowen: A Reputation in Writing
By renée c. hoogland

Lesbian Erotics
Edited by Karla Jay

Changing Our Minds: Lesbian Feminism and Psychology
By Celia Kitzinger and Rachel Perkins

(Sem)Erotics: Theorizing Lesbian : Writing
By Elizabeth A. Meese

Bisexuality and the Challenge to Lesbian Politics:
Sex, Loyalty, and Revolution
By Paula C. Rust

The Search for a Woman-Centered Spirituality
By Annette J. Van Dyke

I Know My Own Heart: The Diaries of Anne Lister,
1791–1840
Edited by Helena Whitbread

No Priest but Love: The Journals of Anne Lister, 1824–26
Edited by Helena Whitbread

Heterosexual Plots and Lesbian Narratives

Marilyn R. Farwell

NEW YORK UNIVERSITY PRESS
New York and London

NEW YORK UNIVERSITY PRESS
New York and London

Library of Congress Cataloging-in-Publication Data
Farwell, Marilyn R.
Heterosexual plots and lesbian narratives / Marilyn R. Farwell.
p.   cm.—(The cutting edge)
Includes bibliographical references and index.
1. Lesbians' writings, American—History and criticism.
2. American literature—Women authors—History and criticism.
3. English literature—Women authors—History and criticism.
4. American literature—20th century—History and criticism.
5. English literature—20th century—History and criticism.
6. Lesbians' writings, English—History and criticism.   7. Women and
literature—History—20th century.   8. Man-women relationships in
literature.   9. Heterosexuality in literature.   10. Sex role in
literature.   11. Narration (Rhetoric) I. Title. II. Series:
Cutting edge (New York, N.Y.)
PS153.L46F37   1996
810.9'9206643—dc20   95-41751
CIP

New York University Press books are printed on acid-free paper, and their
binding materials are chosen for strength and durability.

Manufactured in the United States of America

10 9 8 7 6 5 4 3 2 1

For Kay

Contents

Foreword

Despite the efforts of lesbian and feminist publishing houses and a few university presses, the bulk of the most important lesbian works has traditionally been available only from rare-book dealers, in a few university libraries, or in gay and lesbian archives. This series intends, in the first place, to make representative examples of this neglected and insufficiently known literature available to a broader audience by reissuing selected classics and by putting into print for the first time lesbian novels, diaries, letters, and memoirs that are of special interest and significance, but which have moldered in libraries and private collections for decades or even for centuries, known only to the few scholars who had the courage and financial wherewithal to track them down.

Their names have been known for a long time— Sappho, the Amazons of North Africa, the Beguines, Aphra Behn, Queen Christina, Emily Dickinson, the Ladies of Llangollen, Radclyffe Hall, Natalie Clifford Barney, H.D., and so many others from every nation, race, and era. But government and religious officials burned their writings, historians and literary scholars denied they were lesbians, powerful men kept their books out of print, and influential archivists locked up their ideas far from sympathetic eyes. Yet some dedicated scholars and readers still knew who they were, made pilgrimages to the cities and villages where they had lived and to the graveyards where they rested. They passed around tattered volumes of letters, diaries, and biographies, in which they had underlined what seemed to be telltale hints of a secret or different kind of life. Where no hard facts existed, legends were invented. The few precious and often available pre-Stonewall lesbian classics, such as *The Well of Loneliness* by Radclyffe Hall, *The Price of Salt* by Claire Morgan (Patricia Highsmith), and *Desert of the Heart* by Jane Rule, were cherished. Lesbian pulp was devoured. One of the primary goals of this series is to give the more neglected works, which constitute the vast majority of lesbian writing, the attention they deserve.

A second but no less important aim of this series is to present the "cutting edge" of contemporary lesbian scholarship and theory across a wide range of disciplines. Practitioners of lesbian studies have not adopted a uniform approach to literary theory, history, sociology, or any other discipline, nor should they. This series intends to present an array of voices that truly reflects the diversity of the lesbian community. To help me in this task, I am lucky enough to be assisted by a distinguished editorial board that reflects various professional, class, racial, ethnic, and religious backgrounds as well as a spectrum of interests and sexual preferences.

At present the field of lesbian studies occupies a small, precarious, and somewhat contested pied-à-terre between gay studies and women's studies. The former is still in its infancy, especially if one compares it to other disciplines that have been part of the core curriculum of every child and adolescent for several decades or even centuries. However, although it is one of the newest disciplines, gay studies may also be the fastest-growing one— at least in North America. Lesbian, gay, and bisexual studies conferences are doubling and tripling their attendance. Although only a handful of degree-granting programs currently exists, that number is also apt to multiply quickly during the next decade.

In comparison, women's studies is a well-established and burgeoning discipline with hundreds of minors, majors, and graduate programs throughout the United States. Lesbian Studies occupies a peripheral place in the discourse in such programs, characteristically restricted to one lesbian-centered course, usually literary or historical in nature. In the many women's studies series that are now offered by university presses, generally only one or two books on a lesbian subject or issue are included, and lesbian voices are restricted to writing on those topics considered of special interest to gay people. We are not called upon to offer opinions on motherhood, war, education, or on the lives of women not publicly identified as lesbians. As a result, lesbian experience is too often marginalized and restricted.

In contrast, this series will prioritize, centralize, and celebrate lesbian visions of literature, art, philosophy, love, religion, ethics, history, and a myriad of other topics. In "The Cutting Edge," readers can find authoritative versions of important lesbian texts that have been carefully prepared and introduced by scholars. Readers can also find the work of academics and independent scholars who write about other aspects of life from a distinctly lesbian viewpoint. These visions are not only various but intentionally contradictory, for lesbians speak from differing class, racial, ethnic, and religious perspectives. Each author also speaks from and about a certain moment of time, and few would argue that being a lesbian today is the same as it was for Sappho or Anne Lister. Thus no attempt has been made to homogenize that diversity, and no agenda exists to attempt to carve out a "politically correct" lesbian studies perspective at this juncture in history or to pinpoint the "real" lesbians in history. It seems more important for all the voices to be heard before those with the blessings of aftersight lay the mantle of authenticity on any one vision of the world, or on any particular set of women.

What each work in this series does share, however, is a common realization that gay women are the "Other" and that one's perception of culture and literature is filtered by sexual behaviors and preferences. Those perceptions are not the same as those of gay men or of nongay women, whether the writers speak of gay or feminist issues or whether the writers choose to look at nongay figures from a lesbian perspective. The role of this series is to create space and give a voice to those interested in lesbian studies. This series speaks to any person who is interested in gender studies, literary criticism, biography, or important literary works, whether she or he is a student, professor, or serious reader, for the series is neither for lesbians only nor even by lesbians only. Instead, "The Cutting Edge" attempts to share some of the best of lesbian literature and lesbian studies with anyone willing to look at the world through lesbians' eyes. The series is proactive in that it will help to formulate and foreground the very discipline on which it focuses. Finally, this series has answered the call to make lesbian theory, lesbian experience, lesbian lives, lesbian literature, and lesbian visions the heart and nucleus, the weighty planet around which for once other viewpoints will swirl as moons to our earth. We invite readers of all persuasions to join us by venturing into this and other books in the series.

Marilyn Farwell's *Heterosexual Plots and Lesbian Narratives* is the first book in this series that consists of lesbian interpretations of ostensibly nonlesbian material. In her analyses of the works of Margaret Atwood, Anne Sexton, Ursula Le Guin, Leslie Marmon Silko, Marion Zimmer Bradley, and Gloria Naylor, as well as movies such as *Aliens,* Farwell shows how a lesbian perspective has enabled both critics and lovers of fiction to "read against the grain," locating enabling narratives

Acknowledgments

Because this project has involved over ten years of my professional life, I can only begin to single out the people and institutions that deserve my thanks. Ten to twelve years ago the study of lesbian issues in literature was not a "hot" academic topic, and, as a result, I am especially grateful to those who encouraged me early. First I extend thanks to former graduate students who, like Susan Bowers and Mary K. DeShazer, were my real colleagues in the earliest years of the feminist movement. They were the ones who encouraged me when I was the only feminist faculty member in the department. Lynda Koolish's early faith in my work provided another important catalyst, and departmental colleagues George Wickes and Molly Westling encouraged me by expressing, at crucial times, faith in my work. Later, Karla Jay, the editor of this series, continued to press me for material when I seemed to drop out of sight, and Niko Pfund, editor in chief of New York University Press, always gave cheerfully of his time.

I am especially grateful to the University of Oregon's Center for the Study of Women in Society for its early and consistent financial support of my work on lesbian topics. While the views in this book are not necessarily those of this research institute, it supported my work long before queer theory came into existence.

To these acknowledgments I must add my special thanks to those who combined encouragement, humor, and technical expertise during the actual writing of this book. Those who kept me aware of other issues in life, my dear friends Barbara May and Linda Danielson, deserve my hearty thanks. My thanks, too, to Marylynne Diggs for her expert editorial eye. To Anne Laskaya I owe thanks for reading early drafts, proofreading with unmeasured accuracy, and encouraging me at much appreciated lunch breaks. To Monza Naff I owe more thanks than I can express for her many years of steady support, animated discussions, and editorial and proofreading skills. She supplied these in abundance, not only for this book but also for every academic manuscript I have written. Finally, for the support during the final months of writing, when I could not give her the attention she deserved, I thank Kay King. She provided the space where creativity could flourish. Without her quiet steadiness, ready humor, and willingness to take up slack on the domestic scene, this project would still be dormant.

Finally, the projected audience is a dilemma for any writer. I have imagined a reader somewhere between the general academic audience seeking an introduction to questions about lesbian literature and the more specialized scholar of feminist and lesbian narratives. For the former I have eliminated footnotes in order to summarize in my text the parameters of the current debate; for the latter I have felt compelled to include most of the current commentary on these issues. In one sense, the current debate *is* the topic of my book and thus needs to be an integral part of my text. My hope is that this book will widen the debate and the number of participants. (Note that in all quotations in this book, italicized words or phrases indicate the emphases of the original author.)

Portions of chapters 2 and 3 appeared as "The Lesbian Narrative: 'The Pursuit of the Inedible by the Unspeakable,'" in *Professions of Desire: Lesbian and Gay Studies in Literature,* edited by George E. Haggerty and Bonnie Zimmerman and published by the Modern Language Association of America. Portions of Chapter 3 first appeared as "Toward a Definition of the Lesbian Literary Imagination," *Signs* 14:1 (Autumn 1988), 100–18; and portions of chapter 5 appeared as "Heterosexual Plots and Lesbian Subtexts: Toward a Theory of Lesbian Narrative Space," in *Lesbian Texts and Contexts: Radical Revisions,* edited by Karla Jay and Joanne Glasgow and published by New York University Press.

Grateful acknowledgment is made for permission to reprint the following material:

Excerpts from "The Images" are reprinted from *A Wild Patience Has Taken Me This Far: Poems 1978–1981* by Adrienne Rich, by permission of the author and W. W. Norton & Company, Inc. Copyright © 1981 by Adrienne Rich.

Excerpts from "The Burning of Paper Instead of Children" are reprinted from *The Will to Change: Poems 1968–1970* by Adrienne Rich, by permission of the author and W. W. Norton & Company, Inc. Copyright © 1971 by W. W. Norton & Company, Inc.

Excerpts from "Transcendental Etude" and "Twenty-One Love Poems" are reprinted from *The Dream of a Common Language: Poems 1974–1977* by Adrienne Rich, by permission of the author and W. W. Norton & Company, Inc. Copyright © 1978 by W. W. Norton & Company, Inc.

Excerpts from Anne Sexton's *Transformations*, copyright © 1971 by Anne Sexton, are reprinted by permission of Houghton Mifflin Co. and by permission of Sterling Lord Literistic, Inc. All rights reserved.

Excerpts from Margaret Atwood's "Circe/Mud Poems" are reprinted from *Selected Poems: 1965–1975*, copyright © 1976 by Margaret Atwood, published by Houghton Mifflin Company (U.S.), Oxford University Press (Canada), and Virago Press (England), by permission of the author.

Excerpts from Marilyn Hacker's *Love, Death, and the Changing of the Seasons*, copyright © 1986 by Marilyn Hacker, are reprinted by permission of William Morrow & Company, Inc.

ONE

When Is a Lesbian Narrative
a Lesbian Narrative?

Precisely because it is motivated by a yearning for that
which is, in a cultural sense, implausible—the subversion of male homosocial desire—lesbian fiction characteristically exhibits, even as it masquerades as "realistic" in surface detail, a strongly fantastical, allegorical,
or utopian tendency.   —Terry Castle,
                               The Apparitional Lesbian

The Well, published in the same year as *Orlando* . . . is,
like *Orlando*, a "lesbian novel."   —Marjorie Garber,
                                      Vested Interests

As a not-so-closeted lover of opera, I sometimes imagine what a lesbian
opera might look like. The prospects are dim. Nineteenth-century romantic opera celebrates excessively and ecstatically heterosexual romance in a way that tests one's feminist let alone one's lesbian politics.
Woman is both the object of adulation and of erasure in this strange art
form that idealizes Maria Callas's ability to sing triumphantly about the
victimization of Lucia di Lammermoor. As a feminist critic, I know that
opera is about a plot and that the Western plot is male and heterosexual.
In a book about opera libretti, *Opera, or the Undoing of Women,* the
French feminist Catherine Clément warns of the danger of such stories
when coupled with beguiling music: "The music makes one forget the
plot, but the plot sets traps for the imaginary" (10). Like Hélène Cixous,
her partner in other theoretical writings, Clément sees safety in the space
of alterities, in sorceresses, "madmen, Negroes, jesters" (119); only in
those spaces can "women win" (130). While this French feminist reading
rescues some opera plots, the maternal subtext that writers like Hélène
Cixous and Julia Kristeva identify is not synonymous with a lesbian plot
or subplot. Nor can I find solace in the music if I believe feminist

1

musicologist Susan McClary, for music itself partakes of narrative and is subject to traditional plot structure. McClary warns that Western music operates according to "narrative demands of tonality" (14) in which the main theme or key is pitted against a subtheme, usually in a minor key. Using Teresa de Lauretis's feminist theories of narrative, McClary identifies this struggle as a battle between male and female elements (14–15). It is no wonder, then, that Carmen is given those slithering chromatics and that the whole opera ends on an improbable chord of resolution (54–67). Nor is it strange that the love story of *Tristan und Isolde* is told in five hours of unrelenting chromaticism and one moment of mystical, sexual, and tonal resolution. For one seeking a lesbian opera, then, there is no escape from the narrative institution which posits subjectivity for the male and marginality for the female in a heterosexual relationship that assures his triumph, usually over her dead body. I would have to conclude, then, that opera doubly inscribes the Western narrative as unleashed heterosexuality and anti-feminism. It would seem to leave the lesbian opera fanatic in alien territory.

At the same time, opera is often considered the province of gay male culture. Wayne Koestenbaum's recent book, *The Queen's Throat: Opera, Homosexuality, and the Mystery of Desire*, breaks open the operatic closet with a postmodern, impressionistic reverie on gay culture's love of the opera's camp and of the feminine, especially of opera divas. Koestenbaum ostensibly includes lesbians in his construction of gay culture, but his primary concern is to articulate the affinity gay males have for opera through the congruence of the "flamboyant, narcissistic, self-divided, grandiose, excessive" (85) elements of gay male culture and of an elaborate nineteenth-century art form kept anachronistically alive in the late twentieth century. If we add to Koestenbaum's perceptions Eve Kosofsky Sedgwick's theory (using René Girard) that male bonding is at the core of many heterosexual stories, even when the male-male connection is antagonistic (*Between Men* 21), then those rivalries between the tenor and the baritone are not about a Lucia or a Leonora, but about themselves. I must, then, conclude that opera plots are either a heterosexual institution which represents the ecstatic and transcendental union of opposites or a gay male province which plays to male bonding and sometimes, as in the case of Benjamin Britten's operas, to male homosexuality. My search for a lesbian opera seems doomed.

In an effort to find a lesbian opera, I often resort to redefinition, and because I have been a feminist and lesbian critic for twenty years, I am practiced at rereading and rewriting texts. I search for whatever or, more likely, whoever can be identified as lesbian. The one lesbian character of which I am aware, the Countess Geschwitz in Alban Berg's *Lulu,* is intriguing because she is the only loving figure in an otherwise selfish, self-centered world of men trying to win sexual favors from the aloof and self-absorbed "femme fatale," Lulu. But most often operas offer no literal lesbian characters. Then I resort to the ambiguity, intended or otherwise, inherent in one of opera's quaint traditions: the trouser role. These are male parts—usually young boys on the verge of manhood— sung by mezzo-sopranos. For instance, in the first scene in Richard Strauss's *Der Rosenkavalier,* the young nobleman, Octavian, and the female lead, the Marschallin, are found in most contemporary productions embracing in bed as the curtain rises to explicitly sexual music in the orchestra. Octavian is a trouser role. In a wonderful twist of fate, the eighteenth-century male roles created for the castrati—originally men with surgically induced treble voices, often alto, employed by a church that excluded women from participating in its ritual—are now played by women. Other operas intentionally assign the part of a young man to a lower-voiced woman. Famous male lovers such as Orfeo in Glück's *Orfeo ed Eurydice* and Romeo in Bellini's *I Capuletti ed i Montecchi* have been played by mezzos like Janet Baker, Marilyn Horne, or, my favorite, the late Tatiana Troyanos, making the lovers, under their costumes, two women. Terry Castle coins the term "gynophilia: exaltation in the presence of the feminine" (230) to describe the lesbian potential in this situation. At other times, I rely on Adrienne Rich's well-known metaphor of lesbian as the "primary intensity" between two women ("Compulsory" 648) in order to secure my chances of finding a lesbian opera. Bellini's *Norma* contains such potential. The two Druid priestesses, Norma and Adalgisa, sing a duet of reconciliation in the second act that appears to position them as lovers rather than rivals. Marilyn Horne's and Joan Sutherland's memorable characters embraced in a way that confirms this reading. Although this situation lasts for only a moment, it is a satisfying one. In order, then, to find a lesbian opera, I must first determine what or who in the text can be termed "lesbian," particularly who or what can be called a "lesbian subject."

Although this task is formidable in opera, it is no less problematic in literature. At first glance, lesbian literary narratives appear to offer no major definitional problems. Identifiable lesbian characters, themes, and authors inhabit much of the twentieth-century literary landscape. In fact, a comparison of operas of the nineteenth century and lesbian literary narratives of the twentieth century might be called a comparison of apples and oranges. But several points of intersection are significant. Both areas—opera and literature—rely on a system of narrative meaning informed by the same gender and sexual ideology, an ideology that discourages, subverts, and buries lesbian concerns. The lesbian subject, variously defined, appears in a number of coded, indirect, and subversive as well as literal ways. As a result, both forms provide the reader or listener with abundant definitional problems. Instead of a recognizable genre, lesbian literary narrative is, in reality, a disputed form, dependent upon various interpretive strategies. In fact, the definition of a lesbian narrative is as problematic and requires as many interpretive skills as my search for a lesbian opera. The ultimate question for both is where and how to posit the "lesbian" in a lesbian text.

Understandably, then, literary critics offer a variety of possibilities, some contradictory, for the definition of lesbian narrative. Marjorie Garber's distrust of any definition is apparent not when she connects two different novels as lesbian, *The Well of Loneliness* and *Orlando,* a common juxtaposition, but when she encloses the genre in the ubiquitous, ironic postmodern quotation marks (135). For literary criticism, a lesbian narrative is a problematic category because it involves two contested terms: lesbian and narrative. What would, on the surface, appear to be a simple issue—a lesbian narrative is a story about women who are sexually attracted to other women—has become over the last twenty-five years a complex theoretical problem dividing current literary critics and theorists, pitting anti-essentialists against essentialists, pro-narrative against anti-narrative factions, and political lesbian-feminists from the 1970s and their descendants against queer theorists of the 1990s. In this atmosphere, the word "lesbian" remains an elusive term that, as noted over ten years ago, is "plagued with the problem of definition" (Zimmerman, "What" 456) and more recently has been called the "hub of conflicting intellectual and ideological interpretations" (Palmer, "Contemporary" 60). After the explosion of narrative theory in the last half of this century, theorists also debate the relative worth of popular, realistic narrative structures versus the more avant-garde, postmodern narratives. Traditional lesbian theory treats the lesbian narrative as a text determined by the shared experience among identifiably lesbian authors, readers, and characters and treats narrative itself as a relatively neutral tool into which lesbians can be written;

postmodernism treats lesbian as a fluid and unstable term and the narrative as a powerful if not closed ideological system into which lesbians enter only to be entangled in a heterosexual, male story. Traditional lesbian theory validates traditional narrative structures like quest stories and detective fiction as potentially lesbian; postmodernist theory valorizes only the nonlinear disruption of the "master plot." The definition of a lesbian narrative is caught in the crossfire of these contending theories, leaving, for example, a film like *Desert Hearts,* based on Jane Rule's novel *Desert of the Heart,* an exciting lesbian story under one set of rules and inadequate, and therefore not really lesbian, under another. Perhaps for this reason or in spite of it, Terry Castle calls lesbian fiction "somewhat undertheorized" (67).

One reason for this claim is that contemporary criticism and theory have treated the lesbian narrative as a marginal form. Earlier critical interests steered away from lesbian fiction because, in the 1970s and 1980s, lesbian fiction was equated with popular novels, a form that seemed to lack literary depth. Instead, lesbian theory doted on the fine lesbian poets of the time, Adrienne Rich, Audre Lorde, Olga Broumas, and Judy Grahn, among many others. In the mid-1980s, studies of women's fiction became central to feminist criticism, but in recent reviews of critical studies of women's fiction, both Ellen Cronan Rose (373) and Carolyn Allen ("Review" 233) note that these studies offer less than substantial attention to lesbian narratives. Recently, studies of gay male literary themes dominate much of the theorizing about homosexuality and literature, notably in Eve Kosofsky Sedgwick's and Jonathan Dollimore's work. In fact, the new emphasis on gay and lesbian studies downplays the specificity of lesbian theory and literature in favor of an inclusive queer theory. This inclusivity is often illusory. In a recent article in *PMLA,* Gregory W. Bredbeck identifies homosexual theory as a complement to feminism: "Feminism, one might say, has launched a first-strike frontal assault on the privileging of the phallus. Homosexual semiotic theory can bolster the battle through a subsequent attack from the rear (*every* pun intended)" (269). But because this "homosexual semiotic theory" relies exclusively on male imagery, lesbian theory is absent. At the same time, queer theory privileges drama as a genre because poststructuralism puts a premium on performance as a means of highlighting the artificiality of essentialist categories like gender. In this current climate, lesbian literary narratives are again marginalized. As the generational and theoretical gaps grow wider, the need for critical and theoretical attention to the lesbian narrative grows stronger.

The definition of a lesbian narrative, however, has always been in crisis, for unlike other minority literatures, lesbian texts reflect the ability and need of some writers and readers to disguise their sexual identity in order to pass as heterosexual. Furthermore, lesbian writers have not written exclusively on lesbian topics nor straight authors on straight themes. While the parameters of the current debate are unique, they are related to a simple but problematic question that has plagued lesbian literary criticism: where is the "lesbian" in the lesbian narrative? The practical questions are endless once that first question is asked. For instance, must the characters be overtly lesbian? Must the author be overtly or covertly lesbian? Must both be true at the same time? Must there be a lesbian theme and must it be politically acceptable? Must the characters or theme be positive instead of negative? Is, for instance, Virginia Woolf's *Orlando* a lesbian novel when the main character is never identified as lesbian, unlike Stephen Gordon in *The Well of Loneliness?* Sherron Knopp uncovers the lesbian relationship between Woolf and Vita Sackville-West that motivates *Orlando* (" 'If I Saw You' "), but does that context constitute the text as lesbian? Does the mere existence or even the centrality of lesbian characters determine that the novel is lesbian when, perhaps, the author is not? How explicit must a text be to be considered lesbian? Alice Walker created one of the most powerful lesbian situations in contemporary fiction in *The Color Purple* without using the word "lesbian."

Because some African-American critics object to calling this book lesbian, the recent *PMLA* essay on the lesbian elements in Walker's novel emerges as revolutionary (Abbandonato 1108). Is it possible to produce a definition of a lesbian narrative that cuts across racial, class, or cultural differences? On the other hand, what if the writer is lesbian, has written a significant lesbian novel, and chooses to write a book with indirect rather than direct references to lesbian issues? Jeanette Winterson's *Sexing the Cherry* and *Written on the Body* are such books. What if neither the author nor the story is identifiably or literally lesbian? The recent Penguin collection of lesbian short stories includes Isak Dinesen's "The Blank Page," a story not overtly lesbian. The editor, Margaret Reynolds, claims that the story's "real unwritten history is that belonging to lesbians" (xx) because, as she declares of the lesbian implications of *A Room of One's Own,* "It's not explicit. But it's there" (xxii). Although she does not include Dinesen's story in her recent anthology of lesbian literature since the seventeenth century, Lillian Faderman is confronted with a similar issue. Faderman must label as "lesbian," literature that predates notions of sexual identity and that, like Emily Dickinson's and Christina Rossetti's poems, vaguely but provocatively hints of lesbian content and authorship. In order to include the variety of lesbian literature she finds in these four centuries, Faderman admits in her preface to an enlarged definition of the term "lesbian": "By dubbing such writers and characters 'lesbian,' I am employing the word most familiar to our era to signal content about female same-sex emotional and physical relationships" (ix). From these anthologies, then, we might ask if it is possible for a text to contain a lesbian theme without clearly identifiable lesbian characters or a lesbian author.

Because many lesbian writers have been closeted and silenced by a patriarchal system that coordinates its oppression of women and lesbians, the lesbian nature of their works is problematic. Because silence is not simply the space in language which women are accorded but also the lived experience of writers like Willa Cather and Elizabeth Bishop, is a critic justified in reading their works as coded lesbian texts? Is the use of codes acceptable or unacceptable? Is Bishop's poetic distance a function of being a sexual outsider as Adrienne Rich argues (*Blood* 129)? Is there, as Sharon O'Brien suggests, a "lesbian subtext" in some of Cather's fiction (593)? Other critics go further. In reading Ivy Compton-Burnett, Susan Crecy suggests that while her works cannot be read as "coded references or suggestive metaphors to evoke the sexuality which literary decorum decreed could not be openly expressed" (13), her writing is relevant for lesbian studies because of her nightmarish treatment of the heterosexual family (22). With these difficulties in mind, the reader might become the locus of the lesbian in the lesbian text. In fact, for some critics, the reader is the only locus of the lesbian text. From that perspective, Diana Collecott calls for a "revision of reading practices" (104), and Sally Munt, using Roland Barthes' distinction between readerly and writerly, highlights the "lesbian culture's ability to be so *writerly*" (xxi) because lesbian readers must rewrite texts, heterosexual or lesbian, as they read.

Employing codes enables critics to discount the need for either a lesbian writer or a literal lesbian character in determining whether a text is lesbian or not. The definition of lesbian in the works of Adrienne Rich and Audre Lorde, Judy Grahn, and Olga Broumas became, in the 1970s, the theoretical center of a rich metaphor for the space every woman could occupy. These theories and some versions of French psychoanalytic feminism expand the definition of the lesbian subject; no longer only literal, it can be a metaphor for women's primary relationships with one another and for a political stance a woman takes toward other women rather than, as the culture demands, toward men. Adrienne Rich's notion of a *"lesbian continuum"* as the "primary intensity between and among women" ("Compulsory" 648) and Monique Wittig's description of her intent in *The Lesbian Body* to "lesbianize the men and the women" (*Straight* 87) allow critics to suggest that the disruption of categories of gender, with or without lesbian authors or characters, constitutes a lesbian text. Barbara Smith's well-known analysis of Toni Morrison's *Sula* claims that the novel is lesbian not because Nel and Sula are literally lesbians, which they are not, but because the novel challenges the primacy of heterosexual relationships (189). Can, then, a text like Marion Zimmer Bradley's *The Mists of Avalon* be interpreted from the perspective of the ambiguous lesbian relationship between the main character, Morgaine, and the priestess, Raven? While current queer theorists dismiss this version of lesbian as static and essentialist, the metaphoric lesbian enlarges the potential as well as the problems of reading certain narratives as lesbian.

But current theory entertains the most abstract and the most specific definitions of all. Marked by the relationship of the lesbian body/sexuality and textuality, this theoretical position privileges "a rebellious, subtle, raucous textuality" (Stimpson, "Afterword" 380). Is, then, a textual strategy identifiably lesbian? At times, this approach requires no literal lesbian anywhere in sight. Paulina Palmer, for example, concludes that a collection of short stories by Jennifer Gubb, which has no identifiable lesbian character and contains no lesbian eroticism, can "arguably be called a lesbian text" whereas a Fay Weldon novel with a lesbian narrator cannot be called lesbian because Gubb "gives the impression of writing from the margins" and Weldon does not ("Contemporary" 45–46). Before feminist thinking became enamored of continental theory, Bertha Harris, one of the earliest and least recognized lesbian writers of the current era, prefigured the modern emphasis on subversion when she claimed that "if in a woman writer's work a sentence refuses to do what it is supposed to do" then we have "innately lesbian literature" (cited in Smith, "Toward" 175). These approaches eliminate the need for a lesbian subject, even broadly defined, as central to a lesbian text. On another level, Judith Roof and Elizabeth Meese ask whether it is possible to narrate lesbian in a plot system which is already overdetermined as male and heterosexual. Meese, in her stunning analysis of the possibility and impossibility of lesbian writing, calls lesbian, paradoxically, a category to end categorization (*(Sem)Erotics* 8). Judith Butler takes this thinking to its logical conclusion: "I would like to have it permanently unclear what precisely that sign [of lesbian] signifies" ("Imitation" 14).

Postmodernism, then, simultaneously enlarges and limits the possibilities for a lesbian narrative. Do these larger definitions of lesbian as metaphor or textuality disparage the "realistic" lesbian narratives that depict "real" lesbians, sometimes negatively, sometimes romantically? Does that redefinition of lesbian exclude the literature which lesbian women most often read and which common sense dictates is lesbian? Is *Patience and Sarah* absent from a list of lesbian literature because its romantic idealism does not exhibit a view "from the margins?" Does this position negatively affect a reading of Adrienne Rich's poetic narrative, "Twenty-One Love Poems" (*Dream*)? Terry Castle's provocative discussion of lesbian fiction as a counterplot to Sedgwick's erotic triangle, however, turns these wider definitions around, claiming that lesbian fiction is best described, even when realistic, as "strongly fantastical, allegorical, or utopian" (88). In her terms, lesbian fiction is identifiable and always noncanonical.

It is no wonder, then, that some readers despair over a definition of lesbian or a lesbian narrative and that others suggest the outrageous. The debates over the definition of lesbian led Sarah Lucia Hoagland, in *Lesbian Ethics*, to refuse to define lesbian because any circumscription, she argues, will be absorbed by the "context of heterosexualism" (8). Frann Michel proposes that Faulkner is a lesbian author because the relationship between "two feminines," the feminized position of the writer and the work of art, which is coded as feminine, makes his writing "a lesbian act" (13) and, therefore, it would seem, his novels lesbian. Finally, Judith Roof declares that the problem resides in the question critics ask because as "part of the lure of identity, definition becomes a critical preoccupation" (167). This position firmly dismisses the earlier concerns with definition and redefinition of words like "woman" and "lesbian." With these extremes, then, any easy assumptions about what books are or are not lesbian are quickly disappointed.

The generational conflict between the lesbian-feminists of twenty years ago and the queer theorists of today stokes the critical fires of contemporary lesbian theory. Each is invested in radically different answers to the above questions about a lesbian narrative because each promotes radically different definitions of lesbian and of narrative. In the simplified terms in which this distinction is made today, lesbian in the 1970s was defined as a disembodied, nonsexualized political stance regulated by a uniform and essentialist identity of woman and lesbian; the postmodern lesbian is defined as an embodied and sexualized figure whose performative identity is never fixed and who therefore allows for a diversity not incorporated into the lesbian-feminist definition. For example, in her most recent book, *The Practice of Love: Lesbian Sexuality and Perverse Desire,* Teresa de Lauretis highlights these generational differences when she declares the goal of her text to be "a theory of lesbian sexuality, not identity" (30). The disagreements about the term "lesbian" are also mirrored in the antithetical views on narrative these critical positions erect. This conflict reflects the twentieth-century distinction between fictional realism and modernism or postmodernism and also embodies the feminist critical conflict between Anglo-American and continental attitudes toward language and narrative. Traditional lesbian criticism has faith in utopian narrative gestures and political and personal relevance; queer theory valorizes only the disruptive potential of postmodern techniques such as nonlinearity and performance. This disparity is also apparent in two seemingly opposed forms of lesbian writing that each group values: popular lesbian fiction published by presses such as Naiad Press on the one hand and, on the other, experimental lesbian writing of a Monique Wittig and a Jeanette Winterson. At first glance, then, the diverse answers each critical approach gives to the above questions seem irreconcilable on political, literary, and theoretical grounds.

Lesbian-feminists, who argue for an essentialist definition of "lesbian," are willing and eager to see narrative as a tool for change if not for representation. They emphasize thematic and imagistic readings of realistic narratives and rely on a theory which casts both lesbian and narrative into relatively unproblematic waters. Both categories should, the argument goes, reflect experiential and political goals. Thus, lesbian is either an unproblematic, empirical category—women who are sexually attracted to other women—or more problematically and yet still reflective of a unified and essentialist identity, lesbian is a political metaphor for women's alliances with one another. Current critics who make these assumptions often align themselves with the lesbian-feminism of the 1970s and ask of a narrative: Does the text have a political purpose? Can we identify the lesbianism of the authors and characters? What do these writers and characters say about lesbianism and more particularly their own lesbianism? Can readers and critics then read literature for political and psychological survival by seeing themselves mirrored and affirmed in language and story? If these critics do not accept simple representation, they still maintain the political nature of the content rather than the form, for like Gayle Greene they believe that realism is a "major literary form for oppressed groups" (22). With the pioneering works of Jane Rule and Dolores Klaich in the 1970s and Jeannette H. Foster earlier, the goal of lesbian criticism became, in Rule's words, "to discover what images of lesbians women writers have projected" and how these women writers have been influenced "by their own personal experience in presenting lesbian characters" (*Lesbian* 3). More recently, Paulina Palmer judges various lesbian detective novels on the basis of the "feminist principles . . . of co-operation and collectivity" ("Lesbian" 16–17). In this context, literature functions as a motivating force, a mirror, a source of identity, in other words as a means of survival. In Alice Jardine's terms, the text is "transparent" rather than "opaque" ("Opaque" 96).

Because of the importance of defining literature from a political per-spective, this approach to narrative did not die with the waves of conti-nental thinking which hit the American shore in the 1980s. Unlike American feminism, which was overwhelmed by these French theoretical concerns, lesbian criticism, like the criticism of women of color, resisted being usurped. For instance, Bonnie Zimmerman, in her important book, *The Safe Sea of Women: Lesbian Fiction 1969–1989,* assumes a position as an active, political lesbian-feminist. Zimmerman demands that, to be included in her study, a lesbian novel be thoroughly self-conscious, that it have "a central, not marginal, lesbian character, one who understands herself to be a lesbian," that it put "love between women, including sexual passion, at the center of its story," and also that it have self-conscious lesbian writers and readers (15). Lesbian narratives function as "a *mythology* for the lesbian community" (16) and therefore work didactically, serving lesbians better than patriarchal stories (25–26). By using the notion of myths, Zimmerman also accepts as viable traditional formal structures such as the quest story. Zimmerman believes that stories can be retold, can be fashioned to fit although not necessarily mirror lesbian experience, and can therefore be used for survival.

The postmodernist, on the other hand, believes that narrative is a system that constructs rather than reflects experience and that it is already constituted as male and heterosexual. The disruption of the traditional structural elements of the narrative are, therefore, central to if not constitutive of a lesbian narrative. These disruptive narrative techniques, associated by the Lacanian French feminists with the linguistic disruptiveness of the maternal subtext, become for the queer theorists homosexuality's performative interrogation of the naturalness of the gender categories embedded in narrative. Lesbian is the image of the disruptive and indefinable and ultimately of the impossibility of narrative. Like Hélène Cixous's notion of the *"other bisexuality"* (254), queer theory's goal is to stir up rather than solidify sexual and textual differences. The ideal lesbian text opposes, as Susan Stanford Friedman states, the tyranny of narrative sequence to lyric discourse, which "in women's writing is inevitably pre-Oedipal and homoerotic" ("Lyric" 179). Like Bertha Harris's earlier idea, the challenge of the homoerotic breaks the narrative sequence and therefore interrupts the male and heterosexual binary system that anchors that sequence.

Postmodern lesbian theory situates the definition of the lesbian narrative on the back of the unstable category, "lesbian." The lesbian subject enacts an excess, specifically a bodily and therefore a textual excess, which subverts categorization itself. For instance, Sue-Ellen Case theorizes that the butch-femme couple, in its constant refusal of identity and gender alliances, becomes a postmodern performance which defies identity by conscious artifice, by the "discourse of camp" ("Toward" 286). The disruption of gender boundaries in the clothing—metonymically the body—of the butch-femme subject signals a multiplicity of subject positions that constitutes freedom from gender binarism. With this position in mind, the butch-femme couple, like the other postmodern image of the lesbian, the vampire, is the lesbian as a sacred monster, the grotesque version of the woman's body exceeding the boundaries assigned to it by culture, discourse, and the narrative. It thus enacts what Foucault terms a " 'reverse' discourse," "whereby discourse can be both an instrument and an effect of power, but also a hindrance, a stumbling-block, a point of resistance and a starting point for an opposing strategy" (101). From this postmodern perspective, then, a lesbian narrative is fashioned by unstable textual boundaries rather than by the existence of a lesbian author or a lesbian character. The extreme of this position is Reina Lewis's definition of "lesbian texts as a genre, something that can be analysed structurally regardless of the author's gender or sexuality" (26–27). Faulkner, then, can be a lesbian author, or more accurately, can write a lesbian text.

Textuality as the source of a lesbian narrative, of course, privileges postmodern nonlinear narratives. As a criterion, nonlinearity puts at risk a host of what we have traditionally termed lesbian narratives, not only the popular ones like the lesbian detective stories of Katherine V. Forrest but also lesbian classics like "Twenty-One Love Poems" and *The Color Purple*. Judith Roof illustrates these dangers in her provocative book, *A Lure of Knowledge: Lesbian Sexuality and Theory*. Roof's argument verges on the paradox that absence rather than presence of a lesbian character creates a successful lesbian narrative. The direct representation of lesbian characters in the movie *Desert Hearts,* she argues, is self-defeating because these images are immediately appropriated by the heterosexual nature of the narrative and made into fetishes "that phallicize and control the sexual activity of the scenes" (67). A more subtle movie, *I've Heard the Mermaids Singing,* is a powerful alternative because the lesbianism is not presented directly. It is always off the screen and therefore never entangled in the narrative system. A successful lesbian narrative, Roof argues, happens when the narrative is detached from the image (84).

The contest between these two schools of thought is generational as well as theoretical. At present, it is uneven. Current theory often portrays itself as the end product, the redemptive conclusion in a progressive narrative that overcomes the earlier theory's reliance on notions of self-identity, gender essentialism, and experience, and on a seeming indifference to the specificity of lesbian desire and sexuality as well as to differences among women. Lesbian-feminism's generalizations about the lesbian courted, it is argued, philosophical naïveté. Current thinkers want above all to take into account differences of race, class, and sexual orientation and to emphasize the body and sexuality as constitutive of lesbian identity. They assert these revisions of lesbian-feminism by resorting to poststructural notions of infinite difference and the free play of the signifier. When current theory privileges the postmodern, it sometimes sets up the lesbian-feminism of the 1970s as a strawperson and often oversimplifies its thought and literature. The tone of the attack found in such popular texts as *Sisters, Sexperts, Queers: Beyond the Lesbian Nation* (Stein) is reminiscent of Toril Moi's derisive comments on American feminist criticism's theoretical naïveté in *Sexual/Textual Politics*. In a more measured response, Shane Phelan privileges the anti-essentialism of current theories because "not only are [they] more 'faithful' to the texture of lesbian lives than are earlier theories of lesbian identity but [they] also provide stronger support for political change" (766). When set in a progressive narrative, current theories ironically contradict the anti-narrative stance assumed by many of the same theorists, but more important, by too easily dismissing the insights of its direct ancestor, lesbian-feminism, current lesbian theory is left to reinvent the wheel. I believe that the current dualistic thinking is itself naïve and that we need an alternative approach.

Another way to approach this impasse is to refuse the either/or gambit that current oppositional thinking encourages, what Teresa de Lauretis calls "the agonistic narrative structure" ("Essence" 10) of current feminist thinking and more recently of lesbian theory. Instead of setting postmodernism against the essentialism of cultural feminism, and lesbian-feminism against queer theory, Zimmerman suggests that "we need not accept a cleavage between essentialism and anti-essentialism, or between lesbian as sign and lesbian as historically constituted subject" ("Lesbians" 10). Nor, I think, should we accept the antithesis of narrativity and anti-narrativity, literary realism and experimental writing. In other words, I believe that lesbian criticism must find a way to accommodate some of the revolutionary postmodern insights of feminist and lesbian thinking on textuality and at the same time validate both traditional and nontraditional stories as lesbian and as disruptive. Narrative is a textual system but not, I will argue, an unchangeable leviathan or a frozen ideological form amenable only to breaking the sequence. As Patricia Yaeger writes about women and language, "we have focused on women's discursive limitations rather than exploring the language games women have invented in the past" (18). Lesbian theorists can validate the utopian gestures of the lesbian-feminists without being dismissed by reductionist notions of essentialism and can argue that lesbian narratives are constituted by textuality without privileging postmodern texts. My concern, then, is to develop a textual theory of narrative in order to uncover the potentially disruptive elements in traditional plot lines and to underscore the traditional aspects of experimental writing. Lesbian theory, as Jonathan Dollimore suggests for gay and lesbian theory, must rethink current theoretical oppositions (26–27).

In order to forge such an approach, I assume, first, that narrative is an ideological system against which the lesbian subject, what I will develop as a complex trope of twentieth-century writing, must be and has been written. This narrative system—more historical than Platonic—can be disrupted and its elements realigned by means other than the postmodern insistence on breaking the sequence. Narrative, especially conventional narrative, is governed by paradigms and codes that are not innocent; in order to understand what Susan Winnett calls "the determinants that govern the mechanics of our narratives" (516), I will rely on two crucial paradigms developed by feminist narrative theorists. In the initial pattern, feminist theories dependent on linguistic, psychological, or sociological parallels to narrative differentiate two coded positions, male and female, through which the narrative privileges male individuation and defines closure—either in marriage or individual triumph—as the resolution or transcendence of the tension of gender separation. Teresa de Lauretis, for instance, analyzes these codes of power as "positionalities" (*Alice* 143) related to desire within the narrative organization, and Rachel Blau DuPlessis parallels these codes to the " 'social script' " (2). Both writers conclude that the narrative is heterosexual as well as male. At the same time, Eve Kosofsky Sedgwick's influential book, *Between Men: English Literature and Male Homosocial Desire*, exposes the male bonding that underlies another but related narrative pattern: the erotic triangle. Although Sedgwick distinguishes male homosocial from male homosexual desire, particularly for the twentieth century, she also provides the theoretical possibility to conclude that narrative institutionalizes male homosexual bonding using the same pseudo-heterosexual positioning of woman as Other. Because both patterns identify narrative positions of subjectivity, I will develop my theory through certain elements of narrative mechanics such as narrator, narratee, protagonist, focalizer, and closure, that final arbiter of subject positions. Traditional narrative structure, then, posits an oppositional and hierarchical relationship of male and female as the foundation of both heterosexual and male homosocial or homosexual plots, and as a condition of those structural alignments, disrupts or prevents female bonding. In other words, narrative is everything but lesbian.

This exclusion, however, is more than an oversight; it is the result of structural codes that, as Marilyn Frye notes, make the lesbian "logically impossible" (*Politics* 159). The lesbian subject appears to be a narrative impossibility; "she" is the most silenced and the most threatening figure for narrative representation because "she" exceeds the constructed boundaries for woman's otherness. The narrative, then, works to prevent and exclude primary female bonding. But instead of proving the lesbian subject's non-narratability, this exclusion of the lesbian from narrative paradigms demands that we analyze instead its unique relationship to the narrative system. Like other patriarchally defined systems of meaning, narrative is not an impregnable fortress, for, as Alison Booth notes, "There never was the perfect patriarchal closed circuit" (4). Positing the lesbian subject in this system, I argue, reorders both the narrative codes and the values on which the system rests. Unlike the heterosexual woman as narrative subject, the lesbian subject becomes an aggressive agent which, to revise Alicia Suskin Ostriker's well-known title, *Stealing the Language,* steals the narrative. But this theft is never without a challenge, for while the narrative system is not impregnable, it must be considered a system of power relationships that does not easily abide change.

The entrance of the lesbian subject into the narrative system redraws the subject positions allotted by gender—primarily the positionalities of subjectivity developed in the protagonist and narrator and the final alignment of subject positions in the closure. The lesbian subject functions as a powerful disrupter of the narrative because, particularly in these last twenty-five years but also since the late nineteenth century, the term "lesbian" has been stretched to mean more than a woman who is sexually attracted to other women; instead, the term has acquired larger implications, in some cases functioning as a metaphor for the feminist woman or for an autonomous female sexuality or body and in other situations as a harbinger of the future or as a revised textuality. Unlike de Lauretis, who recently argued against the "assimilation of feminism to lesbianism" (*Practice* 184) under the metaphoric umbrella of "lesbian," I argue that the development of a metaphoric lesbian subject is a powerful and necessary response to and the "reverse discourse" of the negative construction of the lesbian by male writers of the nineteenth century. From Baudelaire's notorious description of the "Femmes damnées" as a representation of modernism to Richard von Krafft-Ebing's paradigm of the lesbian subject's journey into nonfeminine monstrosity, the lesbian has represented a female figure of disruption, horror, and bodily grotesqueness. These constructions have remained culturally formative, for, in the words of Susan J. Wolfe and Julia Penelope, "since then, Lesbians have lived under siege . . . simultaneously locking several Lesbian generations into their [the sexologists'] discourse framework" (20). But, at the same time, theorists in the early twentieth century and especially recently have reformulated this image of the lesbian into a figure of revolution and change; and, like the early twentieth-century thinker Edward Carpenter, they have described homosexuality as a healing of the alienation of the sexes or, like Gertrude Stein, in a reversal of the negative descriptions of the female body, as a sacred monster (Stimpson, "Somagrams" 41).

From the pens of women writers of the last twenty-five years, the lesbian subject appears as a powerful discursive and political tool for challenging the asymmetrical gender codes in the narrative and the trap of male homosociality and homosexuality. In these years, the energy around lesbian as a metaphor was insistent and influential. The definition of lesbian included a trope for female agency and freedom and, in Adrienne Rich's terms, a figure representing the creativity in all women (*Lies* 201). Queer theorists argue that they have abrogated this essentialist definition of lesbian, but neither the butch-femme couple nor its counterpart, the vampire, is radically unlike the lesbian-feminist lesbian subject against which it positions itself. In narrative, these constructions of the lesbian subject become positionalities which function in both utopian and deconstructive ways. Although far from identical, the postmodern lesbian subject, like the lesbian-feminist lesbian figure, is a disruptive hero in the cultural wars. Put in an historical context, then, the difference between lesbian-feminism and lesbian postmodernism is less than absolute. These lesbian subjects have become, in this last quarter century, the most interesting and powerful contemporary strategy for women writers who intend to challenge the traditional narrative system.

This metaphoric lesbian subject works on two separate but related levels: as a bodily or a nonbodily figure. Each figure contains utopian as well as deconstructive gestures and each, I will argue, functions as a figure that primarily expands the "discursive boundaries" of woman (de Lauretis, "Feminist" 4). Like de Lauretis's argument that "the single English word *motherhood* has been significantly expanded and shifted by Adrienne Rich's book *Of Woman Born*" (4), so lesbian has been expanded in the twentieth century to represent the woman who exceeds discursive and narrative boundaries. Lesbian as a metaphor for woman expands and shifts the narrative codes by securing a place for female narrative agency in the narrative roles of protagonist and narrator. The nonbodily lesbian is the trope for female psychic autonomy and creative agency, while the bodily figure depicts, often although not solely in parody, the patriarchal construction of the excessive and sometimes grotesque female body and its reconfiguration as a desiring rather than desired body. Virginia Woolf's notion of androgyny in *A Room of One's Own* is a precursor of the nonbodily, utopian space of Adrienne Rich's depiction of the lesbian as a woman "choosing oneself" (*Lies* 200). Woolf's surprisingly different but not incompatible version of androgyny in *Orlando* looks forward to Monique Wittig's postmodern text, *The Lesbian Body*, because both construct the lesbian body and psyche as the parody and excess of the patriarchally constructed female and the original, diseased somatic formulation of the lesbian. Like Rich's stretching of the "discursive boundaries" of motherhood, then, the metaphoric lesbian subject stretches the narrative boundaries by the tension it creates between form and content, between the conventional system and its text images. It is the primary way in which women writers of the last twenty-five years have engaged female subjectivity in the cogs of narrative because it is the only term that structurally realigns the gender asymmetry of the narrative system. Since I believe that we live and are constructed by linguistic categories and, most profoundly, by narrative itself, disruptive elements such as the lesbian subject become agents of a realignment of the power-inflected boundaries of gender and sexuality.

Nor can lesbian be separated from gender as a category of analysis. While gender and desire may be separate categories, they are not arbitrarily related. Rather than seeing the term "lesbian" in postmodern, queer terms, as "not at the site of gender, but at the site of ontology" (Case, "Tracking" 3) or separating gender from sexuality as does Michèle Aina Barale (533), I prefer to argue that the lesbian subject of this century is dependent on the expansion of the narrated and linguistic categories of woman. Theorizing a genderless homosexuality is, as Jacquelyn N. Zita claims, "the luxury of a singular cause" ("Gay" 260) which gay male academics have prescribed for theoretical correctness. When gender and sexuality are disconnected, as they are in these postmodern theories, male centrality is reinvented. Gender can remain a category of analysis if we heed Linda Alcoff's words: "If we combine the concept of identity politics with a conception of the subject as positionality, we can conceive of the subject as nonessentialized and emergent from a historical experience and yet retain our political ability to take gender as an important point of departure" (433). The lesbian subject's repositioning toward other women confirms identity as relational rather than as either isolated or alienated. In this argument, then, I will defend the need for a radical sense of lesbian identity rather than, in postmodern terms, a deconstruction of identity. As Patricia Waugh impressively argues, feminist criticism needs, more than a deconstruction of identity, a "*reconstruction, the production of alternative modes and models of subjectivity*" (20). To ignore the possibility of lesbian identity, even if defined as a discursive position, is to capitulate to Western culture's systematic ignorance of, and more pernicious, current theory's erasure of lesbian. If my position risks the "feminist bugaboo about essentialism" (N. Miller 115), then it risks a strategic essentialism that affirms the interrelationship of symbolic constructions of woman and lesbian and of experience in systems of meaning.

While each element—narrative as a system and lesbian as a discursive construction—is primarily textual, I will also insist that each, at the same time, is profoundly political and related to experience. Narrative is the way we give meaning to life, the way we order the chaos of events. As Susan S. Lanser notes, critics must "recognize the dual nature of narrative" and "find categories and terms that are abstract and semiotic enough to be useful, but concrete and mimetic enough to seem relevant for critics whose theories root literature" in real life (344). While I will use certain narrative categories and theories that have been associated with narratology, I assume that the structural parallel on which narrative operates is more social than linguistic, and as a result narrative is not a closed or absolute system of meaning. Nor is the discursively constructed lesbian divorced from women who live as lesbians in a world that despises them. These textual constructions are what confine and, at the same time, reposition real human beings. Postmodernism's tendency to divorce textuality from experience, its denial of identity in theories either of cultural construction or the textual free play of the signifier, and its refusal of agency, thus its refusal of feminism, ignore the real people who are oppressed by textual constructions. In this context, we should take heed of Marjorie Garber's warning that "in political and social terms, in the lives of real people, male and female, straight and gay, there is finally no 'free play of the signifier' " (161). The development of the metaphoric lesbian and its deployment in varied narratives of disruption have served both purposes—the development of an identity category and the deconstruction of restrictive categories of sexuality and gender. With de Lauretis, we need to argue that the "relation of experience to discourse, finally, is what is at issue in the definition of feminism" ("Feminist" 5) and lesbianism.

The six literary texts I analyze from this perspective present a number of critical challenges. Two of the narratives contain what Catharine R. Stimpson calls "severely literal" ("Zero" 244) lesbian characters, themes, and authors. The four other texts fall into the various problematic categories noted at the beginning of this chapter: a lesbian author but no lesbian character, neither an identifiable lesbian author nor a literal lesbian character, or negative lesbian characters. In terms of narrative construction, most but not all of these stories are traditionally linear, but this stark dualism will prove illusory, for linearity can, like essentialism, be used in a strategically disruptive manner. I also divide these six texts according to two related types of narration—the romantic story and the heroic or quest story. Yet the questions that unfold in each instance are similar: How does the lesbian subject, as defined above, invade the narrative positions and reorder crucial narrative elements? How does this alien figure, no matter how realistic or empirical, redistribute elements of the narrative? How does this figure, in effect, create a narrative space—or function—that I will call a lesbian narrative space, different from the two or three primary positions allotted to gender asymmetrical structures? The lesbian subjects range from single figures to couples to communities, from the literal subjects of lesbian love poetry which rely on the metaphor's vehicle, to the purely symbolic, nonempirical figures which exploit the metaphor's tenor. Some of the lesbian figures are construed in nonbodily terms, others in excessively and identifiably bodily terms; at times these images intersect. In all cases the metaphorical lesbian subject disrupts narrative through the structural realignment of the narrative's subject positions, first through the disruption of male bonding (Castle 86) and the repositioning of any remaining male character and second through a "radical shift from gender opposition to gender likeness as a governing narrative and aesthetic principle" (McNaron 293). As a result, these changes alter narrative structure's implied thematics of conflict, individuality, and domination. These structural realignments are the direct result of the lesbian subject that bears more weight than transparent literalness.

In the first instance, I examine the romantic narrative through the unusual but significant form of the poetic sequence. Adrienne Rich's

"Twenty-One Love Poems" and Marilyn Hacker's *Love, Death, and the Changing of the Seasons* reflect the authors' positions as white, middle-class writers who have often taught in academic settings. Their polished poetic forms and language and their literary allusions recall the Renaissance sonnet sequences of which Shakespeare's homosocial or, in some critics' eyes, homosexual sonnets, are the most recognizable. In fact, the connection of these lesbian sonnet sequences to Shakespeare's sonnets helps to differentiate between lesbian and gay male narrative structures. First, Rich and Hacker constitute their primary lesbian subject as the couple, the lover and beloved, or in narrative terms, the narrator and narratee. On another level, the lesbian subject is the individual, nonbodily narrator/poet who uses her positionality as a narrative agent to claim the power to create and who addresses another reader: a community of women. Although Rich's sequence posits, with one crucial exception, a nonsexualized lesbian couple, her concern is to redefine the female body through a normalization of the lesbian body; Hacker's poems revel in the centrality of the sexual and bodily lesbian subject. The speaker of each sequence, then, is both the lover who positions herself differently in relationship to the beloved and the poet who, as female, claims the autonomous power to invent but only within and related to a community of women.

In the chapter on the quest story, I look at two types of literary heroes, the single quest hero and the communal hero. Neither author nor text calls attention to any lesbian status, yet the development of a metaphorical, nonbodily lesbian subject in each case warrants its inclusion as a lesbian narrative. Racial difference also demands interpretive attention for anyone wishing to provide a single definition of a lesbian narrative. The narrative issue is the repositioning of a female subject in the male narrative role of protagonist and narrator. As an example of an individual quest story, Marion Zimmer Bradley's *The Mists of Avalon* provides a classic linear trajectory based on one of the great heroic legends of white, Western culture, the Arthuriad. As a Euro-American writer, Bradley is known as a popular American author of fantasy books, but while the setting in this text is based on fantasy, the tone and linearity signal realism. Bradley's heroine, Morgaine, cannot be called literally lesbian, but because of her intense connection with the priestess, Raven, and the resulting repositioning of narrative agency, Morgaine must be designated a lesbian subject. Morgaine is also the problematic narrator of this story, including in her voice other women's voices as narrators and focalizers. These multiple narrators reposition the lesbian hero in what appears to be a conventional quest narrative. The communal hero is a strong part of African-American writers of the 1980s, and in the case of Gloria Naylor's *The Women of Brewster Place,* like Alice Walker's *The Color Purple,* the lesbian subject is a potent force that turns the women's community into an autonomous narrative agent. Although I will concentrate on Naylor's text, Walker's more popular and more controversial book offers an instructive parallel. Lesbians appear directly in both books, although they are depicted differently— Naylor's figures in nonbodily terms and Walker's couple, Shug and Celie, in earthy, bodily language. Both writers, however, determine the narrative agency of the women's community from the disruptive position of the lesbians in their midst. In fact, in a move different from many white women writers, Naylor, like Walker, positions the lesbian subject not only at the center of the women's community but also at the center of the African-American community as a whole, including men in a revised notion of the lesbian community. The inclusion of men in lesbian space is not solely the property of women of color—Monique Wittig, for instance, appears to include men as potential lesbians when she defines lesbian as a positionality (*Straight* 87)—but, I will argue, men and women occupy this space differently. The resultant community as a lesbian subject is depicted structurally by the complex narrator's voice in the last chapter. The realistic writing and the linear story in each text, including Bradley's story, reaches a closure that is reminiscent of Terry Castle's contention that lesbian fiction "often looks odd, fantastical, implausible" (91).

Jeanette Winterson is an experimental British writer whose texts are exempla of postmodernism's effort to challenge the illusion of realism. In particular, her writings address the issue of closure and postmodernism's desire to deny the reader's expectation that the end of a story will satisfactorily round off any plot line. Winterson is also a lesbian writer who is probably best known for *Oranges Are Not the Only Fruit.* But her latest works, *Sexing the Cherry* and *Written on the Body,* are experimental texts that neither directly address lesbian issues nor contain any conclusively identifiable lesbian characters. But the characters of the fantastically enormous Dog-Woman of *Sexing the Cherry* and the diseased beloved, Louise, in *Written on the Body* are female bodies in excess, lesbian subjects as grotesque bodies. Their literal sexuality is problematic, however. Dog-Woman, except for a few failed heterosexual attempts, is asexual; the narrator of *Written on the Body* never reveals its gender, although the beloved is clearly female. These lesbian subjects gain agency through the play of multiple narrators of a quest fantasy and through the ungendered, twentieth-century narrator's multiple revisions of the romance story.

The challenge, then, for reading this literature is to identify the similarity in the diversity. The discursively constructed lesbian subject enters diverse narrative structures—realistic or experimental, romantic or heroic—and interrogates the gender positioning of the narrative elements. It undermines gender opposition and hierarchy and also male bonding, structural elements which combine to form the ideology of Western narrative. The lesbian subject refuses and repositions the constricted narrative stance of woman, creating what I call a lesbian narrative space. It therefore works in both a utopian and a deconstructive fashion, what Sally Robinson, in a description of women's fiction, calls a "double movement: simultaneously *against* normative constructions of Woman . . . and *toward* new forms of representation" (11). In the twenty-five years of writing covered in this book, the lesbian narrative replots itself in dialogue with its adversary, the traditional narrative structure that both ignores and erases the lesbian subject.

Making the lesbian subject, however expanded and textually defined, the locus of the lesbian narrative invites several problems. The first is that, by adopting the semblance of a unified subject, I am guilty of essentialism. Although I stress the need to define the lesbian subject as a textual strategy and to distinguish sameness from identity, I do not want to use those arguments as antidotes to essentialism. I embrace essentialism and identity politics as strategic necessities along the lines of Diana Fuss's argument in her excellent book, *Essentially Speaking*. In fact, Fuss contends that "essentialism underwrites theories of constructionism and that constructionism operates as a more sophisticated form of essentialism" (119). The alternative is what Susan Bordo calls postmodernism's "dream of being *everywhere*" (143). My description of the lesbian subject as the locus of the lesbian narrative acknowledges the need for the centrality of a textual approach in the definition of the lesbian narrative but also refuses to be caught in the trap that decrees lesbian as undefinable and therefore the lesbian narrative as indefinable. Thus, while lesbian-feminism ignored the need for a sophisticated concept of textuality, its insistence on a lesbian subject as the core of its thinking is historically viable and crucial to a definition of the lesbian narrative. Secondly, because I define the lesbian subject broadly and not literally, I might be accused of ignoring lesbian specificity and inviting meaningless generalizations. Under these conditions, Faulkner indeed may be a lesbian author—a serious problem. In reading Sarah Orne Jewett's *Deephaven* as a lesbian text, Judith Fetterley cites two reasons— her own personal history and Jewett's life—as controlling contexts that predispose her to such an interpretation (164–65). These contexts help to limit any possible slide into meaningless generalizations. My context will be the broadly defined lesbian subject which, if used to call a narrative "lesbian," must be surrounded by a context which would justify that interpretation: a lesbian author as in Winterson's novels, undeniable lesbian erotic scenes as in Bradley's book, or lesbian characters, central or marginal. This position refuses a broadly defined existence of two feminines as a qualification for a lesbian authorship or textuality. On the other hand, my position allows the possibility that not all lesbian characters constitute a lesbian subject. This conclusion is accurate, although the concentration on a lesbian subject rather than on a vague lesbian textuality minimizes that possibility. Because the lesbian subject as the locus of a lesbian narrative must subversively reposition central narrative elements, the mere existence of a lesbian character is not enough. The risks of a naïve essentialism or philosophical vagueness that may overcome my interpretive efforts are risks I will take rather than accept lesbian as only a literal, empirical figure or an unstable and therefore indefinable term. Each of these categories restricts too sharply what might be called a lesbian narrative and does not do justice to the variety of literature that otherwise has used that umbrella term.

One academic generation's critique of another's theories often points out weaknesses and excesses to which earlier adherents were blind. Lesbian-feminism and the feminist theory of the 1970s naïvely generalized about all women and sometimes about all lesbians, usually from a white, middle-class position and without acknowledgment of the myriad differences of race, culture, history, and ethnicity. Postmodernism took up this cause and succeeded in making essentialism a four-letter word and erasing the need for categorization and gender difference. Instead, we might take as a precedent Teresa de Lauretis's description of Italian feminism's "notion of the symbolic mother [which] permits the exchange between women across generations and the sharing of knowledge and desire across differences" ("Essence" 25). Formulating a theory of the lesbian narrative that addresses both sides of this issue is one step toward healing this fractious dispute which refuses to see the continuity between yesterday's lesbian thinking and today's. That kind of separation for women and lesbians has always meant disaster, for which we must usually wait another generation or two to heal. The alternative is not to erase all difference between two seemingly opposed philosophical positions but to explore the similarities and connections that have been heretofore ignored.

Narrative: The Elastic Project

All classes, all human groups, have their narratives,
enjoyment of which is very often shared by men with
different, even opposing, cultural backgrounds.
—Roland Barthes, *Image, Music, Text*

No repetition can ever be identical, but my story carries
with it their stories, their history, and our story repeats
itself endlessly despite our persistence in denying it.
—Trinh T. Minh-ha, *Woman, Native, Other*

When seen as a set of ideological codes, narrative is an institution but
not an innocent one, an artificial system but not an arbitrary one. It is a
complex system that encodes both sexuality and gender, both of which
rest upon male centrality, but it is an historically determined structure
rather than a Platonic absolute. Those writers who have, in recent
years, explored its gender and sexual biases have identified two primary
patterns: the heterosexual, asymmetrical gender pattern and a pattern of
male bonding which, according to Eve Sedgwick, is also heterosexual
and dependent on a female Other. Western culture's two most prominent genres, romantic and heroic stories, depend on these gender and
sexual alignments. Lesbians are neither an integral nor structural part of
either genre. Feminist writers of theory and literature have probed the
recesses of how stories operate in our culture, and while many have
despaired of narrative's power, others have recognized the means to
challenge it. It is easier to despair. In what Gayle Greene might call
"feminist metafiction" (1), Anne Sexton and Margaret Atwood have
proffered poetic narratives which depict women in the stranglehold of
the narrative system—Atwood of the heroic narrative, Sexton of the
romantic narrative. While neither is a postmodern theorist or a narratol-
ogist, each of their poetic interrogations of the Western narrative is as

astute and as thorough as anyone who has wielded the terms "subjectivity" and "narrativity." But while each looks for an alternative story, and while the narrative is elastic enough to encompass other possibilities, neither can imagine that story as a lesbian narrative.

In "Circe/Mud Poems," Margaret Atwood retells Ulysses' sojourn on Circe's isle from Circe's point of view. As a reader of the West's urnarrative, of its primary quest story, Circe is aware of being trapped in a story—and an island—not of her making or telling, and, as she says late in this sequence of poems: "It's the story that counts. No use telling me this isn't a story,/or not the same story" (221). It is the sameness of this story, a story which has been repeated from pre-history to the feminist 1970s (the poems were published in 1974), that traps the female speaker, "and the story is ruthless" (221). In positing a female speaker attempting to understand the inevitability of a system that has determined the positions Ulysses and she are to occupy in the heroic story, Atwood posits this repeatable story as a violent, anti-feminist system. In effect she analyzes the narrative system which determines how stories are told in our culture—who tells them and who acts in them. The tone of despair that inhabits this poetic sequence tells its own story of a crushing system that is almost beyond transformation.

Anne Sexton in *Transformations* provides another kind of analysis because she examines the fairy tales that traditionally idealize heterosexual romance and marriage. Often seen as the inversion of the quest story, romance represents the stories our culture codes as female instead of male. Sexton agrees with Rachel Blau DuPlessis that the romance narrative is dangerous and constrictive. While DuPlessis in the 1980s is able to formulate a theory of "writing beyond the ending," Sexton, in 1971, is unable to perceive the system's potential for change. The romance story includes the same seemingly neutral elements—problem, complication, resolution—that define all narratives and at the same time traps the female in a fatalistic apparatus. Like Atwood, Sexton brilliantly exposes the terror, violence, and anti-feminism of the narrative system that demands that woman be muted, silenced, and violated when she enters the time-line that forces her into the sexual story. Of the most familiar fairy tales, "Cinderella," "Snow White and the Seven Dwarfs," and "Briar Rose (Sleeping Beauty)," the latter two are positioned at the beginning and end of her book of poems. Each tells of the young girl's maturing into sexuality, menstruation, adulthood. It is time and its representative, the narrative, that are her enemies. The story inevitably forces the young girl to grow up, to get married, to become a woman. Sexton characterizes this movement as death.

In both cases, the poets view narrative as a system of codes that transcends the specific stories, and they recognize with Annette Kolodny that "insofar as we are taught how to read, what we engage are not texts but paradigms" (151). They also agree with what we now take for granted: that literary conventions are not neutral, that they are imbued with the culture's social and political ideology. There are, in other words, thematic implications of structural codes. Atwood is particularly aware of the hierarchical gender positions of the characters and narrator and of the violence perpetrated by narrative structure. Sexton is more concerned with narrative time, with the young girl violently caught in the movement of the plot and its closure. As a result of their perceptions, neither poet chooses to revise the stories with simple role reversal. Atwood does not offer a Ulyssea as Wittig suggests in *The Lesbian Body* (21), nor does Sexton imagine a princess rescuing a forlorn, captive prince. Without these easy but problematic alternatives, each has difficulty imagining another narrative possibility.

What both Atwood and Sexton know, then, is that narrative is a system of power relationships not easily challenged. It is a story that has as part of its system an alignment of gender into opposite and hierarchical categories. At the same time and in a more subtle way, it guarantees male power through male bonding, either homosocial or homosexual. The only way a woman can enter this system is in relationship to a man. If change is possible, these writers seem to say, structural as well as thematic elements must be challenged. Each poet makes a gesture in the direction of thematic and structural change. The unrelenting cynicism of Circe's victimization is relieved only in the last poem in which Atwood imagines another island, another story. It briefly, too briefly, tells the story of a different journey from the one Ulysses takes ten years to complete, one that this time includes Circe and moves less violently to its conclusion. Sexton interjects an identifiably lesbian alternative. The poem "Rapunzel" tells the story of a short but significant interlude of lesbian love also in a narrative in which separation and violence are abated. But Sexton concludes that this alternative is unrealistic and ultimately unnarratable. Both poets' inability to tell a new story, particularly a lesbian story, reveals the problem of the lesbian in relationship to narrative and its ideology.

Sexton's and Atwood's insights reflect twentieth-century narrative theory's desire to identify an abstract story, which conditions our reading expectations, and the actual text, what Seymour Chatman calls the "mere manifestations" (16) and what Teresa de Lauretis terms the "text-image" (*Alice* 119). Although this formulation, in Barbara Herrnstein Smith's terms, constitutes a "naive Platonism" (213), it is helpful to understand narrative as a system of meaning that has developed in Western culture and that determines readers' expectations rather than as an arbitrary collection of characters and events. Narrative is a system of plot movement—beginning, middle, and end, or problem, complication, and resolution—arranged either chronologically or logically and "subject to teleological determination" (Culler 209). Both quest and romance narratives—as well as any other story—partake of this elemental structure. On this theoretical level, characters are figures or functions of the plot rather than transparently self-conscious human beings. In Mieke Bal's theory, "an *actor* is a structural position, while a *character* is a complex semantic unit" (*Narratology* 79). From this perspective, it is the character's positionality that determines its meaning rather than its textual manifestation. Within this formalist context Hamlet is less a person with recognizable human emotions and a human dilemma with which we can identify than an actant that causes and, more often, reacts to events. This distinction between the system and its manifestation is fundamental to understanding how women writers like Atwood and Sexton despair over changing the story. For despite the commonsense assumption that this abstract system is neutral, Atwood and Sexton both believe that traditional narrative is a "self-regulating" system of meaning which "maintains and closes itself" (Chatman 21).

The questions, then, are at what narrative level—the abstract system or the textual manifestation—is ideology inscribed and at what point is disruption possible. If, as Christine Brooke-Rose maintains, the abstract system is "not innocent of subjectivity" (289), then ideology is a function of the seemingly neutral system of plot movement and subject positionality. If that is the case, then the central question for the critic interested in disruptive narrative techniques is whether the text image— e.g., a female or lesbian character—can challenge that ideologically inflected system or whether only structural changes such as nonlinearity can effect transgression. For instance, many touted the movie *Aliens* as feminist because Sigourney Weaver as Ripley portrayed a strong, action-oriented heroine. If one, however, accepts the notion of narrative as a system which determines the character and not vice versa, it is easy to argue that the existence of a strong heroine does nothing to change narrative as a system. Ripley simply occupies a traditional male position while the same story is told. We have at best only "another normative narrative wrapped around the thematics of liberation" (de Lauretis, *Alice* 156). But if the existence of a woman in the traditional male narrative space challenges that structure because women heroes are differently related to the system, then the system itself has been forced to stretch.

I would argue both positions. Ripley both shapes and is shaped by the protagonist's space she occupies. To deny the power of either the abstract system or the text image would be to ignore the complex interaction of these two narrative levels and would be to accept the abstract system as an innate product of the human mind rather than an historically contingent system of Western culture. This position refuses narratology's view that narrative moves by an internal logic parallel to grammar or the Lacanian-influenced notion that this internal logic is controlled by Oedipal desire. Both views reify narrative as absolute. Instead narrative is a system parallel to the social structures that are embedded in categories such as narrator and actor. Because the abstract system is not inevitable but the result of history, tradition, symbolic connections, and reader expectation, it is conditionally male-defined. From this position, it is also possible to argue that both traditional, linear narrative movement as well as nonlinear plotting are potentially disruptive and therefore to undermine twentieth-century theoretical antithesis between realism and modernism/postmodernism. Like Mieke Bal, then, I believe that "narrative is a system, but is not ahistorical, collective but not unchangeable, regulated by abstract rules but not uninformed by concrete uses and adaptations of those rules" ("Point" 737).

We must, however, not abandon specific narrative categories, for these are the site both of ideology and potential disruption. If narrative is not a neutral organization of story events but a system that is, within the Western tradition, authoritative, it is in the construction of subjectivity in certain narrative functions, particularly in the subject or protagonist, the object of the protagonist's attentions, the narrator, the narratee, and the figure who sees the events or action—the focalizer—that the magnitude of the Western narrative as a power-inflected system is apparent. Each of these categories is encoded with power and desire before a specific character enters the picture; at the same time, as I will try to show, the character who moves the story along, who narrates it, the character who sees, and the one who is seen can challenge these codes. In the traditional narrative system, these positions assume a unitary subject who acts on others as objects. In feminist terms, each narrative category that pertains to what we usually call character, and to what I will call categories of subjectivity, becomes susceptible to a power dynamic of male centrality over female marginality if not female erasure, a perspective of which both Sexton and Atwood are aware. These mechanics also encode a heterosexual relationship between the noninnocent gendered categories, but also, in a more subtle move, encode male bonding as a crucial if not the central relationship. The result is that the institution appears to encode heterosexuality and male bonding in its very mechanics. As a result, some of narrative's most forceful themes include individualism, conflict, tension, violence, and transcendence.

In one of the strongest feminist revisions of formalist narrative theory, Teresa de Lauretis exposes the inscription of gender hierarchy and heterosexuality on a structural level. In *Alice Doesn't,* she identifies two primary narrative codes, the active and passive "positionalities of desire" (143) which, for de Lauretis, are always gendered. Using Yuri Lotman's reduction of the narrative to two functions—the active, mobile protagonist and the passive, immobile boundary space—de Lauretis forces narratology to accept its own gender biases (118). The female function as the boundary figure, the frontier or the object from which the narrative subject must separate himself, encodes violence and oppression as part of the structural apparatus of narrative. He, the desiring subject, must not only define himself as a knower who is separate from the desired object of knowledge, the teleological space of closure also gendered female, but he must also pass through a figure or space that will secure his identity. The separation of sexual categories into a hierarchy assures male dominance and the "exchange of women." This movement often calls for violence, or perhaps one can say, violence is inherent in the narrative categories. Only in the adventure story and in the quest narrative is this violence made overt. Catherine Keller boldly describes the inherent violence of the narrative as the need to establish male hegemony through "perpetual decapitations" (58) of the female. In her reading of the Perseus/Medusa myth, it is matricide that creates the gender dichotomies; for "it is by 'killing' the monster that the male establishes her monstrosity and his heroism" (62). The hero's violent decapitations produce the isolated and boundaried individual who rises above society.

De Lauretis's argument genders these narrative spaces or positions rather than a specific character: "In this mythical-textual mechanics, then, the hero must be male, regardless of the gender of the text-image, because the obstacle, whatever its personification, is morphologically female and indeed, simply, the womb" (*Alice* 118–19). Moreover, the separation of the text into male and female functions also assumes a heterosexual plot movement in which the male endlessly takes and overcomes the female. Using Lotman's definition of plot as " 'entry into a closed space, and emergence from it,' " de Lauretis exposes his inherent gender bias through a direct quote: " 'In as much as closed space *can be interpreted* as 'a cave', 'the grave', 'a house', 'woman' . . . entry into it *is interpreted* on various levels as 'death', 'conception', 'return home' and so on; moreover all these acts *are thought of as mutually identical*' " (her emphasis 118). The plot, not just the act of reading, becomes a ritual enactment of intercourse, perhaps of rape. Atwood's Circe sees Ulysses' story as destructive of everyone involved, and her identity with the mud woman of the central poem places her in the position of an always and forever raped woman.

The narrative boundary is fixed not only as female but also as the bodily female, nature, the mud woman, sexuality. The boundary is Circe's island and her sexuality; it is Shakespeare's Forest of Arden or the woods of Athens; it is the American frontier. It is, symbolically, the woman's body. Again, de Lauretis provides the account of the hero of the story taking over the woman's body in his quest. In describing a shamanistic ritual for a good childbirth—noted in Lévi-Strauss—the shaman "seeks to sever [the birthing mother's] identification with a body which she must come to perceive precisely as a space, the territory in which the battle is waged. The hero's victory then results in his recapturing the woman's soul" (*Technologies* 45). This entry into the woman's body indicates not only the importance to narrative of the female passive position but also of the control of the female body.

If the Western narrative intends to create sexual divisions, it also maintains bodily distinctions. In our culture, that means making distinctions between pure and impure bodies, natural and unnatural bodies. The female body in Western culture is associated with what Julia Kristeva calls the "abject," which she defines not as a "lack of cleanliness or health . . . but what disturbs identity, system, order. What does not respect borders, positions, rules" (*Powers* 4). The body that violates rules is one that exceeds itself by exuding some form of culturally defined filth, "the object jettisoned out of that boundary, its other side, a margin" (69). The two defilements that Kristeva identifies—excrement and menstrual blood—"stem from the *maternal* and/or the feminine, of which the maternal is the real support" (71). Although M. M. Bakhtin's notion of the grotesque is more positive than Kristeva's category of abjection, Bakhtin also associates the grotesque with natural functions of the body, of which female reproductive activities are central: "acts of defecation and copulation, conception, pregnancy, and birth" (21). The construction of the woman's body as the grotesque or abject cultural body focuses on, in both accounts, the maternal. Like the grotesque mother insect in the movie *Aliens* who uncontrollably oozes eggs, which are in turn replanted in human carriers who undergo an horrific and deadly pregnancy and birth, Kristeva and Bakhtin emphasize female reproduction as a central image of cultural horror. Barbara Creed argues, using Kristeva, that "when woman is represented as monstrous it is almost always in relation to her mothering and reproductive functions" (7) rather than her sexuality. In her examination of monstrous women in horror films, even the lesbian vampire threatens as a mother rather than as a sexual creature: "where the vampire is female, we are made more aware of the dependent relationship between the vampire as mother and her lover as child" (70).

But female sexuality is also a source of cultural fear, for an uncontrolled female sexuality spells chaos and destruction in the patriarchal mind. The myth of the *vagina dentata* is only one locus of this fear; the other is a woman's control of her own sexuality, her willingness to use it for her own pleasure and purpose. For example, in using Bakhtin's distinction between grotesque and classical bodies, Peter Stallybrass analyzes Shakespeare's Desdemona in terms of the Renaissance's fear of a woman's unregulated sexuality, part of a larger Western assumption that the woman's body—including her sexuality—is by definition grotesque, always and "*naturally*" on the verge of "transgressing its own limits" and therefore in need of constant policing (126). The lesbian is the core of the culture's fear of women's sexuality, for it is lesbian sexuality that is ultimately unregulated by men or by reproduction. For this reason the early sexologists connected criminal activity and sexual aggression. As Lynda Hart notes in her study of lesbian sexuality and aggression, it is the lesbian act of desiring rather than being desired that "inextricably bound [her] to the perpetration of violence" (10) in the mind of the late nineteenth-century sexologists. The body, then, that transgresses boundaries is, by definition, female; it is this body in all its symbolic guises that the narrative system attempts to police. One example, then, of female body in narrative is Atwood's mud woman, the always controlled, always violated, always mute figure who can be transgressed and possessed at will, at the male's desire.

The two other narrative categories of subjectivity—the narrator and the narratee—occupy a similar relationship of coded power. Although more problematic than the categories de Lauretis discusses, these narrative positions mimic the structural division between active and passive narrative spaces identified above. The narrator, especially when this figure coincides with the protagonist, positions itself as the owner of language and the shaper of the objects of narration. The decades-long feminist argument for the gendered nature of speech can be seen both as an argument about the gendered position of the writer—which Sandra Gilbert and Susan Gubar definitively labeled as male in *The Madwoman in the Attic*—and, more problematic, the gendered position of the narrator. The narrator and the writer both appropriate language and narrative to themselves and therefore, as Emile Benveniste argues, constitute themselves as subjects, for "It is in and through language that man constitutes himself as a *subject*" (224). In fact, "Language is so organized that it permits each speaker to *appropriate to himself* an entire language by designating himself as *I*" (Wittig, *Straight* 226). But women, argues Monique Wittig, using Benveniste's theory, cannot become these universal "I's" because as soon as they speak they must identify themselves as marked rather than unmarked (81–87). Wittig explains that her fictional works are attempts to break the male centrality of the "I" with a new lesbian subject, the only means by which, she believes, a female subject can attain universal subjectivity (87). The narrator as well as the author, then, becomes a positionality that appropriates language as a universal subject with the right to speak. Both Atwood and Sexton use narrators who are commentators on the plots they are delivering, but because they are identifiably women their form of narration is hesitant, qualified, indirect. The dilemma of each narrator, apparent in the poem's tone, arises from the difficulty each has in usurping a universal subjectivity.

As a corollary to the narrator, the narratee is that figure within the fiction who is addressed directly. The narrator and narratee are the speaking equivalent of the active and passive positions de Lauretis identifies, especially when identified as the lover and beloved in the romantic narrative. Gerald Prince in his *Dictionary of Narratology* defines this narrative position most succinctly: "The one who is narrated to, as inscribed in the text" (57). As a character in the text, which Prince distinguishes from the real or the implied reader, the narratee is in a position of being addressed, not of speaking. In love lyrics, for example, and particularly in narrative sonnet sequences, the narratee is the beloved who is addressed as "you." In the context of de Lauretis's gendering of the two basic narrative spaces or functions, the mobile and immobile, the narratee logically occupies the immobile, feminized space. In traditional sonnet sequences, the narratee as the beloved—Petrarch's Laura; Sidney's Stella—is the object upon whom the speaker/lover constructs his subjectivity. Women writers have, at times, intervened in these dualistic positionings. Robyn R. Warhol, for instance, challenges the division between narratee and reader, claiming that "not every narrator who intervenes to address a narratee does so to set the actual reader apart from the 'you' in the text" (811). In the rhetorical structure of the lesbian essays that I analyze in the following chapter, the beloved is positioned as the narratee, as the auditor of the theorizing who becomes, in a revisionary way, part of the theory. These possible revisions of the narrator/narratee relationship are not a part of Atwood's or Sexton's texts.

The figure through whose eyes we see the narrative action is another important narrative position identified in contemporary narrative theory and one whose potentially gendered position we must consider. Sight, defined as the camera, has been a coded position of male power in feminist film theory for the last decades. E. Ann Kaplan's rhetorical question, "Is the Gaze Male?" and Laura Mulvey's essay, "Visual Pleasure and Narrative Cinema," assume that the camera's and the male viewer's gazes are one because they both objectify the female body and provide the lens for the reincorporation of "her" into his story. But the assumption of who owns the gaze is not limited to film theory. Luce Irigaray argues that the male gaze, the "eye-penis," is the site of power that forges the "envy and jealousy" (47) Freud placed on little girls. But without the benefit of this psychologizing, the gaze is male because men have the physical power to reinforce their subjectivity in places like construction sites. But is the narrative position of what Gérard Genette calls "*the character whose point of view orients the narrative perspec-*

tive" (*Narrative* 186) inherently powerful and male-identified? Mieke Bal, for instance, identifies focalization in active and passive categories as "the relationship between 'vision,' the agent that sees, and that which is seen" (*Narratology* 104) but assumes that these positions, as she does of narrative as a system, are neutral. But as with the active and passive categories of narrative movement and narrative speech, focalization is not innocent of subjectivity or of power, primarily because sight is not a neutral position. While this simple dualism, as absolute in its immobility as de Lauretis's active and passive narrative spaces, has been challenged recently in a collection of essays on popular culture, *The Female Gaze* (Gamman and Marshment), the connection of sight with male power over the female is fundamental to the cultural construction of power positions, including those set out in the traditional narrative. As John Berger notes, sight is about control, about "Men look[ing] at women" and "Women watch[ing] themselves being looked at" (47). It is not surprising, then, that the image of sight has become one of the fundamental contemporary ways to define the metaphorical lesbian.

The structure of what Atwood calls the "white plot" ("Circe" 217) bears out the most dismal of de Lauretis's warnings: that all stories are divided into gender-defined active and passive spaces which control the figures in those spaces. Circe's positions are predictable and, at the same time, contradictory. Circe's roles as both narrator and character are ironic because she is speaking a story in which she is neither the narrator nor an actor. She is the narrator telling someone else's story, unable to move her own plot; she is, in the original and in Atwood's poems, the boundary space through which he will move toward his own goal, and she envisions herself as the closure, the end, the resting place for his story, where all desire is met. She is all women in "The Story." As such, she is aware that power and subjectivity are embedded in the narrative paradigm and that they belong to Ulysses and not to her. Her complaint is about the irony of the power assigned to her. The original story gives Circe the power to change men into animals, but here Circe claims, "I made no choice/I decided nothing" (205). Unlike Emile Benveniste's speaker of language, Circe tells a story that has already been told, with a different narrator, with her as a figure/island through which Ulysses, the "real" actor in the story, moves. Her sense of powerlessness is an extension of her ironic speaking position as a narrator who cannot tell a story. She often complains of her lack of control over language, of her dumbness: "I did not say anything, I sat/and watched" (203). Atwood underscores Circe's alienation from the "received language" (204) that she cannot speak or that has no real power when coming from her lips, even though the story attributes magical powers to her. Circe also exists as its boundary figure or closure, for as she says later, "but I am the place where/all desires are fulfilled" (220). Ulysses, too, is caught in the power of the story, but it is, after all, his story.

She must be raped, taken, possessed, moved through, in order for the heroic narrative to be realized. The discomfort we feel from the monotony of Circe's complaint arises from her inability to move the plot along, to create a tension from her own narrative movement. In fact, the sequence of poems is a cry of despair against Ulysses' ultimate control of the story she is trying to tell. The tension is palpable, for Circe's story is static. In the poem that gives the sequence its name, Atwood underscores the woman's powerlessness: she is the story and her body its text. In this poem's story, which is more like prose in its form and telling, two boys construct a woman out of mud. She is without a head because "they stuck to the essentials" (214). Each sun-filled day they go to the island to have intercourse with her, finding her perfectly amenable and welcoming to both. The story has a double narrator, for Circe repeats a story told "by another traveller" (214), one of the boys, passing through her island, like Ulysses. The same story, the same traveller. Of course, the mud woman is perfect because she is static; she cannot speak, cannot respond, or talk. It is understandable that "no woman since then has equalled her" (214). Circe asks, trying desperately for some agency in all of this objectification: Do you really want me to be like this?

Atwood is also aware of the violence inherent in this story, a violence which, ironically, turns on the perpetrator. Ulysses, too, is bound to repeat the endless quest cycle: "Don't you get tired of killing" (206). But while he, too, is doomed to repeat the story, it is, after all, his story and his language. He, for instance, is writing a book and is unaware of the quicksand of the story itself, a knowledge that Circe would like to share with him but to which he is deaf. In this poem, Ulysses retires every day to write his travel story, oblivious to anything around him, especially to her. With the traditional things, like food, that women have always provided for the male writer, Circe brings him warnings about the danger of this story, but he refuses to listen. As Catherine Keller notes, this heroic story is a "secret matricide" (57), for his subjectivity depends on the "violent defeat of the values and claims of the female power" (62).

Circe does imagine an alternative to his story, a story "which includes, instead of excluding, herself" (Ostriker 212). It contains no lesbian possibilities. Instead, it is a heterosexual love story that moves the female character into a position of equality but not into her own quest story. As noted by numerous feminist critics, the romantic plot often overcomes the woman's quest story, leaving the heroic tale to the male protagonist. In Atwood's last poem, written in italics, she posits the possibility of two islands, of two stories, of two endings. This second island we "*know nothing about/because it has never happened*" (222). But the new story is heard in a "few muted syllables" (204) from nature, from the stones and the shrubs. This gesture to the natural world is common with American women writers of the 1970s such as Susan Griffin and Adrienne Rich. The appeal to nature is an appeal to its immediacy of communication, its seeming naturalness. Atwood conceives of language and narrative as barriers between the sexes; thus, on this other island, the language is direct, physical, and animal in character: "*We lick the melted snow/from each other's mouths*" (223). Because the narrator attempts to speak the new story, the tone is less strident or defensive. Much like her description of mythical coupling in her novel *Surfacing,* Atwood's answer to a story or language in which the heroine does not fit is to appeal to the mute power of nature. In the novel, the unnamed heroine takes on power when she moves her lover out into nature to make love and puts a premium on the fact that they do not speak (189–91). In both texts, Atwood paradoxically mixes the five senses. In *Surfacing,* for instance, the heroine says, "My tentacled feet and free hand scent out the way, shoes are a barrier" (161). Atwood's solution to the gender asymmetry of narrative is to imagine an equality of the sexes through the mediation of nature, a stance which ironically undermines the woman's power of speech and action.

Ursula Le Guin's short story, "She Unnames Them," provides a direct parallel to Atwood's narrative solution and to the problems inherent in this alternative. Le Guin imagines a point at which Eve leaves Eden and Adam's company, but Eve takes her leave only after she gives back to Adam and God her name and all the animals' names. After the animals have returned their names, Eve describes her congruence with them: "They seemed far closer than when their names had stood between myself and them like a clear barrier" (27). Like Atwood's projection of a new island, Le Guin's last paragraph inaugurates a new, metaphoric language dependent on connection rather than separation: "My words now must be as slow, as new, as single, as tentative as the steps I took going down the path away from the house, between the dark-branched, tall dancers motionless against the winter shining" (27). Because narrative has traditionally allowed few alternatives for female agency, both Atwood and Le Guin invent the proscribed by separating the female from the male, at least temporarily, and tempering the solitude with a connection to a mute partner, nature. But because this invention occurs as narrative closure, the female figure is repositioned but allotted only the potential not the reality of narrative agency. As Margaret Homans points out in *Women Writers and Poetic Identity,* women writers' identification with the immediacy of nature is often self-defeating (17).

Atwood also assumes that heterosexuality is central to the story writ large and to its alternative because her new island and her new text contain no hint of a lesbian solution. The argumentative tone Circe employs with Ulysses in many of the other poems is eclipsed in the last poem by a declaration of "we." The reader must assume the nonantagonist heterosexual relationship of Circe and Ulysses at this point. Feminist theorists have noted that the interdependence of heterosexuality and the narrative structure is a burden that limits the development of female agency. Rachel Blau DuPlessis, for example, argues that "the erotic and emotional intensity of women's friendship cuts the Gordian knots of both heterosexuality and narrative convention" (149) as if the two elements were so intertwined that narrative cannot be written about women without some intervention in the sex/gender structure and convention. Her own sense of rewriting the ending demands a breakup of heterosexual fictional normality using alternatives such as "reparenting, woman-to-woman and brother-to-sister bonds, and forms of the communal protagonist" (5). The same is true of Lee R. Edwards' observation that heterosexuality has exercised a stranglehold on heroines because tradition has "derived female identity from an equation linking limited aspiration and circumscribed activity to institutionalized heterosexuality" (237).

Other theoretical approaches to the narrative, less likely to separate the abstract structure from the text images, confirm the binary and heterosexual centrality of traditional Western narrative codes. These theories posit a narrative based on a societally defined structural relationship such as the heterosexual dyad or the homosocial triangle. At the same time, these social dynamics reaffirm the power relationships among narrative categories of subjectivity, leaving intact a similar ab-

stract system of meaning behind the specific textual images. By paralleling narrative order to social structure rather than the absolutist internal
logic of the sentence or of Oedipal desire, both realism and experimen-
talism can be affirmed as potentially disruptive. Because, according to
these theories, narrative replays social expectations and cultural codes,
societal scripts can be read as a narrative frame, and this paradigm,
unlike the linguistic, depends on the relationship between social and
textual reality and therefore gives significant insight into the larger
workings of traditional narrative paradigms. In the most important
societal parallel, narrative is likened to society's institutions of romance
and marriage. But like de Lauretis's analysis of the active and passive
functions of narrative, this model invokes categories of subjectivity
which privilege the male and assure the hierarchical placement of male
and female in a heterosexual relationship. Those rules and institutions
which ask all of us to marry, to have children, and to assume sexually
oppositional positions become the ideologically inflected, abstract codes
by which genres such as the *Bildungsroman* and the romance or marriage plots tell their tale. Simone de Beauvoir's famous formulation—
"He is the Subject, he is the Absolute—she is the Other" (xvi)—is an
effective way to read the social contract we call marriage, whether we
understand marriage through the medieval and Renaissance model of
the femme covert, the woman who is socially and legally under her
husband's control, or through Lévi-Strauss's notion of the "exchange of
women." Thus, the eighteenth- and nineteenth-century bourgeois novel
becomes, according to Joseph Allen Boone, a limited narrative of middle-class culture which uses the abstract rules of the narrative code
(conflicts ultimately resolved) to encode oppositional and hierarchical
relations between the two sexes and to fashion a "stability, consonance,
or equilibrium" (79) in the narrative closure of marriage. Romantic
stories have no less an investment in the paradigmatic movement from
desire to consummation, although sexual consummation and narrative
resolution might take place in death instead of marriage, as they do in
the Western world's ur-romance, *Tristan und Isolde*. Male and female
characters are positioned accordingly, as Leslie W. Rabine suggests, with
the "totalizing masculine voice of romantic narrative" (8) negotiating
his subjectivity against the heroine's position as the object of his desire,
"the means of his identification with his own ego ideal" (11). Although
definitions of marriage or meanings of romantic involvement change
historically, narrative closure is often defined as a form of consumma-

tion and/or transcendence, whether it is the mystical eroticism of *Tristan und Isolde*, the socially sanctioned marriage of *Jane Eyre*, or the contemporary affair in A. S. Byatt's *Possession*.

The possibility for disruption of this pattern exists and yet is contested by the self-regulating system that provides the framework. Disruption calls for a rearrangement of the heterosexual and homosocial structural relationships, making the binary and gendered power relationships embedded in narrative structure challengeable. Denis Jonnes, for instance, negotiates between his belief that narrative is a semiotic system informed by our social system of families, a "discursive mode both constrained and enabled by events, interactions, relations marked in terms of what happens in or around 'families' " (111) and his insistence that narrative is a self-regulating system which "permits criticism and interrogation as well as the articulation of new configurations and sequences" (120). While "new configurations" appear limited in these theories because the heterosexuality of the family or of marriage and romance asserts itself as part of narrative self-regulation, marginal groups can contribute to what Jonnes describes as a "loosening" of the story form (266). Marginal groups dispute the values of the societal norm and therefore challenge the narrative system which encodes those norms. Both Jonnes and DuPlessis identify homosexuality as one of the ways to open up the gender boundaries of the narrative system. Jonnes, however, appears more inclusive when he quaintly names as marginal "homosexual life forms" (266) while DuPlessis specifically identifies woman-to-woman bonds (5) as one of the new scripts.

This difference is not solely because DuPlessis is writing about women writers and characters; it is also because the dominant patterns of the traditional narrative affirm not only heterosexuality but also male bonding—homosexual as well as homosocial. Jonnes too easily includes all "homosexual life forms" among marginal groups that are "loosening" the narrative. Narrative patterns not only reaffirm male centrality in a heterosexual dyad, but, at the same time, as a condition of that dyad, they also affirm male homosocial bonds, the guarantor of male power. This structural pattern also depends on the disruption or exclusion of female bonding. Eve Kosofsky Sedgwick's incisive description of the male homosocial patterns in novels between 1750 and 1850 argues that the male bond is realized and affirmed within a male-female-male triangle. Within this set of relationships, the homosocial bonds between men are the most crucial; the woman provides the glue as well as the social acceptability of what could too easily slide into a male homosexual relationship. While Sedgwick limits her study to one century of writing, this pattern can be and has been used to describe much more than a century's worth of novels, from Sedgwick's own consideration of Shakespeare's sonnets (*Between* 28–48) to Susan Winnett's discussion of the phallocentric author/reader relationship (507). Although recognizing a continuity between male homosocial and male homosexual desire in historical eras like ancient Greece, Sedgwick emphasizes the separation of these two types of male bonding in the last several centuries, particularly in the twentieth century. Male bonding, especially today, assumes an " 'obligatory heterosexuality,' " and, it seems, "homophobia [as] a *necessary* consequence of such patriarchal institutions as heterosexual marriage" (3). In the contemporary separation of homosocial from homosexual desire, gay men are marginalized along with women, and alienated from the male power that polices the homosexual/heterosexual boundaries. Thus homophobia and misogyny go together as means of drawing lines around that which is male and powerful (216). But, rather than seeing gay men alienated from the male homosocial power system, I believe that the pattern of male bonding through a distant female applies to both homosocial and homosexual male bonding, leaving only the lesbian as untheorized. If male homosexuality were radically forbidden by societal structures, then, in narrative representation, male homosexuality should eliminate the middle term, woman, and challenge the heterosexually driven narrative paradigms. Yet this does not seem to happen. Rather, women are also needed as the Other in order to secure male homosexual identity. If this is the case, then the literary paradigm of male bonding that Sedgwick identifies remains secure in male homosexual writing, for unlike lesbian realistic and experimental fictions which seek to excise male presence, gay male fiction of this century more easily includes women. More stereotypical is the use of women entertainment figures as distant but necessary means of being in contact with that which is female, what one reviewer of Wayne Koestenbaum's book on opera calls "the obsession some gay men have with larger-than-life femininity" (Ross 116). Judy Garland, Bette Midler, and Maria Callas have served that role of "larger-than-life femininity" for a variety of reasons, including their larger-than-life suffering. Lesbians do not flock in discernible numbers and, more important, in culturally identifiable ways, to a Tom Jones or a Placido Domingo or even a Johnny Mathis. Wayne Koestenbaum's book is significant at this point because he identifies his love of opera with his love of the diva, with his act of living through a female voice. He positions his "queeny love of women" in opera through a structural yet distant connection with women (23). Male homosexual discursive identity is forged, then, by the connection with a distant, feminine figure who provides the same sense of otherness that she provides in heterosexual dyads or erotic triangles. Although Bruce Smith's reading of Shakespeare's sonnets ignores the Dark Lady's narrative function, I will argue in Chapter 4 that Shakespeare makes her crucial to the definition of what Smith identifies as a homosexual relationship with the young man (228–70). Although arguing for a differently constructed male homosexuality in classical Greece, David Halperin's reading of Plato's *Symposium* similarly posits Diotima, Socrates' teacher, as the female figure through whom Socrates presents a model of "an ethic of 'correct paederasty' " (113). Her presence works, as it would in a male-dominated heterosexual situation, to assure male authority by endowing "the paedagogic processes by which men reproduce themselves culturally . . . with the prestige of female procreativity" (144). While Koestenbaum and Halperin refuse to regard these male homosexual uses of the female as appropriative, they both posit woman as pivotal, whether discursively constructed or socially available, to the formation of male homosexuality. While the existence alone of male bonding as a narrative paradigm is enough to argue that only women's bonding, lesbianism, is untheorized and excised from narrative, it is even more accurate, I believe, to argue that male homosexual bonding is implied in theories of male bonding. Sedgwick herself points to the uniqueness of lesbianism when she notes that it must be theorized "on different [sometimes opposite] grounds and working through different mechanisms" than male homosexuality (*Between* 25). Like other cultural constructs, then, the narrative system works on various levels to exclude the lesbian, making "her" narrative's most disruptive nightmare.

In this context it is interesting to note that two boys, not one, create Atwood's mud woman. In the central verse paragraph, the protagonist is "they," as the two boys make the woman according to their own specifications, row over to her island, and "take turns" having intercourse with her. Their bond is in part their mutual sexual pleasure, for "they were not jealous" (61). From one perspective, the lack of jealousy arises from the fact that their sexual pleasure is displaced. They are sexually enjoying each other in the act of sexually taking the same hand-made woman. Another literary text underscores the charged sexuality that is a part of male bonding in literature. In A. S. Byatt's tour de force, *Possession,* this bonding is across the century but is nevertheless sexual. The two scholars, Roland Michell and Maud Bailey, become lovers after their lives and work cross as they explore connections between their respective nineteenth-century literary subjects. In discovering the letters and love affair between the earlier writers, Randolph Henry Ash and Christabel LaMotte, the two scholars become pale avatars of their literary heroes. Maud Bailey, it is revealed, is the descendant of Ash's and LaMotte's one night of passionate love. In the last pages, when Bailey and Michell make love, his connection is less with her than with his male literary idol; he seeks Ash through her. It is as he discovers Ash in her features that he begins to touch her, to stroke her hair and touch her face (548). One could, with Sedgwick in the background, argue that when he makes love with her he is making a homosocial bond with his literary love, and, without Sedgwick's blessing, a homosexual connection. That crucial closing, then, confirms two male-dominated sexualities—homosexual and heterosexual—but at the same time erases another. The frail Victorian poetess, whom we imagine as Christina Rossetti, falls in love with the robust Victorian poet, a Robert Browning figure; but she had lived first with a woman who, in her desperation at their heterosexual liaison, commits suicide. The lesbian implications are blatant, and the rejection of them at the end is stirring. In the name of literary and erotic tension, female bonding must be ripped from narratable possibilities. This book mirrors much of the theory that argues the structural necessity of the narrative to position heterosexual and male homosexual as the fundaments of narrativity. The erotic tension of the novel is heterosexual, in fact a heterosexual triumph over lesbian desire, but the closure of the narrative is decidedly male homosocial verging on the homosexual.

The difficulty of narrativizing lesbian desire is clearly depicted in Anne Sexton's poem "Rapunzel." This radical retelling of the traditional fairy tale is juxtaposed to other poems in which Sexton tells the usual heterosexual story. Her conclusion appears to be that the lesbian story is ultimately unimaginable. Her metafictional concern in *Transformations* is the movement of the plot, the traditional movement that dictates a beginning, middle, and end, and the subsequent relationship of cause and effect for the various narrative events. This movement, especially in the fairy tales, demands a closure of heterosexual marriage. Sexton exposes these narrative mechanics as an inevitable doom for the young girls of the fairy tales. In the poems most pertinent to this study and the ones that parallel "Rapunzel" in its theme of rescue by the prince, "Cinderella," "Snow White and the Seven Dwarfs," and "Briar Rose (Sleeping Beauty)," Sexton exposes the macrostory of a young girl's maturation that inevitably traps her in a stifling relationship with a male. The story is as ruthless as Atwood's, perhaps even more ruthless. For the girl to enter into sexuality and adulthood, the tale that these stories variously tell, is to enter into time and as a result into the narrative, to be trapped in a system which will ultimately turn her into the wicked stepmother, the aged and useless woman. The worldly-wise as well as world-weary narrator characterizes Snow White with a detached, biting humor—"The virgin is a lovely number" (3)—pointing both to her vulnerability and position as a commodity. The narrator positions herself on the other side of the story as the older woman who, because she has already entered the story and knows the ironic position of woman in it, speaks with sardonic and cynical humor. The narrator characterizes the young girl as a china doll prior to adulthood, the virgin who has yet to enter time and is therefore forever young and vulnerable. As a virgin, Snow White is "fragile as cigarette paper" and rolls her "china-blue doll eyes" (3), and Sleeping Beauty is a "Little doll child" (107). But her first physical symptoms of maturity—and note that it is the body that determines her entry into adulthood, not an heroic adventure that determines the boy's entry into manhood—place textuality and sexuality in the same breath. The entry into time, adulthood, and narrative, however, brings only another kind of death for the young girl. Instead of the usual happily-ever-after story, Sexton returns to the same images of stasis that characterize her young girl at the beginning: "Meanwhile Snow White held court,/rolling her china-blue doll eyes open and shut" (9). Once caught in the textual/sexual system, she only changes her position of stasis. No longer humorously dead as a virgin, she is now obscurely dead as a married woman. This stasis also exposes the male bonding that forces the girl into relationships with other men. In "Briar Rose," Sexton reveals the exchange of the young girl from father/king to husband/prince as a ritual in which the girl is erased, sometimes violently. In the last scene of this last poem in the collection, Sexton's unraveling of narrativity ends with a vivid and devastating image of incest, revealing the underseams of violence that keep the woman in her place. At the end of her story, Briar Rose is a woman who, after having been awakened from a long sleep by her prince, suffers from insomnia, and whose only memories are of "my father thick upon me/like some sleeping jellyfish" (112).

"Rapunzel" interrupts the expected plot with its first line: "A woman/ who loves a woman/is forever young" (35). Here Sexton gestures toward a lesbian relationship as an alternative story, but cannot follow through. She treats the lesbian story as a nonstory, what D. A. Miller might call the "nonnarratable," not "the unspeakable" but "its incapacity to generate a story" (5). The older woman, Mother Gothel, keeps Rapunzel in a tower and when she asks Mother Gothel to let down her hair, Mother Gothel climbs it to be with her. Their togetherness lasts until the prince comes and breaks this woman-to-woman bond. In their bonding, the female characters refuse to enter time and therefore refuse to enter the plot; for, as Mother Gothel says to Rapunzel, outside of their relationship, death and deflowerment are synonymous: "Let me hold your heart like a flower/lest it bloom and collapse" (38). While, as if to ally herself uneasily with Freud, Sexton perceives this relationship as an immature stage of development, however lovely and enticing, at the same time she eschews her usual satirical tone and instead describes the relationship in overtly idealistic terms of "two clouds/glistening in the bottle glass" (38). The coy phrase for their lovemaking, "mother-me-do" (40), alludes both to a mother-daughter relationship and also to a sense of imprisonment that will justify Rapunzel's "rescue." In the middle of the poem, the interlude of the garden "more beautiful than Eve's" (39), Sexton underscores the aura of unreality yet purity that she associates with one woman's relationship with another woman. But in this Edenic stasis, Rapunzel is lonely, and the prince who rescues her is strangely yet powerfully masculine and "dazzled her with his dancing stick" (41). In the stanza reserved for the story's moral, Sexton ironically dismisses homosexuality as a stage to be outgrown, "just as the fish on Friday" (42), but she also leaves the older woman strangely sentimentalized. The images underscore the Edenic unreality of the witch's garden but also garner sympathy from the reader, leaving her to wonder about the platitudes which describe the necessity of heterosexuality in the penultimate stanza.

In this way, Sexton agrees with much contemporary thinking about the rapacious nature of plot movement, and might, at some level, concur with those who believe that only breaking the sequence will disturb the power of the traditional narrative to exact death from its female inhabitants. For both modernists and feminists the broken sequence becomes the answer to disturbing an ideological monster: the master plot. In the nineteenth-century historical novel, modernists argue, it is linear plotting and its concomitant realism that encodes bourgeois values of universal subjectivity and a normative closure, usually marriage; in twentieth-century women's writing, feminists contend, it is linearity that traps the female figure in male-dominated positions of subjectivity and of closure, always marriage or death. The primary elements of narrative movement—sequences determined by cause and effect, time or verb tenses, and narrative closure—all figure as means of privileging an ideology either of the middle class or patriarchy or both. In fact, Virginia Woolf may have both in mind when she recognizes the potential value of her mythical novelist, Mary Carmichael, in A Room of One's Own: "Mary is tampering with the expected sequence. First she broke the sentence; now she has broken the sequence" (85), but Woolf also adds that Carmichael must do this "not for the sake of breaking, but for the sake of creating" (85). This distinction is crucial, for it is important to look at the various ways in which the sequence can be broken and to what effect.

Readers are conditioned to expect a narrative pattern that sets up a series of events that are logically or chronologically related. This cause-and-effect pattern is not innocent, for it reinvests in narrative form a type of thinking that establishes a logic of consequences and a teleology. This movement is often seen as an emblem of political and ideological control. Fictional realism most directly mirrors this pattern and has therefore been the object of modern and postmodern critiques. Roland Barthes, for instance, associates realism's use of the literary French past tense, the preterite, with a closed and ordered world, a "security system" (Writing 32). It is that tight system of "classical temporality" that Gérard Genette perceives Proust disturbing through his use of "iterative temporality," which "free[s] his narrative forever from the constraints and limitations of traditional narration" ("Time" 118). Feminist theorists, seeing the gendered nature of narrative authority, search for a lyric narrative that Joanna Russ defines as a "mode [that] exists without chronology or causation" (12) and that Susan Stanford Friedman argues "foregrounds a *simultaneity,* a cluster of feelings or ideas that project a gestalt in stasis" instead of "a *sequence* of events that move dynamically in space and time" ("Lyric" 164). The Lacanian French feminists see the two types of narrating—one linear and the other circular—as reflections of the male and female economies of desire. The feminine disruption of sequence, Cixous's *écriture féminine,* at times available to either male or female writers, signals the rupture of the male symbolic order, one defined by gender separation and hierarchy and determined by male desire. Female desire, or the entry of either sex into the realm of the maternal, produces a different text. Both Cixous and Luce Irigaray write in such a mode—in fragments and impressionistic leaps. Both subvert normal sentence order, or as Irigaray rhapsodically demands, "*Overthrow syntax* by suspending its eternally teleological order, by snipping the wires, cutting the current, breaking the circuits, switching the connections, by modifying continuity, alternation, frequency, intensity" (*Speculum* 142). Kristeva sets women's time against "time as project, teleology, linear and prospective unfolding" ("Women's" 17). If the comparison of linearity is not made directly to male bodies, it exists as a comparison to male thinking or patriarchal lineage, what Patricia Drechsel Tobin, for instance, calls "the genealogical imperative" (5). The attack on sequence, causality, and time leads these thinkers to refuse anything that smacks of "another normative narrative" (de Lauretis, *Alice* 156) or to imply, as one of my students jokingly proposed, a "transgression scale," a test by which nonlinear texts send the scale to new heights and traditional story lines fail to move the needle of disruption.

Closure of the normative narrative is posited as the logical result of a series of causes, making narrative a form driven by a teleology. The story's ending is the teleological structure that Culler insists is central to narrative (209–10) and that Frank Kermode sees as part of a "primeval pattern" (31) underlying even the most disruptive of modern texts. Closure is the ultimate place in which subjects are positioned in relationship to one another and to power. But traditional movement toward closure, like linearity, can be interpreted as authoritarian. It is no wonder, then, that closure is the fulcrum of feminist narrative theory, for in closure the female character is finally encased in the authoritative social/sexual/narrative system, never again to escape. If she has rebelled, she is returned to a normality that allows the reader to gain a "sense of an ending." Rosalind in *As You Like It* is allowed that wonderful hiatus as Ganymede but must return to "woman's weedes" and marriage at the end of the play. The alternative to marriage is death. Catherine Clément attributes the numerous deaths of operatic heroines like Carmen and Lucia to transgressions against authority, to "transgressions of familial rules, political rules, the things at stake in sexual and authoritarian power" (10). Death or marriage is the only choice for most nineteenth-century heroines, and so final are those choices that we are tempted to read Edna Pontellier's suicide in Kate Chopin's *The Awakening* as an escape to freedom. DuPlessis's entire book is predicated on the twentieth-century women writers' attempts to write beyond that double bind of death or marriage. If traditional closure "limit[s] the inherent possibilities of fictional narrative and of human desire" (Boone 80), if it sets up as realistic what is artificial, then it becomes one of the crucial arenas for the development of narrative alternatives. Sexton exhibits her uneasiness with traditional closure because she is aware that it reinscribes traditional social codes for women. Sexton signals her dis-ease when she resolves her tales in unfamiliar ways. She refuses closure. Snow White returns to her doll-like stasis at the beginning of the poem, and Briar Rose returns to the incest with her father. Closure for women in this kind of story, Sexton claims, is not to gain or learn anything but to be trapped in a repetition of the same.

Twentieth-century consideration of narrative time and closure draws heavily on the psycho/sexual model of narrative progression. Highly influential but, in the end, more rigid, these theories draw a parallel between narrative and the male psychological maturation process or the male sexual experience, creating a formidable dilemma for those interested in changing the system. By assuming linguistic or narrative meaning to be the result of the internal logic of a system which is made more inevitable by its interconnection with psychological development, the only alternative is to posit an entirely different, alternate arena of meaning. Narrative theorists influenced by Freud and Lacan have compared these different organizations to libidinal drives, both male and female. In terms of the narrative trajectory, plot movement is a simulacrum of the sexual act; it moves from an originary nonaroused but desiring state of the narrative's beginning to the complications and false orgasms of the middle to the orgasm and quiescence of the closure. The ease with which narrative tension is explained in terms of erotic tension is second only to the ease with which erotic tension is described in terms of male experience. Peter Brooks's otherwise fine book, *Reading for the Plot,* is such an example. Insisting that the plot is desire working in the narrative, Brooks implicitly identifies this desire as male desire that "should stretch, extend, and project the self" (51) toward an end which then "foreshorten[s]" (52) the self. In another example, Brooks characterizes the middle of the plot as always on the "verge of premature discharge," fueled by "mistaken erotic object choice," of either the " 'Belle Dame sans merci' variety" or the "annihilatory bride" (109). Brooks realizes this male-centered perspective when he acknowledges a difference between female and male plots and claims that the female plot demands "a reinterpretation of the vectors of plot" (39). In neither of Brooks' imagined narrative trajectories is the lesbian logical.

It is to this commonplace presumption of the universality of male psychological experience that the Lacanian French feminists ardently spoke. If the dominant system of meaning is controlled and fashioned by male desire, how can female desire be represented? What is the female libidinal economy and how would it look in writing? How would the "vectors" of the plot change in a woman's writing? But for these French feminists—Cixous, Irigaray, and Kristeva—the answer to these questions resists the lesbian in favor of the maternal alternative. In fact, the difficulty these thinkers have including the lesbian in their theories is the subject of several critical attacks in current queer theory. In the Lacanian theory that the French feminists privilege, the maternal realm is the pre-Oedipal stage of psychological development dominated by the undifferentiated relationship with the mother and is a stage that remains in the subconscious as it does in the subconscious of language. Upon entering the symbolic world in which meaning is ordered by binary oppositions and by gender difference, the subject comes under the law of the father as a split subject, always desiring and never being fulfilled, always seeking presence in language and always being disappointed by deferral. The presence of the maternal exists as the potential for the disruption of the repressive order of the Oedipal. Upon this Lacanian psychological distinction between maternal and paternal realms, the French feminists devise a theory to represent women's writing as an expression of the female's different libidinal drives and body.

The insistence on a unique female sexuality and female imaginary leads several of these thinkers to consider lesbian as a possible alternative image for women's writing, but with mixed results. Cixous, for instance, calls *écriture féminine* the woman's writing at one with her bodily rhythms, a connection at times determined in relationship to another woman. But the primary other woman for Cixous is the mother: "Everything will be changed once woman gives woman to the other woman. There is hidden and always ready in woman the source; the locus for the other. The mother, too, is a metaphor. It is necessary and sufficient that the best of herself be given to woman by another woman for her to be able to love herself and return in love the body that was 'born' to her" (252). As Toril Moi describes Cixous's position, she "presents this nameless pre-Oedipal space filled with mother's milk and honey as the source of the song that resonates through all female writing" (114) and at times, for Cixous, through some male writing. Yet Cixous's description of the woman-to-woman connection draws on a lesbian possibility, for the maternal can be an eroticized space, but she falls short of exploiting its full potential by what Judith Roof calls "Cixous' neutralization of potentially overt lesbian content" (136). Although other writers at this time, including Adrienne Rich, collapsed the maternal and lesbian, Cixous's concentration on the psychological elevates, in the end, the maternal as the dominant image of this pre-Oedipal space.

Kristeva has the most difficulty accommodating lesbian imagery or experience into her theory because she *opposes* the lesbian to the maternal. She does not privilege the relationship of the woman to the pre-Oedipal, and perhaps as a result she, too, relies on the maternal realm, what she calls the semiotic or the chora, as potentially disruptive of the paternal world of the symbolic. She is less able than Cixous or Irigaray to accommodate the lesbian because, as Judith Butler, Judith Roof, and Teresa de Lauretis have recently illustrated, lesbianism in Kristeva's theory is relegated to the psychotic realm. It is not the lesbian, then, but the maternal space that allows women and, especially in Kristeva's view, also men to challenge the patriarchy.

Irigaray's sexual terminology allows the feminine arena to be potentially lesbian rather than simply maternal, although she too relies on the Lacanian divisions of psychological stages and therefore privileges the pre-Oedipal or maternal as the defining context for the lesbian. When Irigaray says in her chapter, "When Our Two Lips Speak Together," "If we keep on speaking the same language together, we're going to reproduce the same history. Begin the same old stories all over again" (*This Sex* 205), she posits the new story on what appears to be the physical and intellectual exchange between two lesbian lovers. While de Lauretis believes that this chapter has been wrongly interpreted as a theory of lesbian sexuality (*Practice* 175), Irigaray's lyrical and rapturous language leads the reader to imagine a female-female sexuality based on a different system of female bodily pleasure: "I love you: body shared, undivided. Neither you nor I severed" (206). Because the woman's body is more multifaceted and less linear, more connective and less separative than the male body, the new writing reflecting female desire must of necessity deploy a total disruption of syntax, chronology, and order, what Cixous calls a song and what Irigaray touts as lyrical chaos: "Turn everything upside down, inside out, back to front. . . . Reinscribe them hither and thither *as divergencies,* otherwise and elsewhere than they are expected, in *ellipses* and *eclipses* that deconstruct the logical grid of the reader-writer, drive him out of his mind" (*Speculum* 142). In narrative terms, then, the lesbian exists only in the lyrical mode of the pre-Oedipal. Because these thinkers too easily accept the male claim that language and narrative are hegemonically male and incapable of female interjection, they create a sometimes mystical world of the feminine. In fact, one of the central problems of paralleling the narrative system to the different psychological maturation processes or sexual experiences of males and females may be that, in its reductive claims, it accepts the given system as inevitably and unalterably male. If, for instance, narrative tension is always about male sexuality, then the female narrative is doomed to the serenity of Charlotte Perkins Gilman's *Herland.* The French Lacanian feminists appear to accept these premises, but even in their reliance on a different and, in some cases, a utopian female space, the image of the maternal overwhelms that of the lesbian as a descriptor of that space. This utopian space allows for only one kind of writing, the experimental and lyrical, because any writing which partakes of the traditional narrative structure will be absorbed into a male libidinal economy. This psycho/sexual approach also allows, but only intermittently, for one positive definition of lesbian—a space of mystical lyricism.

The solutions, then, offered for the didacticism, authoritarianism, and sexism of traditional plot movement are, at times, extreme. If the system is so rigid as to absorb everything in its way, if linearity is never anything but authoritarian, then only radical dissociation will achieve disruption. In this view, time cannot be represented as a causal relationship among elements nor can closure be final. These are the axioms on the basis of which contemporary theory separates interesting literature from normative narratives. The lyrical novel becomes not one possibility among many but the only way to challenge a power-inflected system. The only problem with the demand for a total break from narrative order is that it risks unintelligibility and elitism as well as its own binary thinking; it risks privileging Woolf's experimental writing *The Waves* and ignoring the powerful but more traditional writings of a Dorothy Allison or a Radclyffe Hall. It also risks defining the potential for disruption in only one way, in terms of plot movement and in terms of a radical undermining of the traditional logic of plot movement. But this way of reading narrative and its alternative depends on a stark dualism. Barbara Herrnstein Smith rejects such an inherent dualism arguing that "by virtue of the very nature of discourse, nonlinearity is the rule rather than the exception in narrative accounts" (227). I would argue the opposite. By the very nature of narrative codes, linearity is always presumed and necessary, even in nonlinear texts. Linearity, then, should not be considered the demonized opposite of the lyrical narrative mode; and if so narrative in its traditional form can be stretched to amend itself.

The stark contrasts between linear and nonlinear stories, between the lyrical and the realistic novel, between the normative narrative and a postmodern narrative are, for some, ethnocentric distinctions. As Karl Kroeber notes, contemporary theories of narrative which presume inclusivity and reject realism depend on ignoring non-Western cultures (2). Kroeber argues that the fundamental truth about stories is not their structure but the fact that they are told and retold (8–9). And in the retelling they are changed. The storytelling techniques of native cultures change with retelling in part to fit new social and cultural contexts. For example, Leslie Marmon Silko's *Ceremony* is about such a change. Interspersed in her tale of a young Native American, Tayo, who is nearly destroyed by his participation in World War II, are ancient stories of the Southwestern Native Americans. Silko's story is a re-enactment of the ancient stories, and only by knowing those stories and retelling and reliving them for this age will Tayo—and the reader—be free. In retelling the story, change occurs to accommodate itself to new situations and new questions. Story, then, is a paradox of telling the already told, of changing the already determined. In Trinh T. Minh-ha's words, "the same story has always been changing, for things which do not shift and grow cannot continue to circulate" (123); in Kroeber's words, narrative is a "dynamic interplay of fortuitousness and inevitability" (59). While this approach often denies the idea of narrative as an ideologically defined institution, this paradox allows us to speak of narrative as an institution which is susceptible to change. It also allows us to see the production of multiple narratives as one of the results of retelling the same story. We can, then, acknowledge the institution of narrative which systematically excludes and silences the lesbian and, at the same time, its potential for change through re-enactment.

In an attempt to find a middle ground, feminist critics have imagined other narrative structures which allow for both familiarity and disruption of the plot movement. When feminist theories suggest alternative narrative patterns for heterosexual women's fiction, they often rely on parallels to heterosexual women's experience, especially passive positions of waiting or reacting. Susan S. Lanser argues that because women's plots are often not progressive or linear in a traditional way, theorists need a narrative model that recognizes plots that have, for instance, "a structure of anxiety and (gradual) relief" or simply "waiting, inaction, reception" (356–57). Peter Brooks defines the different narrative trajectory of the "female plot" as "a resistance and what we might call an 'endurance': a waiting (and suffering) until the woman's desire can be a permitted response to the expression of male desire" (330n). By excluding lesbians, Nina Auerbach's important book on women's communities in literature settles on a definition of those communities as "furtive, unofficial, often underground entit[ies]" (11). Circular patterns often represent an alternative narrative movement—or nonmovement—and provide a popular alternative to linearity. Gayle Greene develops the "pattern of circular return" (14) because such a pattern allows enough recognizable linearity to maintain coherence and at the same time provides a substantial critique of its problems (15). But while different plot trajectories substantially question the narrative system's themes, categories of subjectivity must also be perceived as sites of disruption. The restructuring of subject/character relationships or positionalities is as capable of revising narrative thematics as is a lyrical, destablized narrative movement.

Ursula Le Guin's delightful essay on "The Carrier Bag Theory of Fiction" is one example of an awareness of the system that produces narrative's themes and an example of multiple ways that narrative can be interrogated. Le Guin compares two kinds of narrative order and two gendered types of narrative subjectivity. One evolves, she suggests, from the hunters who went out on their heroic quest, came back, and told their linear story: "the proper shape of the narrative is that of the arrow or spear, starting *here* and going straight *there* and THOK! hitting its mark" (*Dancing* 169). It is the story "about bashing, thrusting, raping, killing, about the Hero" (168). Opposed to this story is that of the women and children who gather food in containers, acts that are devoid of thrusting and raping and of stories dependent on a linear and conflictual tension. The most appropriate shape for the novel is "medicine bundle, holding things in a particular, powerful relation to one another and to us" (169). While this description of the novel depends on the plot movement, it also provides distinctly different narrative subject positions. Near the time in which she writes this essay, Le Guin also writes a novel, *Always Coming Home,* that includes more formal experimentation than she usually allowed herself. Because Le Guin is noted for her brilliant storytelling, her intelligible sentences, and her linear stories, her medicine bundle is not the abandonment of linearity but its periodic disruption, not the destabilization of identity but its redirection. This narrative playfulness with what DuPlessis calls the "habits of narrative order" (34) is overshadowed by her experimental repositioning of the central female character, Stone Telling. Le Guin tells her character's primary story in three sections, interrupted by a long sequence of short stories and poems, each with its own linear structure but juxtaposed to one another in a nonsequential fashion. This story displays Le Guin's usual mastery of narrative tension, a fact which encourages many readers to skip the intervening sections in order to finish, first, Stone Telling's story. She begins her story in the alternative, matrifocal community which orders itself around seasonal, ritual dances. When her foreign father returns, Stone Telling is seduced by his power and love into following him to the warrior culture of the Condors. This culture exaggerates the dualisms that inform the patriarchal system. In an exciting escape and journey home with her daughter and friend/servant, the heroine leaves that gendered, hierarchical society to return to the more egalitarian society of her birth. Stone Telling's journey repositions her relationship to men, but not through a change of sexuality, for there is no question about her heterosexuality. Thus, while Stone Telling's story ends with marriage, it does so as an afterthought rather than as a climactic triumph. Consider her ruminations: "My mothers had not been very good at being married, and I had already had one husband whom I had left without a word or a thought. Alder and I certainly got along well, and by marrying me he could leave his creditors in Chumo fairly and start fresh at the Doctors Lodge in Sinshan. That was a good reason for marrying" (373). The lack of passion affords a different narrative tension and closure, for without a drive toward the closure of marriage, the narrative tension must exist elsewhere. Thus, while contemporary theory privileges plot movement and therefore its disruptions, the study of women's and lesbian texts also demands attention to the categories of subjectivity. In fact, these character and narrator functions must be included, if not privileged, as sites of disruption which loosen the ideological narrative pattern. From this perspective, de Lauretis's separation of male and female narrative functions from the character or text image ultimately tightens rather than loosens the narrative categories of subjectivity. In using Freud to define the narrative as Oedipal, de Lauretis places into narrative Freud's limitations, his assumption that only the male has a libido. "And so her story, like any other story, is a question of his desire" (*Alice* 133). Under this system, the alternatives for a woman in the narrative are pallid. As Jackie Stacey claims of the similarly restrictive feminist psychological theories of Laura Mulvey, women are left with three "frustrating options of masculinisation, masochism or marginality" (120). In this heterosexual positioning, according to de Lauretis, the small place reserved for a female libido is absorbed into a notion of duplicity as the only valid point from which the woman can enter and disrupt this narrative scheme, for the "real task is to enact the contradiction of female desire" (*Alice* 156). In her extreme separation of character image from narrative function, de Lauretis leaves for the critic the almost impossible task of justifying a female protagonist, just as Judith Roof in *A Lure of Knowledge* leaves for the same critic the similarly impossible task of justifying a centrally placed lesbian character.

In her recent discussion of lesbian sexuality, de Lauretis suggests a less rigid view of narrative structure (*Practice 130*), although this current book is not devoted to narrative theory. We can determine an intermediary position by striking a middle course between de Lauretis's early theory of active and passive narrative spaces and Mieke Bal's analysis of the neutrality of the narrative system. In a primer text on narratology, *Narratology: Introduction to the Theory of Narrative*, Bal is aware of the gender implications of narrative while not making this the direct point of her book; but unlike de Lauretis, Bal assumes that the system at its most basic level, as fabula, is ideologically free. For example, she reverses the gender roles in a number of her examples, indicating with some humor in a scientifically rigorous book that role reversal is easily possible. In a number of explanatory scenarios, Bal places "John," narratology's ubiquitous subject/actant, in strange plots: "John was pushing his shopping cart when he suddenly saw his hated neighbour at the check-out counter" (43) and "Sobbing, John sat on his neighbour's couch, pouring out his woes. 'I didn't know, when I married Mary five years ago, that she would sacrifice everything to her work' " (57). Bal, however, goes further than mere role reversal to make her point; in fact, she redefines the active and passive narrative functions. In discussing the power that the plot allots to the active figure and the receiver of action, Bal claims: "Seen grammatically, the active subject is passive in his role of receiver" and "the passive object is also subject, and therefore more autonomous." Therefore, inverting the roles should "give no reason for the 'he' to panic" (29). Perhaps overstating her case, she argues for an equalization of power in the two central narrative positions, while also acknowledging that "he" expects to be the sole possessor of power. While she acknowledges that the position of agency traditionally is a male and not a female province (83), in general the narrative system as system—as fabula—does not contain the ideological determinations that make de Lauretis's version a virtual straightjacket. What I intend to suggest is that, while de Lauretis accurately genders the traditional narrative system on its most basic level, those gendered positions are capable of reformation, capable of the power exchange that Bal indicates because characters, by virtue of different structural alignments with one another, revise the ideology embedded in the traditional narrative system.

If the text image informs and challenges the narrative structure, then the possibility exists that characters and narrators can loosen the plot system. As I briefly noted earlier, *Aliens* is a particularly blatant example of the problems inherent in these theoretical disagreements. Many feminists see Sigourney Weaver's Ripley in the film as a feminist heroine whose heroic exploits make her the equal of any male science fiction hero. Ripley does what any male hero would do: use fire power, stay emotionally distant, enter the cave of the engulfing and dangerous monster and (almost) destroy it in a violent closure. Without taking into account narrative as a gendered system of meaning, this approach hails Ripley as the new liberated female character. But from another perspective, this movie reinstitutes the positioning of "woman" not as hero but as, once again, the monster to be overcome. Ripley steps into a male narrative position and enacts the traditional heroic male quest, thereby underscoring rather than challenging its values. The alien becomes the identifiable female boundary space whose rampant reproductivity threatens humans because the ugly and dangerous half-birthed monsters need a second, a human, "womb" to mature, a process that kills the human in an horrific birth. Ripley attains the status of hero by killing the female-as-alien, thereby confirming her male positioning toward the female. At the same time she is not simply absorbed by the system's gender function but rather modifies it as well, albeit in miniscule ways. In order to justify violence in the hands of a woman, Ripley is given a child to protect. In this nurturing act, Ripley is separated from the other woman on the voyage, the macha Vasquez, whose stereotypical lesbian characteristics make her, in the movie's homophobic humor, more a man than most of the male soldiers. Motherhood, of course, is a stereotypical way to assign strength to women and thereby to justify traditional male heroic characteristics that ascribe to the protagonist agency and violence. At the same time, this role redesigns elements of the viewers' expectations of heroism, stretching it to accommodate female agency. But more problematic as well as more potentially disruptive is Ripley's sexual positioning. The narrative system demands the heterosexual positioning of the female character, even in the pseudo-heterosexual plots of male bonding. The film refuses Ripley a love affair because that would immediately position her as the object of desire, against which the character would have to struggle to maintain her autonomy. Again this characteristic works in two ways, pulling Ripley into the heterosexual system by denying the concurrence of female desire and female agency but also allowing a female text image to control her own sexuality. The ultimate problem, however, is that Ripley is not realigned with anyone else. Thus she is neither totally absorbed by the narrative structure nor does she fully recode it.

The narrative system, even on this simple level of adventure tension, is neither impenetrably nor tyrannically "his" story. If, as Peter Brooks suggests, the dynamics of the plot are related as abstract form and text image (25), character and abstract function qualify one another and ultimately affect plot movement. In his study of recent trends in narrative theory, Wallace Martin also notes a contemporary movement in that direction: "Even theorists who formerly reduced characters to 'actants,' defining them only as byproducts of the functions they performed, have come to recognize that ignorance and knowledge, vested in character as an independent entity, are crucial to an understanding of narrative structure" (117). From this perspective, it is not insignificant that the heroic figure of *Aliens* is female nor is it inconsequential, as Peter J. Rabinowitz proves, that a woman detective, Sue Grafton's Kinsey Millhone, invades the hard-boiled, male-defined genre of detective fiction (331). Theory must accommodate the interrelationship of the abstract narrative level and the particular manifestations in a story, a position, I believe, that refuses to separate so starkly postmodern from thematic readings. It is the tension between the ideologically determined traditional narrative rules, along with subsequent reader expectations, and the particular woman or lesbian who occupies this space that creates the energy in contemporary narratives by women and lesbians. The tension between function and the character permits disruption and a shift in the narrative paradigm itself; for the woman, and especially the lesbian, is by definition a figure marginal to society where the male is always, even in his rebellion, a representative of the culture's values (Edwards 7–9). Thus, when a woman occupies the space of the hero or lover she is differently aligned to power but not necessarily either devoid of it nor necessarily absorbed by the maleness of the binary structure. Neither Atwood nor Sexton successfully imagines what this position might be, but both writers sense that it is necessary to imagine this place for women. The writers of the lesbian narratives of the last twenty-five years, however, have imagined what this position might look like.

How, then, can we think about a lesbian narrative when systematic descriptions of narrative patterns, especially those aware of the gender implications, suggest the hegemony of not only male heterosexual but also of male homosexual/homosocial desire and offer as alternatives plots which rely on heterosexual women's experience and a narrative position related to men? How would a lesbian narrative function as an alternative narrative model? Literary critics of the last twenty-five years have more often provided thematic rather than structural alternatives. Catharine R. Stimpson proposed what has become the classic division of lesbian narratives into "the dying fall, a narrative of damnation . . . and the enabling escape, a narrative of the reversal of such descending trajectories" ("Zero" 244). To these distinctions Terry Castle adds the division between the " 'dysphoric' " story—"female homosexual desire as a finite phenomenon—a temporary phase in a larger pattern of heterosexual *Bildung*"—or the " 'euphoric' " story in which a "new world is imagined in which male bonding has no place" (85–86). On that last description hangs lesbian theory's clearest alternative structural paradigm. Castle proposes that we think of lesbian narratives as "counterplotting" (82). Using Sedgwick's triangle of male-female-male relationships as the master plot, Castle suggests that lesbian novels plot against the normal paradigm by first subverting that triangle with a female-male-female triangle and then by eliminating the male middle. The result is fiction that always has "a profoundly attenuated relationship with what we think of, stereotypically, as narrative verisimilitude, plausibility, or 'truth to life' " (88). While Castle's theory unveils sameness as one structural element in lesbian narratives, Toni A. H. McNaron isolates it as the central dynamic of lesbian literature. In an essay entitled "Mirrors and Likeness: A Lesbian Aesthetic in the Making," McNaron claims that "sexual likeness or mirroring" provides an "alternative aesthetic to the thrust and parry, sticks and bowls school" traditionally favored (305). The subject-other dynamic of language and literature can then be reread in Penelope J. Engelbrecht's terms as "the inter/action of a lesbian Subject and a lesbian Other/self," a relationship in which the two terms "are more than interchangeable; they are synonymous" (86). But McNaron refuses to accept the reduction of sameness to blandness, sexual or aesthetic; in fact, she claims that when "liking is based on likeness . . . , the connection often becomes electric" (294). The resulting literature is not without an aesthetic or narrative tension, but its movement mitigates the oppositional polemics of gender division and, as Mieke Bal illustrates, highlights the narrative's potential to distribute power more evenly. Thus both critics point to structural relationships among characters as central to the narrative's rules and the revisioning of these structural relationships as central to a lesbian narrative.

While my definition of the lesbian narrative depends on both of these astute suggestions, it also attempts to combine and extend the parameters of each. Sameness is differently structured in gay male writing than in lesbian writing, and is not to be equated with identity or with a unitary subject. Sameness is determined by positioning, by a direction rather than by identical somatic or psychic characteristics, and this similar positioning also assumes a doubled positionality of desired/desiring and active/passive wherein each character occupies either both positions at the same time or at different times. Terry Castle's reworking of Sedgwick is seductive, but lesbian counterplotting is not only the elimination of the male figure but also a complex readjustment of male characters. However important the elimination of male bonding or male figures may be to primarily white, lesbian narratives, for women of color the elimination of the male often threatens racial unity, even in their construction of the lesbian subject. More important, because Sedgwick's paradigm exists in conjunction with the heterosexually mandated mechanics of narrative, those gendered positionalities that reside in the interaction of a character and its abstract narrative space, excising a male character from the text does not necessarily change the gendered structure of narrative or, what might be called in a less formalist manner, the reader's expectations about active and passive narrative functions. In fact, as Jeanette Winterson proves in *Sexing the Cherry,* it should be possible to position a male character in a lesbian text that revolutionizes narrative mechanics. Finally, while both Castle and McNaron make possible a reading of the lesbian subject as a metaphor, McNaron creating more potential than Castle, neither emphasizes that as the centerpiece of her theory. It is at this point that my theory of the lesbian narrative begins.

In any definition of a lesbian narrative, the first problem is to explain the various meanings attached to the term "lesbian" and then to construe the resulting possibilities for the lesbian subject in narrative. The narrativized lesbian is not simply a given—a character whose sexuality is obvious or hinted at or even a coded image of two intensely involved women friends—rather, it is a trope, developed in the twentieth century and especially in the last twenty-five years, that functions in a variety of literal and nonliteral ways. This figure, which can function as a single character, as a couple, or as a community, is gendered female, but an excessive or grotesque female because by refusing to position itself in opposition to the male, it exceeds cultural and narrative boundaries. The lesbian subject's gendered excess implies that it is perceived as an ambiguously gendered figure—one that occupies both active and passive positions at the same time or crosses these boundaries. But the narrative consistently attempts to force this figure into recognizable gender categories. If, for instance, a male remains in a traditional story, the narrative—or the reader—will attempt to force the female figure into the narrative space of subordination. Thus the film *Aliens* refuses to allow Ripley to fall in love because she would lose her agency under those circumstances. Like Queen Elizabeth I, who knew that she would lose her power if she were to heed Parliament's directives for her to marry, the writers of this film know instinctively that a love relationship for Ripley will make her less than the actor and protagonist of the story. The lesbian subject, however, is a text image that refuses to align itself with the gendered mechanics and instead challenges those mechanics for its own narrative space, a lesbian narrative space. Because narrative space is, in effect, the structural function of narrative elements, lesbian narrative space is the combination and interchangeability of the conventional active and passive functions that have been strictly divided into male and female and, most often, male and female characters. As a result, the lesbian subject realigns some of the accepted narrative categories, particularly those of protagonist and object, narrator, and closure. In other words, the lesbian subject redraws the gender boundaries in the narrative categories in which subjectivity is posited. The narrative system, then, is unavoidable, but also can be stretched to accommodate different power relations. This approach, I believe, will make easier the identification as lesbian texts that do not contain specific lesbian characters, themes, or lesbian authors and yet not exclude more traditionally defined lesbian narratives.

As an interloper in narrative, the lesbian subject must take on the existing structure, function within some of its parameters, yet question its movement and arrangement of subject positions. This interrogation happens first, when female bonding breaks up male bonding, realigning any remaining male characters; second, when the asymmetrical structural patterns of active agent and passive object are revised by the structural interjection of sameness; and finally, when these changes on a structural level affect the movement and thematics of the traditional narrative. One technique, for instance, that affects these shifts is multiple plots or voices. As Susan S. Lanser notes, "polyphony is more pronounced and more consequential in women's narratives and in the narratives of other dominated peoples" (350). Multiple plots or voices heighten our awareness of the arbitrariness of the traditional plot by either imitating it, or parodying it, or referring obliquely to it, or recalling it through images. It is as if the story is instead a series of stories, telling and retelling itself. These counterplots often occur in the multiple voices of the narrators who direct the story's internal strategy. It is not, then, linearity that is poison to a lesbian subject and therefore to the lesbian narrative, but the lack of structural realignments that in turn affect the narrative thematics. Only when a lesbian character does not effect structural change and is consequently absorbed into a single, linear trajectory does the traditional narrative triumph. The lesbian figure who does realign structural categories is the lesbian subject who represents more than transparent literalness.

THREE

The Lesbian Subject: A War of Images

The lesbian is the heroine of modernism.
—Walter Benjamin, *Charles Baudelaire*

The lesbian is a mental energy which gives breath and meaning to the most positive of images a woman can have of herself.   —Nicole Brossard, *The Aerial Letter*

For it is always finally unclear what is meant by invoking the lesbian-signifier.   —Judith Butler, "Imitation and Gender Insubordination"

In the last one hundred years, three critical moments of theorizing the lesbian subject have put this category into discursive circulation. For some critics, these three moments constitute a progressive narrative. The story goes something like this. In the late nineteenth and early twentieth centuries, male sexologists such as Richard von Krafft-Ebing and Havelock Ellis gained control of the definition of lesbian. From their male and heterosexual perspective, the lesbian was a woman trying to be a man. According to Esther Newton, Ellis understood female desire outside of male control or presence only in terms of "fusing inversion and masculinity" (288). In this paradigm the lesbian is the usurper of male prerogatives; in fact, Carroll Smith-Rosenberg contends that Krafft-Ebing's lesbians "seemed to desire male privileges and power as ardently as, perhaps more ardently than, they sexually desired women" (270). Stephen in *The Well of Loneliness* is merely the outcome of this construction of what Newton calls the "Mythic Mannish Lesbian" (281). Well-situated within the economy of sexual difference, the figure of the lesbian as abnormally male was not a challenge so much as a reinforcement of the sex-gender system. The lesbian writers of the 1920s and 1930s struggled against this myth, sometimes inscribing it as did Radclyffe Hall and sometimes challenging it as Virginia Woolf did in *Orlando*. In this definition, argue some theorists, lesbian as a discursive structure remained firmly entrenched in the system of sexual difference.

In the 1970s, the next great period of theorizing lesbian, lesbian-feminists like Adrienne Rich, Judy Grahn, and Audre Lorde refigured lesbian as woman, as autonomous female desire and agency. The lesbian is not any woman but The Woman because, as Judy Grahn claimed, lesbian is "by extension, every woman" (*Highest* 41). Adrienne Rich, for example, inclusively defined as lesbian the "primary intensity between and among women, including the sharing of a rich inner life, the bonding against male tyranny, the giving and receiving of practical and political support" ("Compulsory" 648–49). Because sexuality and the body had, in the first wave of definitions, been used against the lesbian, limiting her to a masculine sexuality, the 1970s definition of the lesbian erotic often transcended, some would say ignored, the sexual body. At the same time, this perspective produced powerful poetic descriptions of a more inclusive eroticism. Audre Lorde wrote the classic definition: "When I speak of the erotic, then, I speak of it as an assertion of the lifeforce of women; of that creative energy empowered, the knowledge and use of which we are now reclaiming in our language, our history, our dancing, our loving, our work, our lives" (*Sister* 55). Lesbian was a utopian, nonbodily category of sameness, a category of meaning to which any woman could potentially subscribe and which could fully represent what it is to be a woman emotionally and spiritually. This position, it is argued today, replicates the oppositional thinking that defines woman in terms of man because it retains the term and the male-defined concept of woman.

The last step in these three moments of theorizing lesbian—a step that the proponents ironically idealize as the liberatory goal of a progressive narrative—is postmodernism, specifically, queer theory. Emerging from certain elements of French feminist thinking in the works of Hélène Cixous, Luce Irigaray, and the Marxist, Monique Wittig, the postmodernists define lesbian as a figure beyond the phallocentric categories of gender. Teresa de Lauretis uses phrases like "obliterate the boundaries of gender identity" ("Sexual" 159) and "does not deny gender or sex but transcends them" (164) to describe Gertrude Stein and Audre Lorde respectively. The body or sexuality, symbolically extended to clothing, becomes lesbian as the site of difference, rather than sameness. Sue-Ellen Case's influential essay on the butch-femme couple depicts the effect of the re-presentation of heterosexual roles as "the camp space of irony and wit, free from biological determinism, elitist essentialism, and the heterosexist cleavage of sexual difference" ("Toward" 298). Mere Sexual difference is by definition a heterosexual system that must be transcended or it becomes a trap. Thus Nina Rapi speaks of the lesbian as "someone who out of necessity invents herself, fashioning a self in those in-between spaces of the dominant order that have escaped categorization" (148). This position denies gender as a category for understanding the lesbian, dismisses much of feminism as a theory reliant on and therefore subservient to sexual difference, and trumpets gay male camp, irony, performance, and self-invention as the logical stance for lesbians. In this refashioning, lesbian is aligned with gay men rather than other women, especially not with straight women.

As with most summaries, this one is too simple; but, at the same time, the distinctions that I have drawn are often made in this stark fashion. As noted earlier, the successive rereadings of any text—lesbian as a category of meaning is such a text—can repair the myopia of an earlier generation. It can also display its own myopia. Such is the current situation. Current theory's concern with transcending gender is an understandable one and, in some ways, a necessary critique of the previous generation's acceptance of an abstract gender identity devoid of other differences like race, class, and ethnicity. Because of the earlier problematically vague use of the "universal woman," queer theory insists on incorporating a *wider play of differences* in conceptions such as multiple subject positions. High theory is not the only place where this revision takes place. In a reversal of her previous concentration on women's and lesbians' oppression, Adrienne Rich's second collection of prose essays, *Blood, Bread, and Poetry,* calls for a recognition of the "simultaneity of oppressions" (xii) and of the need for a "Politics of Location" (210). More recently, Gloria Anzaldúa constructs an image of the multiple subject, the "new mestiza," based on the woman of color's multiple alliances. As these writers argue, disruption, not re-enforcement, of this patriarchal system must be what lesbian theory proposes, advocates, and disposes.

But while continental thinking of the French feminists, relying on the male precursors of postmodernism like Derrida and Lacan, forges an understanding of the systematic nature of oppression and its entrenchment and reinscription in textual systems, at the same time this theory assumes that the system—textual and social—is a prison house that necessitates as the only alternative a transcendent space of the free play of signifiers. Torley on gender means to remain in that prison house and to repeat the enlightenment philosophies of universality and presence. But such a position also contains contradictions. In her discussion of lesbian-feminism's anti-pornography stance in the "sex-wars" of the 1980s, Elizabeth Meese rightly encourages a more complex consideration of power, difference, and inequality in lesbian relationships. Like other contemporary lesbian theorists, Meese considers sadomasochism a liberatory rather than oppressive sexual trope and practice, not a re-inscription of patriarchal gender categories and dualisms. Sadomasochism symbolizes a more flexible if not indeterminant series of " 'cross-identification[s]' " (*(Sem)Erotics* 110). In other words, s/m confounds the simple subject/object dichotomy of gender prescription. Meese is also aware of potential problems in re-enacting power relationships: "the use of Nazi paraphernalia, recalling the Holocaust; slave/master terminology" which reminds all of "the racial crimes of slavery" (120). But while she is aware of gender-controlled positions such as woman/masochism, she is less willing to condemn them (109).

Gender is a category of interpretation, I believe, that must be affirmed despite the current theoretical climate which posits as ideal the escape from the binary system on which gender difference and heterosexuality depend. Arguing that the lesbian subject is a metaphor for female agency and female desire places this trope in a dual position that demands a delicate balance between freedom from all categories, whether immediate or in the future, and a static, stabilized category which has only served those in power. Without the conscious and strategic use of gender or indeed categorization as a measure of interpretation, we will be oppressed by it. If theory does not include gender in its discussions, it will construct, as I believe has already happened in the fascinating but problematic tomes of Marjorie Garber and Wayne Koestenbaum, another universal male subject, more likely today to be the universal gay male subject. The current theoretical interest in gay male subjectivity is, as it should be, a reaction to the AIDS crisis that has foregrounded gay male sexuality and oppression. The result is both extraordinary analyses of culture such as Eve Kosofsky Sedgwick's *Epistemology of the Closet* in which she posits twentieth-century structures of knowledge at the site of the "chronic, now endemic crisis of homo/heterosexual definition, indicatively male" (1) and an erasure of lesbians and the feminist subject. Lesbians can be ignored when gender is no longer a primary category of analysis. Jacquelyn N. Zita's apt image of current queer theory as "another unhappy marriage" ("Gay" 259) highlights the hidden gender structure of a theory which purports to transcend gender. Desire and gender cannot be arbitrarily related in a world in which power is unevenly distributed. The lesbian subject I describe in the following pages has been created throughout the twentieth century in relation to "woman" and must be analyzed not as an escape from gender but as a challenge to this *traditional* category of gender.

But gender must be analyzed not as a quality but as a positionality. The new lesbian subject position is no longer in relationship to men through asymmetrical difference but in a relationship of sameness, not identity, with other women. Imagine, as Zita does in another essay, "Desire uncoded by adjustments to a male body" ("Lesbian" 334). That is the repositioned lesbian subject. In Linda Alcoff's terms, the "subject as positionality" allows gender a directional rather than an ontological status, for woman is "defined not by a particular set of attributes but by a particular position" (433). In her interpretation of Alcoff's theory, de Lauretis focuses on the difference between internal and external elements as constitutive of gender, allowing gender to exist as a category dependent on women's "sociohistorical location, whereas essentialist definitions would have woman's identity or attributes independent of her external situation" ("Essence" 11). But positionality cannot be totally arbitrary, conditioned only by external elements. The body, however one argues for its constructedness, is more than a surface created by social forces. Instead of functioning as the surface rather than the ground of constructedness, anatomical bodies must be taken seriously. Bodies matter, for it is not arbitrary that social and even physical construction posits bodily females in one positionality and bodily males in another. While many of the characteristics of our bodies are the result of the social mapping that proscribes and inscribes bodily rules, and while it is difficult to tell where that mapping begins and ends, it is in my mind a *reductio ad absurdum* to conclude that nothing remains as the ground on which society constructs its sexual, gender, racial, and class rules. Thus, while positionality is essential to the definition of the lesbian subject, and that positionality is determined in relationship to the gendered positionality of woman, the female body is the ground rather than the surface of these positionings. While males can, in different ways, occupy a female position, they do so differently and with different results from females. When I speak of lesbians, then, I speak of women.

Therefore, I would like to see the possibility of imagining each historical version of the lesbian subject, including postmodernism's, as stretching or realigning gender boundaries as an alternative to the genderless indeterminacy that is idealized in queer theory. The lesbian subject problematizes woman not by denying it in a puff of undecidablity or infinite play but by repositioning it as an excess which disputes the traditional binary gendered positionalities. As the hero of a mini-narrative that challenges the gender system, each version of the lesbian subject realigns the structural position that has forced woman into an oppositional relationship with man. From this perspective, I intend to reread the preceding progressive narrative as a series of moments of theoretical insight into the notion of the lesbian subject, as a series of insights which play off rather than displace one another. The mannish lesbian, the woman-as-lesbian/lesbian-as-woman, and the performative body/desire of the queer theory's lesbian subject are all responses to the initial negative narratives of the sexologists. They share important elements as well as rewrite each other. Thus, instead of one historical construction of lesbian being essentialist and another nonessentialist, I will argue that each historical definition of the lesbian subject enacts what Paul Smith in his characterization of current feminist debates calls a "double-play," a simultaneous deployment of both a fixed subject *and* a decentered subject (151). Diana Fuss contends similarly "that essentialism underwrites theories of constructionism and that constructionism operates as a more sophisticated form of essentialism" (119). Each construction of the lesbian subject, I argue, oscillates between sameness and differences, utopian essentialism and deconstructive nonessentialism, and woman and not-woman. The first two moments of defining the lesbian subject, then, cannot be reduced merely to Irigaray's the *"same re-marking itself"* (*Speculum* 21) and the last to theoretical salvation. The second story of the development of the lesbian subject begins with Virginia Woolf.

In the space of one year, Virginia Woolf published two works that focused on androgyny, *Orlando* and *A Room of One's Own*. In androgyny she found a way to encode lesbianism—then termed sapphism—as a response to contemporary arguments over homosexuality and gender identity. In response to the sexologists' construction of the lesbian subject, Woolf writes the mannish lesbian as both a utopian and a deconstructive figure. In the first instance, Woolf writes the dazzling fantasy of *Orlando* for her lover, Vita Sackville-West—"a biography beginning in the year 1500 & continuing to the present day, called Orlando: Vita;

only with a change about from one sex to another" (*Diary* 161). As Rachel Blau DuPlessis claims, it is in the androgyny of this text that "lesbianism is the unspoken contraband desire" (63). Like the other writing project Woolf discusses in her diary at this time—a fantasy about the ladies of Llangollen—*Orlando* is a work in which "Sapphism is to be suggested" (131). Woolf relishes the combination of male and female elements that makes up Vita's physical as well as mental character. Orlando's body, her physical sex, and her gender-ambiguous as well as gender-specific clothing are at the center of Woolf's parody and satire of the rigidity of gender boundaries.

The second book, published in 1929, seems an entirely different enterprise. Taken from lectures she gave at two women's colleges, Newnham and Girton, *A Room* became the bible of the early feminist literary movement. At first considered a plea to all writers to write not from a gendered perspective but from a transcendence of it, *A Room* has become whatever the current critic wants to exact from it. Androgyny is the sticking point of any interpretation. On the surface, Woolf displays relief when she turns to make the argument for androgyny near the end of her humorous and agonizing exploration of women and writing. Women write too often from anger, men from ego, Woolf says. When we become "man-womanly, and conversely . . . woman-manly" (*Room* 102), those "grudges and spites and antipathies" (58) will disappear into the "incandescent" art of a Shakespeare and an Austen (58). Instead of mocking rigid boundaries, this view of androgyny depends on a clear sense of what is male and what is female. This mental marriage of the two genders, states Woolf, follows from what Coleridge meant "when he said that a great mind is androgynous. It is when this fusion takes place that the mind is fully fertilised and uses all its faculties" (102). Although in the era in which these books were written, "lesbianism remained almost literally unspeakable" (Rosenman 639), the homosexual dimension of this book is not absent, although less commonly recognized than in *Orlando*. When, in her diary, she movingly anticipates the reception this book will have among her colleagues and in the press, she declares that "I shall be attacked for a feminist & hinted at for a sapphist" (*Diary* 262). Jane Marcus's historical reading makes this sapphism more apparent, for *A Room*, she argues, is not only an indirect defense of Radclyffe Hall, whose *Well of Loneliness* was on trial in 1928, but also a love letter to Vita: "Much of *A Room* was meant simply to convert her beloved Vita to feminism, its seductive tone an extension of her love letters" (167). As two love letters to Vita, *Orlando* and *A Room* participate in the developing discourse on homosexuality and feminism that had started in the late nineteenth century. These two books inscribe the nascent lesbian subject in two separate but interrelated metaphoric forms: the utopian, nonbodily figure and the bodily, often parodic, figure.

Since the 1960s, literary critics and theorists have debated androgyny's relation to gender and to sexuality in these two texts. Because androgyny can be interpreted as liberating or constricting, as feminist or anti-feminist, as pro-homosexual or homophobic, Woolf's notion of androgyny in these two books is not universally accepted as a code word for homosexual or as a feminist concept. Opinions range from Carolyn Heilbrun's separation of androgyny and homosexuality (118) to Barbara Fassler's contention that, for the Bloomsbury circle, androgyny connoted homosexuality (246), from Carroll Smith-Rosenberg's reading of androgyny in the early twentieth century as primarily a feminist ideal (276) to Elaine Showalter's reading of it in *A Room* as an "escape from the confrontation with femaleness or maleness" (*Literature* 289). Woolf, to confuse the issue, appears to advocate two divergent concepts of androgyny: either a mixture of two distinct, gendered categories, or a playful disruption of their arbitrary hegemony. I believe that Woolf does both. Woolf presents androgyny simultaneously as heterogeneity and as a combination of fixed gender characteristics, as a utopian category and as a refusal of categorization. By maintaining this combination, Woolf is careful not to deconstruct gender to the point where her feminism turns obsolete.

Androgyny was a problematic term, variously related to gender and homosexuality, before Woolf approached it. Androgyny's long history, beginning at least with Plato's *Symposium,* has many surprises, most particularly its non-neutrality. As I have detailed in previous essays (1975; 1988), androgyny is a term which usually functions to appropriate, with approbation, the feminine to the masculine, but refuses the alternative. It has been a term that, in the words of the title to Kari Weil's recent book on androgyny, encodes a *Denial of Difference.* The stereotypical and hierarchical relationship between the two terms male and female reflects a version of heterosexual coupling. This evaluative and hierarchical structure of its binary content means that androgyny is a more positive ideal for men than for women. The nineteenth century's renewed interest in androgyny did not challenge the relative values associated with the two gender codes; female is still associated with emotion, intuition, darkness and male with reason, light, control. Androgyny remains a way for the male to come in touch with his creative self. Carl Jung embraces this perspective when he claims that a man in touch with his anima opens to his creative side, but the female in touch with her animus becomes an opinionated woman (218). It is no wonder that after an initial flirtation with androgyny, the present feminist movement rejected the idea because, in the words of Adrienne Rich, "The very structure of the word replicates the sexual dichotomy and the priority of *andros* (male) over *gyne* (female)" (*Of Woman* 77n). The more recent revival of interest in the idea coincides with both French feminism's and queer theory's definition of androgyny as the profound disturbance of gender categories, a space that challenges the boundaries that parcel out human characteristics, including physical, to male and female. Weil, in fact, carefully distinguishes between the hermaphrodite and the androgyne, privileging the hermaphrodite over the androgyne because the former figure "reveals both the instability of boundaries between categories of opposition such as masculine and feminine, and the self-serving function of their illusory symmetry" (12); the androgyne, on the other hand, partakes of the binary gender system as "a figure of unmediated expression and projected fullness" (12). Perhaps one of the sources for postmodernism's emphasis on gender undecidability is Plato himself. In the *Symposium*, Aristophanes' famous story of androgyny does not rest on a simple binary system. In his fantastical story, Aristophanes describes the original sexes as not two but three, including an hermaphrodite, the figure that will, ironically, be separated to create heterosexual attraction. When Zeus breaks each of the three figures in two as a punishment for presumption, each half continues to look for its other half, leaving some women looking for men, some for other women, and some men looking for other men (543–44). The homosexual implications of androgyny are, therefore, present from the beginning of Western thought, and it is not unusual to have those implications in the background if not the foreground of any definition. In speaking of the lesbian aesthetic of the theater, for example, Nina Rapi includes androgyny along with the butch-femme couple as a means of " *'distancing' role from 'essential being', and 'woman' and 'man', the social constructs, from male and female, the biological entities*" (157). Wayne Koestenbaum does not hesitate to suggest the androgyne as the analogue if not substitute for the homosexual (218). As we shall see later, the connection of androgyny and homosexuality also comes to the fore in the theories of the sexologists like Havelock Ellis and Richard von Krafft-Ebing.

The contemporary concern to disturb gender with terms like androgyny or homosexual is often dismissive of the gender implications of these moves. Some theorists assume that, by going beyond gender in the play of signifiers, gender discussion is no longer applicable. This position is neither indicative of Woolf's strategy concerning androgyny nor helpful in articulating the full range of contemporary meaning surrounding the lesbian subject. Marjorie Garber's brilliant discussion of the transvestite is a case in point. Although her interest is not in androgyny or homosexuality, her description of transvestism is a contemporary effort to theorize a space free from gender decidability. She employs the same ideas associated with postmodern elaborations of androgyy and homosexuality, although she distinguishes the transvestite from the "instantiated 'blurred' sex as signified by a term like 'androgyne' or 'hermaphrodite' " (11) and considers the homosexual less radical than the transvestite as a challenge to the binary gender system (132–33). Garber argues that transvestism is the " 'third,' " (11), a *"space of possibility structuring and confounding culture"* (17), a description reminiscent of queer theory's insistence that the homosexual occupies this privileged position. Such arguments claim that rather than repeating the same patriarchal binary system, the subject positions of the homosexual or transvestite stir up differences.

While Garber is well aware of gender difference and of sexism, she insists that critics' attempts to read gender into the transvestite neutralize the disturbing quality of its undecidability. Weil dismisses the androgyne because it renegotiates a place along society's gender boundaries and therefore, like the gender system, privileges the male. But she is particularly aware of her paradoxical dilemma: "a feminist who is wary of essentialism, but [who] wishes to speak as a woman" (159). A feminism that is wary of essentialism and that privileges gender undecidability risks not being able to speak its feminism; in fact, it risks its own version of re-marking the same by not acknowledging gender difference.

The refusal to invoke an overtly feminist analysis leaves unsolved problems. The hidden universal male subject is one of them. When Garber argues that all fetishistic performance is predicated on the "ownership of desire," whether it is the woman "who lacks the penis but 'has' the phallus" or the man who having the phallus has "the fetish," the point of reference is the phallus or "No one has the phallus" (120). Like Lacan's similar assertion, this position uncritically leaves the male subject as the point of reference for this new "third" when in fact anatomically and culturally constructed males and females are differently related to "no one having the phallus." But the mixing of gender characteristics was, for Woolf's era, a profoundly feminist and sometimes lesbian issue. Disturbing gender boundaries did not erase gender awareness or feminism. The androgynous cross-dressing of the early twentieth century, as Sandra Gilbert and Susan Gubar explain, constitutes a strong feminist statement, "for it implies that no one, male or female, can or should be confined to a uni-form, a single form or self" (*No Man's* 332). Women's revisionary cross-dressing signifies liberation because women who dress as men occupy a charged cultural space that challenges male authority. But because women's and men's clothing have different evaluative connotations, men who dress as women do not occupy the same cultural space. Thus Carroll Smith-Rosenberg argues that women writers of the 1920s and 1930s "deliberately transposed the male sexual metaphors [of the Mannish Lesbian] into a feminist language" of androgyny, using as their feminist ideal the same image that men had used to negate the New Woman as lesbian (276).

At the same time that Woolf's depiction of androgyny partakes of the feminism of her time, it is also a part of the contemporary debate about the dual nature of the homosexual. Karla Jay points to the interest in androgyny of some early twentieth-century Parisian lesbians, particularly Natalie Barney and Renée Vivien, both of whom were radical in "developing a paradigm for this new sexuality, one which stressed a vital and often unmentioned (and unmentionable) part of the 'third sex,' that is, Lesbianism" (106). Sackville-West describes her heterosexual and homosexual tendencies in terms of a "dual personality . . . in which the feminine and the masculine elements alternately preponderate" (Nicolson 110). Her position relies on the late nineteenth-century sexologists' theories of homosexuality and on later theoretical attempts to use the same language in more positive ways. The sexologists Havelock Ellis and especially Richard von Krafft-Ebing construct a narrative of inversion in which physical and psychological gender violations forge two forms of excess: crime and a lack of sexual control. Krafft-Ebing organizes homosexuality as a progressive narrative of disease, each of four stages dependent on the degree of physical and mental cross-gendering. He terms androgyny a "high degree of degeneration" because the individual displays physical as well as psychic characteristics of the opposite sex (389). He proposes the term "gynandry" for inverted women, in which the disease is the "masculine soul, heaving in the female bosom," enjoying sports and male clothing (399). The ultimate excess is sexual, for, he claims, "abnormally increased sexuality is almost a regular accompaniment of antipathic sexual feeling" (439). Havelock Ellis, a follower and reformer of Krafft-Ebing, describes homosexuality as congenital and therefore not a choice, but he still concludes that female homosexuality is deleterious, the abnormal disturbance of gender boundaries. In his discussion of sexual inversion in women, he is concerned to elaborate the male characteristics which appear or do not appear in women who are considered truly inverted. The tightrope of gender definition is obvious in Ellis's discussion of women who, because they take on certain male tendencies, are more prone to crimes of violence (200–201) and, on a less threatening level, who can whistle (256). Both are obviously considered masculine prerogatives.

Although Ellis does not define the inverted woman in strictly physical terms, for he claims, neither the body nor the psyche can be trusted to give off accurate signals, he easily mixes bodily and emotional characteristics when he describes how a "keen observer" recognizes a lesbian: "The brusque, energetic movements, the attitude of the arms, the direct speech, the inflexions of the voice, the masculine straightforwardness and sense of honor, and especially the attitude toward men, free from any suggestion either of shyness or audacity, will often suggest the underlying psychic abnormality to a keen observer" (250). What the keen observer will discern is excess, is a woman who violates the restrictively constructed female boundaries. The excess is particularly egregious in women because they are usurping male prerogatives. It is no wonder that lesbians are associated with crimes of violence, for it is not that the lesbian is more likely to be a criminal but that her existence must be read as a crime. Even the slightest deviation mapped the lesbian body as criminal and monstrous. Havelock Ellis describes at length the oddity of one lesbian's body: "But with the arms, palms up, extended in front of her with inner sides of hands touching, she cannot bring the inner sides of forearms together, as nearly every woman can, showing that the feminine angle of arm is lost" (229). Despite Gillian Whitlock's revisionary reading of The Well of Loneliness, Radclyffe Hall appears to echo Ellis directly when she describes Stephen as a masculinized female in a tone that assumes we will read her as a hybrid: "the long line of her limbs—she was tall for her age—and the pose of her head on her over-broad shoulders" (26) identify her as masculine.

But this same dualism of "woman-manly" could occasion a narrative of liberation as well as disease, and the late nineteenth century as well as early twentieth century found advocates who turned this narrative of degeneration on its head. Instead of androgyny as the ultimate sign of physical and mental deterioration, it could indicate the creative interplay of male and female principles. While this notion at times inadvertently reinscribes heterosexuality as part of a utopian, homosexual narrative, it also re-encodes the story of homosexuality as a positive excess. The turn-of-the-century gay advocate, Edward Carpenter, believes that people Karl Ulrichs calls Urnings "may have an important part to play in the evolution of the race" (127), reconciling the stark separation of the two sexes. Because for him homosexuality is more about the emotional than the physical being, this version of a hybrid is a positive and energizing blend of two opposites. As such, he directly challenges Krafft-Ebing's assumption that the homosexual is hypersexual. In fact, like Woolf and contemporary writers such as Adrienne Rich, Carpenter steers away from sexual connotations in favor of either a psychological or a spiritual definition of homosexuality. In Love's Coming-of-Age, Carpenter argues that lesbians are not identified by bodily characteristics but by an "inner nature [which] is to a great extent masculine" (138). Instead of Stephen's trapped soul which is forever the source of tragedy, this gender tension fosters creativity rather than self-destruction, and as George Chauncey, Jr., has remarked, a psychic rather than somatic hermaphroditism (132). The tension between the two sexes, in fact, is a fruitful vitality which produces people who mend differences rather than exacerbate them (Fassler 250). Carpenter argues that "through their double nature, [they seem to be in] command of life in all its phases, and a certain freemasonry of the secrets of the two sexes which may well favor their function as reconcilers and interpreters" (140). This figure is the harbinger of Judy Grahn's semihistorical rhapsodizing of the homosexual as the necessary religious mediator between the overly determined and divided worlds of the two genders (Another 11). This figure is also reflected in George Stambolian and Elaine Marks's description of the twentieth-century French concept of homosexuality as "a privileged instrument for analysis, a question to raise questions" (26).

Even the depiction of the lesbian as bodily monstrous, a code for autonomous female sexual desire, gains positive reinterpretation in the early twentieth century. Baudelaire prefigures what becomes for many women writers a sacred monstrosity. Baudelaire is easily the epitome of a male who appropriates the lesbian for his own purposes and, in this case, uses her for what Walter Benjamin calls the "heroine of modernism" (90). At the same time that Baudelaire writes this figure as an object of male erotic fantasy, he also writes the lesbian as an anomaly, outside of and therefore a challenge to cultural demands. In *Les Fleurs du mal,* his shocking challenge to bourgeois culture, Baudelaire depicts lesbian love as monstrous, excessive, and seductive. Almost because of her monstrosity, the lesbian becomes the ultimate male image of cultural disruption. In a move that will be used later by women writers, the lesbian is also a category of meaning that represents freedom from constrictive gender norms. The lesbian monster as a grotesque physical and sexual being becomes—sometimes humorously, sometimes nonhumorously parodic—a staple of women writers' "reverse discourse." Gertrude Stein, claims Catharine Stimpson, writes from a "sense of her own monstrosity in this world—as a sexual being, as a marginal cultural citizen" ("Somagrams" 41). The image of a monstrous woman who defies social and physical boundaries is at once the image of decadence and a trope of the sacred. Often the monstrosity that men delight in voyeuristically becomes for women like Djuna Barnes in *Nightwood* and Colette in *The Pure and the Impure* a coded exploration of difference and secrecy (Benstock 56, 248). Thus, when Woolf speaks of androgyny she puts in play a host of complex notions about sexuality and gender. Her construction of the lesbian subject and its metaphorical possibilities depends on this complex interplay.

Orlando is most directly related to sapphism, for as Sherron Knopp illustrates, the historical situation surrounding this text creates what Vita's own son, Nigel Nicolson, calls "the longest and most charming love letter in literature." But Woolf only hints at the homosexual implications in her playful critique of gender categories. Such indirection leads Smith-Rosenberg to argue that Orlando's androgyny, as a "confusion of categories," is a feminist rather than a lesbian statement that "inverts Krafft-Ebing's dark vision of the 'Mannish Lesbian.' Her joyous androgyne ridicules his decadent hermaphrodite" (276). But it does not take a calculated or ahistorical leap to conclude that by inverting the sexologists' discourse on the lesbian, Woolf also constructs a distinct lesbian as well as feminist subject. At first glance, Woolf appears to keep her characters away from sexual ambiguity. When Orlando is a male, he falls in love with women, especially the Russian Sasha; when she becomes a woman, men are her primary although not exclusive erotic concern, a need fulfilled when she meets Shelmerdine. Only in several limited situations does Woolf allow the trickery of gender ambiguity to initiate the possibilities of sexual ambiguity. One is with the fleeting figure of the Archduke/Archduchess who meets Orlando at different times in her variously gendered life, each time, it seems, as the appropriately opposite sex. At a point half-way through the novel, however, the reader realizes that "he was a man and always had been one; that he had seen a portrait of Orlando and fallen hopelessly in love with him; that to compass his ends, he had dressed as a woman" (*Orlando* 179). When Orlando as a woman tires of the superficiality and anti-feminism of eighteenth-century society, she dresses as a man and picks up Nell, a prostitute. Although this situation does not lead to sex, the narrator sums up Orlando's love life to this point with an ambiguous phrase: Orlando "enjoyed the love of both sexes equally" (221). In the more often cited ambivalence of Orlando's marriage to Shel, Woolf allows no physical confusion. The cry from each, " 'You're a woman, Shel!' she cried. 'You're a man, Orlando!' he cried" (252), refers only to psychological characteristics. But rather than reading this book as a conservative refusal to encounter homosexuality directly, I read this effort as Woolf's attempt to expand the definition of the lesbian subject, as the positive vacillation, both bodily and nonbodily, between two assigned gender roles, questioning, in the process, the boundaries imposed by culture but not obliterating them.

What allows this text to constitute a persistent heterogeneity is the playful vacillation about bodily—sexual and gender—reality. This playfulness is realized in the metaphor of clothing, for like Gilbert and Gubar's description of *Nightwood, Orlando* is "a clothing-obsessed book" (*No Man* 359). Orlando fusses with clothing as both a male and a female while the narrator attempts to explain the cultural oddities that connect gender identity and garments. The questions are obvious, although the answers are not. Is there any real difference between male and female when only a style of clothing separates them? Is clothing more profoundly a metaphor for the body and, if so, is the body the clothing of the soul, as apparently arbitrary as clothing? If one can change clothing and even gendered bodies, as Orlando does, can culture attribute any significant differences to its rigid boundaries between male and female? Are bodies, male or female, as superfluous as clothing; can there be a "third" or "the pure, sexless . . . being behind gender and myth" (*No Man* 346)? If gender difference is arbitrary, is what we would today call sexual orientation also arbitrary? Woolf poses these questions about the gendered and sexual body through images of excess—of bodies, clothing, and sexualities transgressing culture's limiting boundaries. The ambiguously or double-gendered subject is Woolf's answer to the sexologists' degrading depictions of the lesbian subject. But what has been read as a radical act of declaring the artificiality of gender must not lead to the opposite conclusion, that because gender is depicted as artificial it is also arbitrary. Woolf both destablizes gender and defines homosexuality as the mixture of two definable genders whose boundaries are evident but less stable than culture presumes. As Kari Weil notes, throughout its challenges to gender boundaries, *Orlando* "never loses sight of the importance of naming woman" (156). In "naming woman" as a part of the androgynous, lesbian Orlando, Woolf insists that both sameness and differences operate in her construction of the lesbian subject. Orlando, then, becomes the early twentieth-century lesbian subject who radically repositions the female narrative subject.

The new lesbian subject, then, is both a utopian and deconstructive figure, both related to the category woman and outside of it, both essentialist and nonessentialist. The key to Woolf's construction of the lesbian subject is clothing as a trope of the body through which we can maintain both that gender is artificial and, with Ed Cohen, "that bodies do make a (political) difference" (85). There are enormous differences between being in a male or a female body, Orlando discovers. So while clothes, at one point in the book, "wear us and not we them" (*Orlando* 188), leaving gender construction artificial, the narrator immediately retracts this untroubled answer by attaching clothing to the profound differences between the sexes, leaving somewhat stable gender categories in place when she describes Orlando as a "mixture" of "man and woman, one being uppermost and then the other" (189). For, the biographer notes, the "difference between the sexes is, happily, one of great profundity. Clothes are but a symbol of something hid deep beneath" (188). In this section on clothing Woolf refuses to choose one argument or the other. Clothing indeed makes gender arbitrary because it allows so many variations on male and female; yet the body speaks when Orlando is changed into a woman. She is different and, as Woolf continues, "it was a change in Orlando herself that dictated her choice of a woman's dress and of a woman's sex" (188). Bodies are both determined and created, for the Archduchess/Archduke "was a man and always had been one" (179). At the same time that clothing carefully represents gender artificiality, Woolf works to assure the reader that Orlando's clothing rarely violates or transgresses gender norms, for even at the point of her change to a female body, Orlando dresses in "those Turkish coats and trousers which can be worn indifferently by either sex" (139). As Marjorie Garber notes, "Whatever Orlando *is,* her clothing reflects it: the crossing between male and female may be a mixture (a synthesis), but it is not a confusion, a transgression" (135). The same "double-play" is true of Orlando's emotional level. At one point Woolf asks what if anything can be called mentally or emotionally gendered—"men cry as frequently and as unreasonably as women" (180)—and at another point she assumes that being "tolerant and free-spoken" is an attribute of the male (258). The gender categories are neither constantly heterogeneous nor stable; instead they are artificial but not arbitrary, and loose enough to be realigned. The lesbian subject exceeds the culture's gender boundaries, even bodily gender boundaries, but remains female as a newly constructed feminist/lesbian subject.

The lesbian subject is a figure of both sexual and gender excess by being a "vacillation from one sex to the other" so that "often it is only the clothes that keep the male or female likeness, while underneath the sex is the very opposite of what it is above" (189). But rather than suggesting that "all is in flux, no fixed hierarchy endures or should endure" (Gilbert and Gubar, *No Man* 344), Woolf's text insists on a flux that maintains both the artificiality of constructed identities and the stability of certain elements of those categories. Woolf underscores this position by the constant juxtaposition of fact and fantasy, by a narrator who claims to be a biographer and who proceeds to tell a fantastic story with a straight face and an index. The heterogeneity, in other words, is not constant. Orlando must live in a female body but can also transgress the boundaries that separate the female from the male, for she can dress in male clothing as she does in the eighteenth century when she tires of the restrictions of female clothing. Clothing thus becomes the trope for the excessive and transgressive female body and situates Orlando in a different relationship to both men and women. This woman-manly lesbian subject is, in the end, what Vita/Orlando turns out to be, a vacillation within an order, a self within a decentered position. The many selves of the book's ending are recuperated in a single self, "one and entire" (320), at the very end of the tale. Woolf's insistence on fluid gender boundaries, on the "double-play" of being both woman and not-woman, rather than the erasure of all boundaries, indicates a more powerful disruptive performance than the attempt to decenter the subject totally.

A Room of One's Own presents a more stable picture of gender structure, and although Woolf concludes her text with her famous discussion of androgyny, the book is firmly rooted in a stabilized gender difference that Orlando challenges. This book is also more problematically related to the nascent and yet unnamed lesbian subject. Ellen Bayuk Rosenman fashions a strong case for concluding that "contemporary definitions of lesbianism are not applicable to Woolf's work" and that androgyny did not connote lesbianism because androgyny "carried different implications in a historical context that defined 'lesbian' as 'masculine' " (648–49). But while the connection between androgyny and lesbianism is not as apparent in A Room as it is in Orlando, this connection is not arbitrary or ahistorical given Vita's presence, its proximity to Orlando, and the contemporary definitional possibilities surrounding androgyny. What is often considered one of Woolf's feminist treatises also depicts a nonbodily androgyny, but like Orlando, A Room does not allow easy answers. Where Orlando repeatedly stablizes what could be mere performance, A Room complicates the seemingly stablized gender categories through a surprising combination of fiction and fact. In the first two-thirds of the book, gender categories remain unchallenged. Women writers have certain characteristics which make their sentences (80), the size of their books (81), their topics—such as women's relationships with one another (86) and male picadellos, what Woolf calls the "spot the size of a shilling at the back of the head" (94)—different from male writers. These differences are confidently proposed until the final chapter when Woolf tires of thinking separately about the sexes and announces her solution to this division in the idea of androgyny, the "man-womanly" and the "woman-manly." While these descriptions assume a gendered centeredness modified by an overlay or infusion of characteristics of the opposite sex, her solution to gender difference appears to be a radical departure from what has preceded it. As a result, Woolf's concept has been read variously as balancing two static principles (Marder 3), as a play of multiple differences (Moi 2–3), or in Showalter's still valid observation, as an evasion of her "own painful femaleness" (*Literature* 264).

Elsewhere, I proposed an answer to the split between the early and last sections of Woolf's book, the seeming contradiction between women writers' uniquenesses and androgyny as a means of overcoming the separation of the sexes. In 1975, I suggested that while Woolf "consciously argues for androgyny in terms that will be accepted by her male peers, she, like Galileo, seems to whisper a rebuttal" (451). Some elements of that rebuttal could be found, I argued, in the fictionalized nature of *A Room*. Almost twenty years later, I would like to conclude the opposite. Androgyny is not at odds with the previous sections of the book if we accept the association—not necessarily equation—of androgyny and homosexuality. This connection is, as noted above, implied by her era's discourse on homosexuality and androgyny and specifically by the writings of the Bloomsbury group. By relying on a term that could imply homosexuality, Woolf trades on the positive image of the homosexual as a trope of human creativity and partakes of what Susan Gubar identifies as the "lesbian tradition [that] may serve as a paradigmatic solution to the problem creativity posed to nineteenth-century women artists" (62). In terms of women's creativity, the lesbian subject becomes the metaphoric possibility of all women's creative potential. Androgyny, then, is a way to explore difference not primarily by stirring up heterogeneity but by repositioning the woman as the lesbian subject. The key to this interpretation lies within the unique fictive structure of Woolf's work of feminist criticism.

Others have noted that Woolf's deployment of three narrators, Mary Beton, Mary Seton, and Mary Carmichael, determines our critical understanding of *A Room* and especially of the problematic idea of androgyny. However, this critical strategy is often employed to deny Woolf's faith in the conclusion she reaches. How could someone so feminist in the first sections of the book, the argument goes, retreat into the nebulous notion of a heterosexual fusion or relationship between two predefined, stereotypical gender principles? In this argument, androgyny is suspect because it is proposed by one of the fictional characters, Mary Beton, not by Woolf's authorial voice. Using Gayatri Spivak's warning that "I would like to remind everyone who cites *A Room of One's Own* that 'one must be woman-manly or man-womanly' is said there in the voice of Mary Beaton (sic), a persona" (cited in *Crossing* 98), Elizabeth Meese concludes that Woolf's use of the persona "unsettles her persona's utopic resolution" (*Crossing* 99). This narrative unsettling is crucial to a contemporary reading of *A Room*, but the parameters of the unsettling must be expanded.

Woolf declares her fictive enterprise long before she proposes androgyny. In fact, it is within the first two pages that she declares the "I" as "only a convenient term for somebody who has no real being. Lies will flow from my lips" (*Room* 4); this same "I" becomes, several sentences later, "Mary Beton, Mary Seton, Mary Carmichael or . . . any name you please" (5). The persona begins to narrate at that point, and all of her suggestions about the woman writer's characteristics, her history, and uniqueness flow from the same lips, from Mary Beton's. Are we then to discard only the narrator's conclusion and accept the rest of her story unsullied? Rather, I would suggest that the radicality of androgyny is missed if we do not associate it with the lesbian subject, with the homosexual creativity that was assigned to this "third" by Woolf and some of her contemporaries. The consistent narrator, in fact, reinforces the believability of Woolf's recommendation of androgyny, but not as a neutralized image that denies difference rather as one that expands the female images she has already offered. DuPlessis puts this contradiction well when she claims that the "doubled emphasis on woman, yet on forgetting woman, is a significant maneuver, claiming freedom from a 'tyranny of sex' that is nonetheless palpable and dominant, both negated and affirmed" (33). This "double-play" is a way to insist on a different positioning for the woman writer.

Instead of offering a sop to her colleagues and critics, Woolf constructs, through the androgyne, the lesbian subject as the creative woman, the "woman-manly," the Carpenter-inspired vital and creative homosexual. With Vita in the audience, the image of the androgyne as the lesbian subject is not lost. Rather than a figure different from Mary Carmichael, this lesbian subject is Mary Carmichael, who, at one moment, breaks the sequence and, at another moment, writes Chloe and Olivia into fictional history. If, as a writer, it is "fatal to be a man or woman pure and simple" (108), it is also fatal to be neither, to obliterate the categories. In one of her less quoted statements, Woolf substantiates the necessity of sex difference in writing: "But this creative power differs greatly from the creative power of men. And one must conclude that it would be a thousand pities if it were hindered or wasted, for it was won by centuries of the most drastic discipline, and there is nothing to take its place. It would be a thousand pities if women wrote like men" (91). If, then, there is continuity between the androgyne and her ideal woman writer, Woolf allows the simultaneity of a stable category and a destabilized, heterogenous fluidity. The lesbian subject is both and as a result is positioned in narrative or in discourse differently from either the man or the woman.

Virginia Woolf and some of her contemporaries, then, restructures the negative narratives of the lesbian subject that dominated the nineteenth-century determination of sexual deviance. In the new construction, the lesbian subject assumes characteristics beyond the clinical. She becomes a metaphoric figure for women's creativity, for the transgression of restrictive gender boundaries, and, in some cases, for feminism. Woolf herself uses both elements of the burgeoning construction of the lesbian subject—the parodic, excessive body and the utopian, nonbodily creativity. Both constructions refigure the restrictive position of woman. With this history, writers now find it possible to use the monstrous female figure, the excessive female body or female sexuality, as an image of the lesbian subject and vice versa. It is also possible to use the utopian, desexualized woman as a lesbian subject, constructed more by her positioning in relationship to other females than by her sexual proclivities. Both constructions, at times suggested by a simple image of a sacred monster or of a robust woman, are figures which exceed the boundaries of the Other that allow the phallocentric Same to assert and maintain its authority. While, in one sense, these metaphoric qualities surrounding the term "lesbian" might be considered an evasion of lesbian specificity, they also might be construed as an expansion of definitional boundaries. Metaphoric possibilities need not be reduced to a "trope of similitude" (Stanton 161) and thus be dismissed as a trope of identity, but instead should be seen as a "category mistake" that works on the level of similarity as well as difference and essentially " 'redescribes' reality" (Ricoeur 22).

The current debate reflects the parameters of those definitions set up as a result of the medical discourse and the "reverse discourse" of women writers like Woolf. So influential is this larger definition of lesbian that it has occurred in the last twenty-five years not only in literary, theoretical, and critical venues but also in social and psychological studies that are modeled on the empirical sciences. Carla Golden, in a recent psychological essay, admits that "the definition of a lesbian is both problematic and far from unambiguous" (19). What strikes Golden as unique is the "degree of incongruence between their sexual activities and their sexual identities" (30). In most cases the "identity" is more important than the sexual activity. Perhaps because lesbian communities have struggled to create a political group identity, the range of definitions for who is included and excluded is precarious. Yet, as Susan Krieger's social study of women's communities claims, studies in this field "consider lesbianism to be a matter of total personal identity rather than primarily a sexual condition" (95).

One crucial example of this definitional problem in the lesbian community as opposed to the literary community is Joan Nestle's book, *A Restricted Country*. Nestle is a radical advocate of lesbian sexuality, and her book is a partly autobiographical, partly theoretical, partly fictional defense of lesbians as sexual creatures. She claims, at one point, that "we must realize that we no longer have to say that being a Lesbian is more than a sexuality" (119). The flow of this paragraph curiously parallels the definition of the erotic in Audre Lorde's well-known essay, "Uses of the Erotic: The Erotic as Power." In Lorde's terms, eroticism is "the lifeforce of women," a "creative energy empowered" (*Sister* 55). Nestle asserts that sexuality is limited to the physical because it is "a whole world in itself that feeds the fires of all our other accomplishments" (119). As the paragraph proceeds, however, the definition of lesbian becomes larger and larger, rooted in the erotic but also related to the "possibilities of erotic choice and self-creation." Finally, in an improbable move, Nestle returns lesbian to the metaphoric level: "a Lesbian celebrating her desire is a symbol of the possibility of social change for all women" (119).

Nestle, of course, is vigorously responding to the desexualization of the lesbian in the initial 1970s studies and discussions of lesbian existence and history. Historians of the 1970s and 1980s often described earlier female relationships as asexual because no direct evidence to the contrary seemed to exist. While these historical studies uncovered examples of intense women's relationships in women's writings, particularly from the nineteenth century, clear statements of homosexuality were almost nonexistent. For instance, was Emily Dickinson a lesbian because of her close relationship with and passionate letters to her sister-in-law? This tightrope of inference, more precarious than that walked by gay males, often led to nonsexualized definitions of lesbian and, as a result, added fuel to the already well-developed tendency to make lesbian a figure of more than sexual import. Lillian Faderman's influential work, *Surpassing the Love of Men*, concludes that prior to the sexualization of almost everything by Freud and his contemporaries, women's relationships with one another existed in nonsexual, idealized Platonic terms in a context of cultural approbation. Faderman avers that these "romantic friendships" emphasized affection over sexuality. This ambiguity leaves a contemporary and sympathetic historian like Jonathan Katz struggling with definitions. In the introduction to his mammoth *Gay/Lesbian Almanac,* he concludes that while "essential eroticism" must be a part of the definition of lesbian, this sensuality includes "the intense, passionate, physical, but seemingly non-genital friendships of women with women discussed by Carroll Smith-Rosenberg and Lillian Faderman" (11).

Differing definitions, vague references by earlier women writers, and denial by their contemporaries plague the scholar who struggles to uncover the history of women's relationships with one another prior to the nineteenth century. This space of ambiguity has always been both a blessing and a curse. One of the first books of the current era of gay and lesbian studies is John Boswell's monumental study of homosexuality in the Middle Ages. He acknowledges, even apologizes for, the "relative absence of materials relating to women" because, especially at this time, "most of the sources for this (as for nearly all) history were written by men about men, and where they deal with women, they do so peripherally" (xvii). Boswell quotes a moving example of twelfth-century lesbian poetry, but it is the only one. Yet, in the small ranks of women troubadours, the troubaritz, stands Bieiris de Romans, a thirteenth-century woman who expressed her love of another woman in poetry. While much of the poem displays a courtesy and modesty toward a woman in a higher social position and thus a distinctly asexual tone, Bieiris implores her not to give her affection to a man: "I pray you, please, by this which does you honor,/don't grant your love to a deceitful suitor" (Bogin 133). Likewise the seventeenth-century writer, Katherine Philips, is called the English Sappho because of her ardent yet Platonic poems to other women. In Philips's lovely poem, "To My Excellent Lucasia, on Our Friendship," she claims for their love something beyond the heterosexual:

> No bridegroom's nor crown-conqueror's mirth
> To mine compared can be;
> They have but pieces of this earth,
> I've all the world in thee. (870)

If their passion had been sexual, contemporary readers will never know. Faderman summarizes the anguish of historians looking for a lesbian

tradition: "If any women wrote lesbian sex literature during the six-
teenth to eighteenth centuries, it has been lost to posterity" (31). In her
study of an Italian Renaissance lesbian nun, Judith C. Brown portrays
the confusion in the medieval and Renaissance minds: "The conceptual
difficulties contemporaries had with lesbian sexuality is reflected in the
lack of an adequate terminology. *Lesbian* sexuality did not exist. Neither, for that matter, did *lesbians*" (17). In fact, if there is suspicion of
homosexuality, most often contemporaries or critics will find a way to
deny it, as the seventeenth-century poet, Abraham Cowley, did of his
contemporary, Katherine Philips (Andreadis 52). Sappho, of course, is
the most famous example of cultural denial. This erasure leaves current
historians and critics with few details about the female homosexual,
but it also opens the way for codes, expanded definitions, and playful
possibilities, in other words, for the continuation and expansion of the
discursive system already in place.

In this space, constructed both by a history of the metaphorical
lesbian subject and by the vagaries of current empirical studies, the
lesbian subject in the 1970s became a poet's and mythologizer's paradise
and now serves current postmodernists with a space for theorizing the
boundary-defying lesbian body. Each of the contemporary theoretical
moments—lesbian-feminist and postmodern—has produced a lesbian
subject either as a single figure entering a male-defined textual/social
system or as two women who, in dialogue, reconstruct the subject/object
dichotomy. The single lesbian figure often interrogates the language to
claim subjectivity for herself or "she" recognizes herself in another
woman. In what might be called a new genre of literary theory, essays
from both theoretical moments represent the lesbian subject as two
women in dialogue. What the postmodernist Nina Rapi calls an "inter-
subjective reciprocity" (155) and lesbian-feminist Adrienne Rich the
"primary presence of women to ourselves and each other" (*Lies* 250)
becomes for each theoretical position what Rich designates as the "crucible of a new language" (250). But more attention has been paid to the
differences between these two theoretical approaches. The single figure
of lesbian-feminism is characterized as the idealized woman; the single
figure of postmodernism is, in Wittig's terms, "a not-woman, a not-
man" (*Straight* 13). In their ideas about intersubjectivity, lesbian-feminists describe the lesbian as the woman who recognizes herself in her
mirror Other, another woman; postmodernists describe the lesbian as

enacting differences by constantly moving between the desired and desiring, subject and object. But, I will argue, notions of sameness and differences adhere in each just as subject positions are complicated in each. By comparing as well as contrasting these two theories, lesbian-feminism will appear more complex and radical than has been allowed and queer theory more conservative than it wishes to admit. Separately and together they perform the "double-play" of Paul Smith's analysis (151) and the "double gesture" that Diana Fuss finds in Irigaray's simultaneous movement toward and away from essentialism (68–70).

Shaped by the feminism of the 1970s, American lesbian-feminists like Adrienne Rich, Audre Lorde, and Judy Grahn construct the lesbian subject as an autonomous figure which repositions the feminist subject. Starting from the assumption that, as Sarah Hoagland notes, "lesbian existence is connected logically or formally in certain ways with female agency" (6), these writers develop a nonbodily lesbian subject as the image of the unfettered female "self." Because most of the lesbian-feminists were poets, the concept of poetic creativity naturally fit into their narrative of the lesbian subject. "She" is the woman who moves from the prison house of male identity, where creativity is mired in heterosexual and male definitions—dancing dogs, the penis as the pen, the writer's need of balls and the like—to a different subject position. Mary Carruthers describes this new lesbian as a "paradigm [of] the large issues of value in language, of women's psyche and of social transformation, of alienation and apocalypse" (294). Grahn describes lesbian in a woman-centered image of a journey to the new island of Lesbos, a " 'crossing' in which a pair of Lesbians make a perilous modern urban journey" (*Highest* 32). Rich develops several definitions, one as a solitary act of becoming, a "sense of desiring oneself; above all, of choosing oneself" (*Lies* 200) and another as a position from which to stand in relationship to another woman, the "primary intensity between and among women" ("Compulsory" 648).

In its most rapturous guise, the lesbian subject took on redemptive qualities. Although Nicole Brossard is not an American lesbian-feminist, her description of the lesbian summarizes much of the definitional energy of the American 1970s:

> There are lesbians like this, lesbians like that, lesbians here, and there, but a lesbian is above all else the centre of a captivating *image* which any woman can claim for herself. The lesbian is a mental energy which gives

breath and meaning to the most positive of images a woman can have of herself. Lesbians are the *poets* of the humanity of women and this humanity is the only one which can give to our collectivity a sense of what's real. (121)

Brossard's movement back and forth from literal lesbians to lesbian as an image of mental energy to which all women can aspire separates and mixes the two definitions. Both meanings of lesbian—lesbians of the "here, and there" and lesbian as "a mental energy" potentially in all women—are gathered in her final reference to lesbians who are poets. Lesbians as oppositionally constituted fixtures of a sexual landscape are transformed into a creative space for all women. As Alice Parker notes, "Brossard deploys the term *lesbian* to collect the visionary potential of hitherto unexplored female desire" (307). In an equally rapturous account of the lesbian and creativity, Judy Grahn claims that "the Lesbian [poet]—and by extension, every woman" (*Highest* 41) creates a space of possibility through which all women can find a new place or a sense of self. That creativity comes about in interaction with other women and oneself: "Such Lesbian poets [Sappho, H.D.] have the understanding that each woman is her own Muse, and in so doing we have found our sense of place with each other" (43). The lesbian as an image constitutes a place of transformation, redemption, and creativity where lesbian is "seeing the poet in the woman, not as alien or monstrous, but as an aspect of her womanhood" (Carruthers 296). Like Lorde's concept of the erotic, or "the creative energy empowered" (55), lesbian as a trope juxtaposes creativity and autonomous female desire.

In this context, Adrienne Rich's formulation of the relationship between creativity and the lesbian subject is both familiar and, at the same time, in need of re-examination. In her most succinct statement on this issue, Rich contrasts the "dutiful daughter of the fathers in us [who] is only a hack" with the "lesbian in us who drives us to feel imaginatively" (*Lies* 201). As in the quest narrative, the creative woman in Rich's account moves from problematic contingency to assertive potential. Rich summarizes this movement in her own life in the sentence which frames the above description: "Even before I wholly knew I was a lesbian, it was the lesbian in me who pursued that elusive configuration" (200). A number of rhetorically important phrases comprise that sentence. As in the narrative system, knowledge is the goal in the subject's movement from one condition to another. The subject or protagonist who is the "lesbian in me" is both the foundation and motivation for the movement from one position to another, but it is a subject position which Rich deliberately confounds, for it exists simultaneously before and after the goal, what must be known and what is already known. What she defines as that "elusive configuration" leaves the construction of a simple static space for female agency an always-to-be-hoped-for and never-attained utopia. Such concepts refuse any simple essentialism, for the lesbian image becomes both the known and the unknown, the goal and the source of the quest.

This connection between sexuality and imaginative creativity is not foreign to Western images of the imagination, but because no image exists for an autonomous female creativity, the construction of the lesbian as the image of the creative woman is a natural response for women writers of the exuberantly productive and feminist 1970s. As I have noted elsewhere ("Toward"), other images of creativity, like the heterosexual constructs of the female muse and the maternal, nurturing mother, depend on the institutionalization of male desire as constitutive of creativity itself. Most of these images have strong heterosexual, in some cases male homosocial/homosexual, overtones because these images have served to describe what it is like to be male and creative. It is commonplace to argue that many of these images exist as a means to appropriate the envied power of women to create from their own bodies; thus, as men have defined creativity, women have been a necessary but, for the most part, controlled element in the story. The long history of the muse as the source of male inspiration exists as a parallel heterosexual image of creativity. This relationship is particularly fraught with patriarchal circular reasoning, for in communing on a symbolic sexual level—sometimes nonsymbolic—with the Other who does not speak, the poet absorbs the female reproductive function and bears his own literary progeny. As Mary K. DeShazer describes the relationship, "the active male engenders his poetry upon the body of a passive female muse" (10). He not only expends his seed on an object, but he also bears the fruit; in other words, he claims a self-sufficient power to create as a result of appropriating and transcending the material world that the woman represents. The more pernicious image of appropriation is the mother either as a metaphor for birthing a creative work or nurturing it along. Unlike David Halperin's reasoning concerning Socrates' appropriation of female creative power in the *Symposium,* I find problematic male uses of female functions to configure their own productive powers. Halperin argues that we cannot read the feminine in Plato simply "as a symbolic theft of women's procreative authority" (145) because the feminine depends on a male construction of an Other as a " 'pseudo-Other' " (145). But, I would argue, because the discursive is related to experience as a constructor of reality, this discursive "pseudo-Other" helps to formulate women's experience. In *The Madwoman in the Attic,* Gilbert and Gubar elaborate upon the effect of these concepts of male authority on women writers of the nineteenth century. Woman-as-Other is necessary for male constructions of self, creativity, and narrative, usually as a means for his transcendence of the difficult bodily and natural world which the female has been forced to represent. It is no wonder that lesbian-feminists pursued lesbian as an image for autonomous female creativity, a configuration which eliminates the male.

But while the use of the terms like "self," "wholeness," and "woman-as-same" permeate the lesbian-feminist construction of lesbian as literary creator or agent, it should not be assumed that such constructions are simply static. As Patricia Waugh notes, "Even in its 'essentialist' modes, in fact, feminism has radicalized the subject at least as much as postmodernism/post-structuralism" (14). Sameness is less an essentialist identity than a repositioning of the subject in relation to other women, a repositioning which connects the lesbian subject to the categories of gender and, simultaneously, disturbs gender. When Adrienne Rich, whose thinking is central to this formulation of the lesbian subject, proposed the "lesbian continuum" to represent women relating to one another in various ways at different historical periods, she was roundly accused of ahistoricism and essentialism. In response to such criticisms, Rich gradually embraced a more inclusive vision, a "simultaneity of oppressions," to reflect the political conditions to which she was a witness. But her development of the lesbian subject in the 1970s is not only formative for that generation of thinkers but is also more complex than is usually acknowledged. For instance, in the same essay in which she proposes the phrase, the "lesbian continuum," Rich also imagines lesbian as an open-ended term. Rich juxtaposes the "lesbian continuum," "a range—through each woman's life and throughout history—of woman-identified experience," with "*lesbian existence,*" which Rich defines as "both the fact of the historical presence of lesbians and our continuing creation of the meaning of that existence" ("Compulsory" 648). Since this lesbian existence is not set up in contradistinction to the "lesbian continuum" but rather is easily—too easily some may say—interrelated with it, the definition of the lesbian subject remains open to the process of recreating meaning in the midst of politically opposing pressures.

Rich writes a more problematic lesbian subject into one of her most unusual essays, "Women and Honor: Some Notes on Lying." In this early essay, set up as a series of impressionistically related thoughts, Rich describes and even enacts what the "primary intensity" between women means, although she rarely mentions the word "lesbian." I have made the following analysis in a previous essay:

> Here, where her prose strategy, usually highly rhetorical, is poetic, Rich measures the erotic charge between women in their trust of one another. In the patriarchal world, woman's honor is acknowledged only by her sexual loyalty to men; in a brave new world of relationships among women, a new code of honor based on truth and trust can begin to unfold. Trust is the primary way of being attentive to one another, of repositioning the woman in relation to other women, and on this trust, truth is based. Trust, she implies, is another way of making love, a way of allowing the full freedom of imagination and of sexuality. Because truth itself is based on trust and not on mere facts, it is created between two people as they open to one another. ("Toward" 113–14)

In fact, Rich's notion of presence, or what other lesbian-feminists imagine as women's seeing of one another, has larger epistemological and even ontological implications. "We take so much of the universe on trust," begins one paragraph (*Lies* 192). A surprising conjunction of empirical and experiential facts follows: "You tell me: 'In 1950 I lived on the north side of Beacon Street in Somerville.' You tell me: 'She and I were lovers, but for months now we have only been good friends.' You tell me: 'It is seventy degrees outside and the sun is shining' " (192). While we have to depend on the lover's veracity to accept the second if not the first statement, the third statement seems beyond the belief system set out by trust. It is an empirical statement that can be verified. Yet Rich juxtaposes these statements as epistemological equals. The world is created between the lovers: "I allow my universe to change in minute, significant ways, on the basis of things you have said to me, of my trust in you" (192). Two people, two women, existing in the presence of one another, invent the world and the truth of their existence between them. In some ways, it is imperative for women to invent reality because the world they are given does not fit their relationships with one another—honor, for instance, is not a term usually used for a woman's pledge. The reality that two women create depends both on sameness—

their positioning toward one another—and differences—other position-alities for creating meaning.

In this juncture, this "between," creativity itself becomes possible. Because, for Rich, the "liar fears the void" and because the void is "the creatrix, the matrix," women's creativity flourishes only in this relationship of truth. In fact, women's creativity is the crux of Rich's construction of the trope of the lesbian subject. In two other theoretical instances, Rich connects the primary relationship of women to one another with the power of imaginative creativity. At a panel discussion for the 1976 MLA meeting, Rich forges her most unequivocal statement on this subject. In contrasting the patriarchally defined woman as "the dutiful daughter of the fathers in us [who] is only a hack" with the "lesbian in us who drives us to feel imaginatively, render in language, grasp, the full connection between woman and woman" (*Lies* 201), Rich reifies the lesbian subject as the artist's positioning of herself in relationship to men or women. Just as reality is determined by one woman telling the truth to another, language is imaginatively revised and reformulated by the primary presence of one woman to another. In repositioning herself, in looking at women instead of men, the woman writer comes in touch with a creative power that in turn revises the meanings and structures of language and literature that have inhibited her vision. In a 1977 essay on Judy Grahn, Rich claims this power as the "crucible of a new language" (*Lies* 250) or what she earlier in the essay describes as the source for "turn[ing] to the light for new colors and flashes of meaning" old words like love and power (247). Like the earlier, androgynous determinations of the nonbodily lesbian subject as a trope for the new woman's creativity, Rich claims for the lesbian subject a privileged positionality and accords its potential to all women.

But, of course, the lesbian-feminist image also differs from the androgynously constructed notion of women's creative agency. Unlike the advocates of androgyny, Rich and her theoretical colleagues reject any connection with masculine energy. This lesbian subject is no longer an idealized healer of the partition between the sexes; it is, instead, a revision of the referential position a woman is forced to occupy in patriarchal discourse and society. But rather than depending solely on some mystical qualities inherent in womanhood, the lesbian-feminist construction of the lesbian subject concentrates on positionality, on the "between" space and the direction that is revamped when one woman faces another instead of a man. In an earlier image of woman's creativity, Rich does develop an essentialist concept, but even then a fascinating one. She argues that "a radical reinterpretation of the concept of mother-hood is required which would tell us, among many other things, more about the physical capacity for gestation and nourishment of infants and how it relates to psychological gestation and nurture as an intellectual and creative force" (*Lies* 77). When constructing the lesbian image, Rich includes a bodily essentialism with a psychological positioning of the "lesbian continuum." The lesbian is, however, determined less by physi-cal attributes than by her positioning toward other women. One woman's focus, primary focus, on another, has its own creative results; thus Rich makes central the story of Demeter and Persephone, of the mother finding the daughter and of the earth's fertility that follows (*Lies* 115). This con-cept of creativity is not based on an ecstatic, transcendental union that is a part of male, heterosexual images of creativity, a transcendence posited on the resolution or absorption of sexual difference; instead, the lesbian image focuses attention on a revised female positionality.

It is no wonder that the image of sight becomes central to the lesbian-feminist construction of the lesbian subject. In her first collection of essays, Marilyn Frye promotes this image for a lesbian subject who claims agency in a phallocentric world. The lesbian subject, says Frye, is the "woman-seer" (*Politics* 173), the one who, like Rich's figure, reconstructs reality by refusing the male-defined subject position. Of course, the image of sight is not innocent. It, too, has a history, particu-larly in the twentieth century, of representing male subjectivity, and in claiming women's agency through this image, Frye wrenches the sym-bolic system out of its moorings. Like other images of agency, it is connected to male sexuality. Irigaray's *Speculum of the Other Woman* runs rife with the image of sight as a male privilege: "Yes, man's eye— understood as substitute for the penis—will be able to prospect woman's sexual parts, seek there new sources of profit" (145). In fact, Irigaray rejects sight in favor of touch as a possible image of woman's revised subject position. Even more problematic is the monovision that John Berger detects as part of Western thinking, the perspective that "makes the single eye the centre of the visible world" because it is a simulacrum of the single eye of God in which there is no visual reciprocity (16).

The lesbian subject who is repositioned to view women rather than men steals and revises this trope. In Frye's early theory, lesbian is a position from which one can reconfigure reality. The lesbian subject moves in a narrative progression from being seen by and being present to men to looking at women and being primarily present to them. This positional change also entails a different kind of sight, what Frye calls a conversion from the "arrogant eye" to the "loving eye" (*Politics* 52–83), a change that occasions an "ontological conversion . . . characterized by a feeling of a world dissolving, and by a feeling of disengagement and re-engagement of one's power as a perceiver" (171–72). It is a political act which signals the possibility for other women: "That such a conversion happens signals its possibility to others" (172). Frye takes seriously the challenge of women of color to her construction of the lesbian as woman and as universal, the nondifferentiated seer, but Frye's answer in her more recent essay, "The Possibility of Feminist Theory," is not to eliminate sameness as a principle of definition. Rather she speaks of patterns: "Naming patterns is not reductive or totalitarian. For instance, we realize that men interrupt women more than women interrupt men in conversation: we recognize a pattern of dominance in conversation— male dominance. We do not say that every man in every conversation with any woman always interrupts" (*Willful* 65). Sameness need not preclude differences, nor vice versa. Her conclusion is apt: "Perhaps eventually the category *woman* will be obsolete. But perhaps not" (71).

Audre Lorde works from the beginning of her writing to relate the women-as-same to women-as-different. Lorde is one of the first feminists to insist on revising unitary notions of woman's or lesbian's identity that plagued lesbian-feminism, and because of her insistence on the "creative function of difference in our lives" (*Sister* 111), she has been one of the few lesbian-feminists appropriated by postmodernists. But Lorde maintains her theoretical distance from a single identification with either group by her insistence on the importance of difference as well as sameness. In a published conversation with Adrienne Rich, Lorde answers Rich's question "Who is the poet?" with seemingly essentialist response: "The Black mother who is the poet exists in every one of us" (*Sister* 100). Although she does not easily reify lesbian, she implies the theory of sameness in her lengthy description of the erotic. At the end of an earlier quoted passage, Lorde asserts that "more and more women-identified women [are] brave enough to risk sharing the erotic's electrical charge without having to look away" (59). Here she underscores the lesbian-centered nature of this metaphoric energy and, at the same time, the importance of the imagery of sight. The erotic, then, like the "women-identified women," does not simply coincide with a sexual orientation but with a position or space from which one perceives the world. From her awareness of differences among women, however, she reverses the imagery of sight. In her significantly titled essay, "Eye to Eye: Black Women, Hatred, and Anger," Lorde speaks of the difficulty black women have looking at each other, of seeing each other through fear and anger: "As we fear each other less and value each other more, we will come to value recognition within each other's eyes as well as within our own, and seek a balance between these visions" (*Sister* 173). Differences between women, in fact must be "seen as a fund of necessary polarities between which our creativity can spark like a dialectic" (111). Difference, in fact, is erotic, and it can lead to an "unthreatening" "interdependency" (111). Erin G. Carlston thus describes Lorde's complex views in *Zami* in postmodern terms of plural but individual identity: "To the idea of coalition between individuals Lorde adds the concept of 'positionality,' or individual identity as an unstable construct, constantly (re)produced both by and within the social matrix, and by the subject's conscious creation of her self" (226). Thus while lesbian-feminists point the lesbian subject in a utopian direction, they imply and at times articulate a more problematic lesbian subject, one whose definition is not enclosed or finalized but in process, a figure whose sameness with other women does not preclude differences, and a subject who is defined as much by a change in the direction of attention as by a psychic or somatic identity.

If lesbian-feminists like Rich and Lorde have deconstructive moments, then postmodernist theorists of the lesbian subject have essentialist moments. In the first place, postmodernists, like lesbian-feminists, represent a broad spectrum of thinking. While all postmodernists are united in their opposition to stable identity categories, the degree to which they refuse efforts of categorization differentiates them. Many, for instance, refuse the label of feminism because it depends on the theoretical assumption of sexual difference and a stable category of "woman." In fact, the very conjunction of feminism and postmodernism exists as a question rather than as a fact (Suleiman 181–205). Shane Phelan identifies as extreme " 'postmodern' purity" (778) what she calls Judith Butler's "refusal to draw lines or name names" (779); in my view, the same purity resides in Judith Roof's insistence on lesbian sexuality as a site of total undecidability—"a configuration that stands for unfixity in relation to mastery" (36). But this "purity" is not necessarily shared by all thinkers who could be called postmodernists. For example, Phelan argues that, except for the few purists, "recognition of [the] provisional nature" of categories of identity is "a key element in both postmodern and poststructuralist theories" (779). In this vein, Teresa de Lauretis entitles one of her essays in decidedly unpostmodern terms: "The Essence of the Triangle or, Taking the Risk of Essentialism Seriously." In it she asks academic feminism to look more carefully at recent Italian feminist theory which, she argues, addresses "the constitutive role of sexual difference in feminist thought" (3). Maintaining a notion of sexual difference does not constitute "a biological or metaphysical essentialism, but a consciously political formulation of the specific difference of women in a particular sociohistorical location" (31). Addressing sexuality in this context "is not merely against, but in part owing to, the very strength of its theory of sexual difference" (31). De Lauretis's willingness to "name names" leads her to this configuration of lesbianism: "What is meant by lesbianism, if it is not a female sexuality unfettered or autonomous from masculine desire and definition?" (30). In these statements de Lauretis is willing to name such categories as "female," "lesbian," and "feminist," categories that purists refuse. But even purists cannot escape categories, for in their efforts to posit lesbian as a site of undecidability, a site of confusion which calls into question the system that tries to control it, they paradoxically set up a utopian space within and outside of the system they revile. Ironically, this utopian space of undecidability is its own version of an essentialist category, an insight that Diana Fuss makes the starting point of her book. Each postmodern version of the lesbian subject, then, enacts the "double-play" I have identified in other twentieth-century constructions of the lesbian.

Monique Wittig can be called an anti-essentialist postmodernist with essentialist moments. A number of critics view Wittig as the archetypal postmodernist, refusing narrative order and mastery in favor of what Martha Noel Evans calls "a disjointed and perpetually changeable confluence of parts" (186) and what Namascar Shaktini terms a position "outside of the presence/absence and center/margin dichotomies" (39). More recently Judith Butler notes an inconsistency in Wittig's writing: Wittig "calls for a position beyond sex that returns her theory to a problematic humanism based in a problematic metaphysics of presence. And yet, her literary works appear to enact a different kind of political strategy" (124). This dilemma, I would argue, is less a flaw in her deconstructive theory than the "double-play" that is the inevitable outcome of constructing a lesbian subject as the implied hero of a disruptive narrative. Wittig's lesbian subject occupies simultaneously the contradictory positions of utopian essentialism and deconstructive nonessentialism, or as Diana Fuss notes of Monique Wittig, only her essentialist moments "demonstrate that constructionism is itself a fluid and unstable category, a constantly shifting and often contradictory position" (45). Fuss, however, advocates a paradox: only some form of essentialism saves nonessentialism from pure essentialism. In this opinion, fluidity is enhanced by a strategic essentialism while still retaining fluidity as a utopian goal. Rather than resolving the binary essentialism/nonessentialism, I would prefer to let the two positions remain problematically intertwined, leaving essentialism as inescapable in our thinking as nonessentialism and thus leaving gender an issue with which we must contend. Wittig becomes a primary example of a postmodern thinker who cannot escape categories nor, it seems, does she try.

In both her theory and in her fictional writing, Wittig's goal is to make the marginal universal, to find an "axis of categorization from which to universalize" (*Straight* 61). The source of oppression is gender, what Wittig calls the artificial categories of man and woman that "conceal the fact that social differences always belong to an economic, political, ideological order" (2). Man has always been accorded the position of the universal; only woman must exist under the sword of gender as the marked category. Lesbian is the only word or space she knows that obliterates gender, the only space in which woman is not dependent on man. In "The Mark of Gender," Wittig carefully describes her efforts to displace the phallic subject of language with a narrative of her own in which the lesbian subject attains this space of universal subjectivity. Constructed in the various experimental pronouns of her first three books, the "I" of *The Opoponax*, the "elles" of *Les Guérillères*, and the "j/e" of *The Lesbian Body*, the lesbian subject supercedes the categories of gender in a space beyond the system of sexual difference. Her use of the "j/e" is a "sign of excess" that "has become so powerful in *The Lesbian Body* that it can attack the order of heterosexuality in the texts and assault the so-called love, the heroes of love, and lesbianize them, lesbianize the symbols, lesbianize the gods and the goddesses, lesbianize the men and the women" (87). In a nondeconstructive mode, Wittig assumes, as Butler rightly notes, a "prior ontological reality" and equality "to exercise language in the assertion of subjectivity" (*Gender* 117). The lesbian subject realizes this equality and appropriates subjectivity in language and narrative as her right. Wittig also seems to suggest that this space of lesbian subjectivity is a space for all human freedom, a space that both men and women can occupy outside of the system. In either case, Wittig creates a narrative of liberation using the lesbian subject as the protagonist who occupies a position in relationship to language that allows her a utopian, universal subjectivity.

Wittig's lesbian subject is also constructed in relationship to woman, the very gender category that lesbian also deconstructs. Critics and theorists often proclaim Wittig's iconoclastic book, *The Lesbian Body*, as the ultimate lesbian postmodernist text. Like the earlier descriptions of the lesbian subject as a sacred monster, Wittig figures the lesbian lovers as monstrous bodies, the beloved as the "adored monster" (35) reveling in the excessive and grotesque female body. Diana Fuss argues that the body is one of Wittig's most problematic issues. In Wittig's effort not to be essentialist, Fuss argues, she avoids "precisely a material-ist analysis of the body *as* matter" (50). Rather, I would argue, Wittig distinguishes between two female bodies, the domesticated female body of the gendered system and what Elaine Marks calls the "undomesti-cated" lesbian female body ("Lesbian" 372). In *The Lesbian Body*, Wittig startles us with a poetic description of the lover ripping apart her beloved's body. In the first section we are greeted with passages like "But/you know that not one will be able to bear seeing you/with eyes turned up lids cut off your yellow smoking/intestines spread in the hollow of your hands your/ tongue spat from your mouth" (13). Like so many postmodernists, Wittig makes the physical body a trope for the textual body, and, thus, to tear at the fabric of the constructed female body is to rip apart, necessarily, the textual structure that defines her only in terms of male, heterosexual desire. Thus Hélène Vivienne Wenzel notes of Wittig's narrator: "The lover *j/e* in *Le corps lesbien* is also the writer whose violent lovemaking both as subject and as object with *tu* is a metaphor for the craft of the writer" (284). Challenges to the struc-tural certainties of narrative and language are metaphorically set out in what appears to be a violent act of lovemaking that also challenges the tastes of most readers. It is this idealization of fragmentation that usually characterizes Wittig as nonessentialist.

But the lesbian subject of this fictive work forges a new positionality by remaining identifiably female and establishing fragmentation as its own utopian space. Maintaining gender as a category of identity puts into play sameness as well as differences in Wittig's construction of the lesbian subject. The revision of the heroic epic in *The Lesbian Body* details a journey from the "black continent of misery" (24), a play upon Freud's depiction of woman, to the "dark and gilded Lesbos" (24). The beloved is both a warrior and an object of desire, but always identifiably, bodily female: "you come towards m/e with adorable precipitancy, orange flashes coming from your breasts surround you, series of suns are setting in gold green saffron" (23). The great epics and their heroes are revised with new, feminized names—"Ulyssea" (21), "Achillea" (32)—and the great female figures of myth and history—Sappho (55) and Aphrodite (67)—are lionized. The new lesbian subject destroys the constructed woman of literary texts but forges a new set of boundaries, on her own terms.

Other Wittig texts do the same—refusing the domesticated woman for the undomesticated female. In a book written with Sande Zeig, *Lesbian Peoples: Material for a Dictionary,* Wittig distinguishes between the female as mother and as amazon. The mothers are the betrayers of the undomesticated amazons because they remain in the city as the "static mothers" who watch "their abdomens grow" (108–9). In *Les Guérillères,* Wittig employs the rarely used feminized form for the third-person plural in French, *elles,* arguing that she thus universalizes the marginalized. She also adamantly objects to its translation as "the women" (*straight* 86). But *elles* is circumscribed elsewhere as female, as the countless female names spotted through the text attest, and, as well, *elles* becomes a new space of identity. This "double-play" belies critical efforts to see her fictional or theoretical works as only an infinite play of parts, a comedic undercutting of gender boundaries, or a repetition of liberal humanist assumptions.

Wittig's "double-play" anticipates queer theory's revision of the lesbian subject in one of its most powerful images, the butch-femme couple. Twentieth-century's third moment of theorizing the lesbian subject is, in one prominent image, touted as a lesbian couple performing differences instead of sameness. Refusing the nonbodily version of the lesbian subject, this butch-femme couple reinvests lesbian in the body as sexuality. On the one hand the butch-femme represents a "severely literal" body and sexuality because the lesbian-feminist subject becomes "a monochromatic type whose sexual (or asexual) virtue is overwhelming" (Meese, *(Sem)Erotics* 104); on the other hand, this body, like the similarly constructed lesbian postmodern image of the vampire, represents a play of positionalities and textuality. As a parody of sex-gender alignment, the single subject of the butch-femme couple enacts the artificiality of gender difference through clothing and positionality. Clothing in particular becomes a trope for the artificiality of a gender system based on "natural" bodies. Both members of the lesbian couple cross-dress, not only one as masculine, but also the other as an exaggerated version of the feminine, with lipstick, high heels, and a short skirt. Ripe for metaphorical implications, the butch-femme couple is culture's version, its nightmare, of the female grotesque body, appropriating all sexuality to its sphere and control. The butch appropriates male positionality by defying culture's restrictive dictum concerning which bodies may don which kind of clothing. The femme, on the other hand, lavishly exaggerates the culturally condoned relationship between a sexually marked body, gendered female, and its appropriate clothing, and positions herself as a female relating to a male who is not a male. In the sexualization of parodied differences, this postmodern lesbian subject becomes a privileged site of inquiry which interrogates the gendered system of meaning. As Judith Butler argues, it is "only *within* the practices of repetitive signifying that a subversion of identity becomes possible" (*Gender* 145), and the lesbian subject becomes this subversive parody through the parodic performance of the "natural" gender binaries. Perhaps this lesbian subject and its postmodern counterpart, the lesbian as vampire—an image that I will discuss in Chapter 6—are what Mary Russo contemplates when she imagines a "category [of the female body as grotesque that] might be used affirmatively to destabilize the idealizations of female beauty or to realign the mechanisms of desire" (221).

But this play of differences does not exist without, acknowledged or otherwise, the qualification of sameness, although where this essentialism resides is a theoretical sticking point. One possibility is the body, for the irony in the gender play of the butch-femme is the knowledge of most observers and certainly of the participants that under the marked clothing exist two female bodies. But for postmodern purists, identity posited in the body is problematic because the body itself is not a foundation of meaning but, like gender, a site of performance or social construction. The body is not a "natural" entity upon which the artificiality of gender is enacted through different clothing, but rather a site at which the arbitrary conjunction of clothing suggests the constructedness of the body. Written upon the shimmering surface which is never finally constituted as originary, identity, even bodily and sexual identity, is unstable and ungraspable. In such a view, there is nothing on which culture writes itself, for the subject is all culturally written. The body for

Judith Butler is not the ground of identity, but "a variable boundary, a surface whose permeability is politically regulated, a signifying practice within a cultural field of gender hierarchy and compulsory heterosexuality" and thereby gender becomes "*a corporeal style*" (139). Garber concludes similarly: "this is the subversive secret of transvestism, that the body is not the ground, but the figure" (374). The body, in effect, is all surface; if anything it follows upon desire.

Thus sameness in lesbian postmodern theory is more precisely identified as sexual desire, but, I would argue, it becomes its own essentialist category. In repositioning lesbian desire, the lesbian body takes on crucial imagistic functions, for a desire not within the sexual system of signification needs representation through a grotesque or excessive body. In Jacquelyn N. Zita's analysis of three contemporary lesbian autobiographies, she states that "the claim to some lesbian commonality" is in "the primacy of sexual desire and pleasure" ("Lesbian" 340). Queer theorists concentrate on lesbian desire or sexuality rather than the female body as the core of lesbian "identity" because gender must come into play if the body becomes a site of analysis. Fear of essentialism privileges sexuality over identity and desire over the body. In recent writings such as Judith Roof's *A Lure of Knowledge: Lesbian Sexuality and Theory*, Teresa de Lauretis's *The Practice of Love: Lesbian Sexuality and Perverse Desire*, and Lynda Hart's *Fatal Women: Lesbian Sexuality and the Mark of Aggression*, lesbian sexuality is, in fact, contrasted to lesbian identity. De Lauretis, for instance, insists that her "goal is a theory of lesbian sexuality, not identity" (30). This gesture also refuses metaphor. De Lauretis rejects both the maternal metaphor of the French feminists and the image of woman-identification in Adrienne Rich's writings of the late 1970s in which "lesbian existence occurs within a female continuum that sustains the trope of woman-identification and aligns it with what I have been calling the maternal metaphor" (192). To construct the lesbian as a desiring subject, de Lauretis argues, "she" must be theorized as part of the symbolic rather than pre-Oedipal order, as her reading of Helene Deutsch allows (58–65). Sexuality, in this argument, remains fluid, "less a stable structure . . . than a relatively open-ended *process* of *sexual structuring*" (261). De Lauretis's construction of lesbian desire is neither utopic nor gender-bound, but in these theoretical moves her theory cannot escape essentialist categories. The fluidity of lesbian sexuality described in many postmodern theories has become its own essentialist construct, as essentialist as the metaphoric ideals of Adrienne Rich and the French feminists. When Annamarie Jagose, for instance, critiques the "logic of lesbian utopics" in Monique Wittig and Bonnie Zimmerman, she, without irony, proposes her own category instead: "Indeed, the category 'lesbian' is not essentially anything. It does not have a fixed valence, a signification that is proper to itself" (9).

But while desire in these theories is often represented as the grotesque or excessive body because it is outside culture's gender boundaries, neither transvestism nor the butch-femme couple would exist as ironic if it were not for the fact that literal bodies, on some level, do matter. Clothing repositions bodies as desiring subjects, but only ironically, leaving women cross-dressers in a different subject position from male cross-dressers. The anatomical body need not be read as destiny to make this argument but only as the site of a consistent cultural positioning. Such positioning does not erase the possibility of sameness but does not necessarily allow it to reside in anything natural or irreducible. De Lauretis, for instance, refers to an autonomous "female sexuality" ("Essence" 30) without essentializing her definition of lesbian but also without erasing all categories. It remains true in either approach that certain bodies are positioned in one way and other bodies in another way, and that gender, homosexuality, heterosexuality, and subjectivity have different meanings for those in differently deployed bodies. In an ironic way, then, the female body is crucial to the postmodern construction of lesbian desire.

But while positing sameness in the body may or may not be problematic, sameness does constitute part of the dynamic of the postmodern lesbian subject. The gender sameness is, I would argue, posited in terms of the subject's positionality in relationship to a system of meaning which constricts gender definition in heterosexual terms. Thus, while differences are enacted in the butch-femme couple that mocks and appropriates heterosexual constructions of desire and bifurcated, gender-defined clothing, sameness asserts its authority as part of the sexual and symbolic dynamic. The male/female posturing is also belied by the potential for each person to become the lover and the beloved, the subject and the object. Although not cast in butch-femme terms, Penelope J. Engelbrecht's reconstruction of subject/object dichotomy as the "Subject and Other/self" projects a similar play between differences and sameness: "they are simultaneous, coexistent, even identical in essence, yet different, because they denote different modes which fluctuate from moment to moment" (92). Although highlighting differences, the postmodern moment of theorizing the lesbian subject incorporates sameness as part of its construction, at times in the body, at times in positionality.

The postmodern lesbian subject emerges in its most playful theoretical form in a unique rhetorical genre. Through this form, the lesbian subject is characterized not by male postmodern alienation but by an identity more closely associated with the lesbian-feminist subject—identity in relationship. Not unlike Rich's rhetorical experiment in "Women and Honor," both Luce Irigaray's lyrical conclusion to *This Sex Which Is Not One* and Elizabeth Meese's *(Sem)Erotics* develop theory through a semifictional dialogue of a speaker/theorist/lover with a beloved Other. Because this form of theorizing walks a fine line, if that line exists any longer, between imaginative literature and the essay, these writers structure a narrator and narratee as part of the semifictional construction of the lesbian subject. This genre is, in many ways, a narrativizing of theory and a structuring of a metaphorical lesbian subject in the relationship of the lover and beloved. The old story, the essay, is told from the single vision of one author (God, man) with the reader as a passive, feminized Other, the receptacle of omniscient thinking. The construction of the postmodern lesbian subject depends on breaking this gendered positioning, assuming instead that thinking happens and reality is constructed as an interchange between two repositioned subjects. Meese and Irigaray forge subject positions that are dependent on reinventing the story in order "to escape from their compartments, their schemas, their distinctions and oppositions" (*This Sex* 212). As such, the experimental theoretical form, like the experimental narrative, attempts to escape gender. In discussing writers like Djuna Barnes, Meese argues that "these anti-gender novels also result in anti-genre texts, as though, among these lesbian writers, the anti-gender stance demands an anti-genre text" (*(Sem)Erotics* 57). This intentional confusion of gender also exists in her own book, where theorizing occurs in letters to a lover intermixed with more recognizable rhetorical discussions of texts and authors. The beloved, the narratee, like Gertrude Stein's Alice, becomes "the site of composition" (75), and like the same confusion of subject and object in the butch-femme couple, the beloved and lover exist as a necessary complement: "Who speaks this text of seduction? I can write it without you, but not without 'you.' Can there be a schizophrenia of desire in which I play both parts (woman and woman, lover and beloved)?" (86). Irigaray resolves her dilemma of the two in multiplicity:

"You? I? That's still saying too much. Dividing too sharply between us: all" (218). But neither thinker leaves gender far behind. Although unlike the essentialism of Irigaray's female body which speaks "our body's language" (214), Meese's lesbian subjects are also implicated in gender. In Meese's formulation, the break from the patriarchally constructed woman is another woman: "Lesbianism installs an un-utterable difference of difference—'I'/'me' and 'my lover,' 'she'/'me'—in the woman, as a double woman, a double subject: 'she' and 'she' " (17). If there is essentialism in such a designation, it is justifiable in Diana Fuss's terms by "*what motivates its deployment*" (xi) and by what Linda Alcoff calls the "conception of the subject as positionality" (433).

Women of color have become some of the most important theorists of the postmodern subject, defining the multiple subject positions on the borders of races, genders, and sexualities. Some Euro-American postmodern articulations of multiple subject positions rely on—if not appropriate—women of color's theories of racial, gender, and class positioning. In fact, "woman of color" has become in some theories a construct of its own. In her classic, "A Manifesto for Cyborgs," Donna Haraway uses Chela Sandoval to argue that the term "woman of color" lacks any unitary definition because of "the lack of any essential criterion for identifying who is a woman of color" (73); thus it "does not replicate the imperializing, totalizing revolutionary subjects of previous Marxisms and feminisms" (74). Haraway sees the "woman of color," like the cyborg, as a construction which challenges identity by being "a sea of differences" (73). Gloria Anzaldúa's much praised work, *Borderlands/La Frontera,* provides the most intriguing trope for this new subject in the "new mestiza," whose origin is never one, whose allegiance can never be singular, who, being both Indian and Spanish, is constantly on the border: "Living on borders and in margins, keeping intact one's shifting and multiple identity and integrity, is like trying to swim in a new element, an 'alien' element" (Preface).

But this formulation of difference is not always without a reference to gender categories and therefore to identity and sameness; nor is gender always divorced from sexuality. Like Audre Lorde, Anzaldúa is not fundamentally bothered by gender dualism but instead by the ways in which Western thinking has structured it. In her descriptions of being lesbian, Anzaldúa points both to her culture's condemnation of deviance and its belief in the "magical aspect in abnormality" (19); it is this latter belief that Judith Raiskin compares to Edward Carpenter's attribution of "spiritual and mystical properties" to the homosexual (160). Like Judy Grahn's earlier description of the sacred character of gay people in tribal cultures because "Gay culture acts as a buffer and a medium between clashing worlds and helps effect the transitions of power and knowledge from one sex to the other" (*Another* 11), Anzaldúa is not afraid to speak of the intriguing combination of male and female: "I, like other queer people, am two in one body, both male and female. I am the embodiment of the *hieros gamos:* the coming together of opposite qualities within" (19). Balance rather than destruction or transcendence of these opposites is her goal. In another recognition of gender difference, women of color, particularly African-American women writers, theorize the lesbian subject not as a separatist category but as one that refuses to exclude men. This position, as we shall see in Chapter 5, is central to Alice Walker's definition of "womanist," the woman "who loves other women, sexually and/or nonsexually" and who is "committed to survival and wholeness of entire people, male *and* female" (*Search* xi).

When gender and sexuality are separated, as they often are when postmodernism encourages gender undecidability, we risk the ironic reinstitution of the central male subject. As if to prove Irigaray's contention that "any theory of the subject has always been appropriated by the 'masculine' " (*Speculum* 133), the reference point for the lesbian subject is that mythical but, at the same time, all-too-real Lacanian phallus. In Sue-Ellen Case's "Toward a Butch-Femme Aesthetic," the parodic camp of the butch-femme relies on "penis-related posturings" in which the primary question is " 'penis, penis, who's got the penis,' because there is no referent in sight; rather, the fictions of penis and castration become ironized and 'camped up' " (291). Like Marjorie Garber's analysis of the transvestite, meaning is constructed only in relationship to male subjectivity. One must then ask whether gender is as profoundly disturbed as the postmodernists intend or whether it is implied all along but never acknowledged and therefore never analyzed. Gender, I would argue, creeps in unexpectedly because it is constantly shoved aside as a category of analysis. A more profitable course would be to acknowledge that lesbians are differently related to gender undecidability, to cross-dressing, and to sado-masochism because they are also positioned as women in relationship to cultural systems of meaning.

Postmodernism's lesbian subject is, like the lesbian-feminist lesbian subject, a figure that repositions itself in the cultural system of meaning and a figure that lends itself to metaphoric implications. The metaphoric potential of the postmodern lesbian subject resides in images like the vampire and, more importantly, in the close connection it maintains between textuality and sexuality making the lesbian body and lesbian sexuality—even the butch-femme couple—the textual body. In some ways, the postmodern lesbian theorizing leads to the broadest of metaphorical referents, for, when Catharine Stimpson asks in an afterword to *Lesbian Texts and Contexts*, "Is lesbianism a metaphor?" she answers in both lesbian-feminist and postmodern terms:

> For "lesbianism" might signify a critique of heterosexuality; a cry for the abolition of the binary oppositions of modern sexuality; a demand for the release of women's self-named desires; a belief that such release might itself be a sign of a rebellious, subtle, raucous textuality. 'Lesbianism' might represent a space in which we shape and reshape our psychosexual identities, in which we are metamorphic creatures. (380)

The postmodern lesbian subject trades on the image of a monstrous, bodily figure beyond the pale of "normality" and, like Orlando and even Baudelaire's "Femmes damnées," is a protagonist in a liberatory narrative. The grotesque body, the body out of control, and particularly the female grotesque body, becomes the ground for figuring metaphoric possibilities. The lesbian subject, then, will function, at times, on the level of the metaphorical tenor—as female sexuality outside of "natural" gendered categories and as an excessive, grotesque female body.

The postmodern lesbian subject is related to, as well as different from, its lesbian-feminist counterpart. It is different because its images are bodily rather than nonbodily and its discursive form is dramatic rather than rhetorical. It is also true that the postmodern lesbian subject, unlike its lesbian-feminist counterpart, emphasizes the deconstructive side of the combined utopian and deconstructive gestures that I have assigned to twentieth-century constructions of the textualized lesbian subject. To claim these radically different projects as identical would be theoretically irresponsible. But the similarities are also striking, particularly as they affect the project of feminist and lesbian writers who want to challenge the traditional Western narrative system. An argument that claims a connection between two diverse systems of thought cannot be blind to the differences. My intention is not to claim that the postmodern lesbian theory is the same as the earlier lesbian-feminist positions against which it sets itself. My argument is that the connections between the two, and therefore the continuity of lesbian theory, have been displaced by a grand and ironic narrative of liberation that obscures lesbian-feminist thought in the swirling dust left by postmodernism. We need instead to emphasize connections as well as disconnections.

In the poem "The Images," Adrienne Rich describes women's struggle against patriarchy as a "war of the images" (*Wild* 5). What has been read as a war of images among contesting lesbian theories needs to be reformulated as a succession of theoretical moments. The real war of images must be waged with the true enemy, not with each other. In the century-long rebuttal of the nineteenth-century sexologists, the postmodern lesbian subject is one in a line of metaphorical constructions. It is, like its earlier counterparts, also a subject constructed in relationship. The three related metaphoric projections of the lesbian subject have always been about redefining woman, stretching the "discursive boundaries" that affect anatomical women so deeply, refusing easy categorization, and offering new alignments and positionalities. Often these images defiantly and sometimes joyously take on the excess that is needed to stretch gendered boundaries. Based on the "double-play" which each theoretical moment enacts, these images posit radical concepts of identity which we should not shy away from in the face of lesbian erasure by previous theories or by current ones. These are the lesbian subjects that women writers of the last twenty-five years have used and have developed further as a strategy to challenge the narrative system.

FOUR

The Romantic Lesbian Narrative: Adrienne Rich's "Twenty-One Love Poems" and Marilyn Hacker's *Love, Death, and the Changing of the Seasons*

> If then, the subject of one's biography will neither love
> nor kill, but will only think and imagine, we may con-
> clude that he or she is no better than a corpse and so
> leave her. —Virginia Woolf, *Orlando*

Sappho's lyrical poems and Shakespeare's sonnets are considered problematic homosexual texts. Vast intellectual effort has been expended to
prove that these two paradigmatic poets of Western love lyricism did not
write on homosexual topics despite the seemingly obvious indications to
the contrary. Joan DeJean in her book, *Fictions of Sappho,* catalogues,
among other topics, historical commentators who deny Sappho's homoerotic poetic subjects and some who even "find themselves in the delicate
position of attempting to disprove Sappho's homosexuality without actually naming that which they claim she was not" (2). Dolores Klaich
uncovers a more recent scholarly attempt to argue for Sappho's "purity." In *Woman + Woman,* she quotes David M. Robinson's tortuous
argument which assumes that it is against nature for a woman to give
" 'herself up to unnatural and inordinate practices which defy the moral
instinct and throw the soul into disorder' " and at the same time to write
verse, as Sappho presumably did, " 'in perfect obedience to the laws of
vocal harmony.' " Moreover, he continues, " 'A bad woman as well as a
pure woman might love roses, but a bad woman does not love the small
and hidden wild flowers of the field, the dainty anthrysc and the clover,

as Sappho did' " (Klaich 145). Shakespeare's sonnet sequence is also the object of ingenious denial. Many of us who studied the sonnets in Renaissance literature classes were subject to the experience of my own graduate career. The professor reviewed lesser-known Renaissance poetry before we read the great sonnet sequences of Philip Sidney, Edmund Spenser, and Shakespeare. He reserved one sentence, in fact one word, for Richard Barnfield's blatantly homoerotic *The Affectionate Shepheard:* "Disgusting." When we turned to Shakespeare and his poems, two-thirds of which are written to a beautiful young man, praising love, friendship, and, perhaps, male homosexuality, the professor praised their dramatic power and lyrical intensity. Instead of disgusting, these poems constituted a mini-drama illustrating the imaginative power of the world's greatest playwright. They were a work of art and not a disgusting display of the libido gone wrong. Shakespeare was redeemed because his sonnets were better as poetry and because he portrayed the difference between Platonic and blatantly physical love. Of course, we never read Katherine Philips's poems to her beloved woman friend, Lucasia, which have also been, at times, vigorously excluded from complicity with homosexuality.

The critics of the future, however, will not have the luxury of ambivalence when they turn to the recent poetic sequences of Adrienne Rich and Marilyn Hacker. Like other lesbian poets of the last twenty-five years, they leave no room for ambivalence. Adrienne Rich's and Marilyn Hacker's openly lesbian poetic sequences tell the story of love found and love lost. They—especially Hacker—spare no sexual explicitness. They also both harken back, directly and indirectly, to the Renaissance sonnet sequence, especially to Shakespeare's, and both are aware of putting their stories not only into lyrical form but also into a recognizable romantic narrative. With that awareness we can begin to understand how they dare the love narrative to harbor a lesbian subject. The lesbian lover and beloved, the traditionally defined spaces of narrator and narratee, are described in both bodily and nonbodily terms, and together the narrator and narratee constitute one of the lesbian subjects in the sequences. The second lesbian subject is the poet/narrator as a nonbodily creative agent whose narratee is both the beloved and a community of women readers. Despite the literalness of the poets' images and the linearity of their stories, these lesbian subjects challenge two crucial areas of narrative mechanics. They upend the narrative's dependence on the positioning of the lover and beloved, the narrator and narratee, in structural terms of sexual difference, and they refuse the traditional love narrative's dependence on inevitability created thematically by passion and structurally by the positing and then transcendence of sexual difference.

Looking at these poems from the vantage point of narrative is rare but can be illuminating. Lyrical works are not divorced from narrative prescription, which includes "a prodigious variety of genres" (Barthes, *Image* 79). While we may, then, accept reading these poems from the point of view of narrative, the poems do not, at first glance, challenge traditional narrative structure, especially linearity. Thus, Jan Montefiore argues that Rich's poems might "be construed as attempts at the forging of new forms (although, compared with *The Lesbian Body,* they look positively conventional)" (165). It is true that the narrative trajectory of both sequences moves relatively smoothly and conventionally from the joy of love found, to complications from within and without, to a painful separation and, in the last poems, to the speaker's resolution to persist alone in Rich's sequence and the speaker's desolate loneliness in Hacker's sequence. Of course, as poetic sequences, there are ellipses of time between the poems, but these do not constitute a significant narrative disruption. The challenge to the narrative happens, for the most part, on the more subtle level of repositioning the relationships between the lesbian subject as narrator—lover and poet—and the narratee as the beloved and as the creative community. This repositioning allows the poets to use linearity strategically.

Both writers either explicitly or implicitly recall the Western romantic narrative told in the great sonnet sequences of the English Renaissance. This fact demands that we carefully analyze these predecessors, particularly the ambiguously homosexual sequence of William Shakespeare. In fact, a thorough consideration of Shakespeare's sequence is crucial to my effort to distinguish between male homosexual and lesbian narratives. The Renaissance sequences harken back to the classic nonmarriage love stories wrought in Western history by the courtly love tradition of the Middle Ages and the Petrarchan tradition of the Renaissance. The Renaissance love stories of Shakespeare, Sidney, and Spenser are conditioned by courtly love's idealization of passion and Petrarch's sublimation of it. The Renaissance sequences exhibit the mechanics of narrative that are thoroughly gendered and fit the pattern we have already identified. The male speaker or narrator is the mover of the plot by virtue of his right to speak and woo; the passive female figure is the recipient of that wooing and often the narratee. The English Renaissance poets depend on wittily replaying and retelling this old romantic plot, what Philip Sidney calls "Petrarch's long-deceased woes" (325). In it the lover's passion, most often rejected by the lady, becomes the dross transmuted into poetic gold or in some cases spiritual enlightenment. Transcendence either in a heterosexual union or in the enlightenment of male poet provides the narrative closure. Petrarch wrote of his love for a woman, Laura, he never met; Sidney wrote of his lost love, Stella, Penelope Devereux; Shakespeare wrote of love for a young man and lust for a woman they shared. Only Spenser's *Amoretti* chronicles a love relationship with a real woman, Elizabeth Boyle, whom the author will marry. Because the love story as a narrative structure is a male story, defined by what Leslie W. Rabine calls the "totalizing masculine voice of romantic narrative" (8), fitting a female voice, and especially a lesbian voice, into it is a challenge.

In the traditional Renaissance sequences, the narratee as female Other and especially as the female body occupy a special narrative position. Hers is a silent position except for the important and enabling word, "No," which in turn causes and inspires the lover's many poems on love's anguish and the transcendence of his sexual obsession. In one famous poem modeled after Petrarch, the early English Renaissance poet, Thomas Wyatt, describes his many love afflictions and ends with one line for his beloved, "And my delight is causer of this strife" (198). As Bruce Smith notes, the goal of the Petrarchan sonnet was to "turn the woman with her disconcerting *otherness* into a managable image in a poem" (259), an image for the construction of the poet's persona. She is the boundary which the speaker/lover must cross. The female body, however, is often described in great detail, and as Nancy J. Vickers has noted, is most often fragmented (96). Spenser's catalogue of his beloved's beauty is not unusual:

> Ye tradefull Merchants, that with weary toyle
> Do seeke most pretious things to make your gain,
> And both the Indias of their treasures spoile,
> What needeth you to seeke so farre in vaine?
> For loe my loue doth in her selfe containe
> All this worlds riches that may farre be found:
> If Saphyres, loe her eies be Saphyres plaine;
> If Rubies, loe hir lips be Rubies sound;
> If Pearles, hir teeth be pearles both pure and round;
> If Yuorie, her forehead yuory weene;

> If Gold, her locks are finest gold on ground;
> If siluer, her faire hands are siluer sheene.
> But that which fairest is but few behold,
> Her mind adornd with vertues manifold. (364)

The female body is not only fragmented, its parts listed and apostrophized, but this body is likened to precious commodities which are bought, sold, and traded. It is upon this transaction that the poet builds his persona. Shakespeare's Dark Lady sonnet mocks the idealization of the female body, but still leaves it in fragments. But, of course, Shakespeare's love is not the Dark Lady, it is the young man, and his poetic struggle is to redefine the feminized object position of the narrative to accommodate a male rather than a female. He accomplishes this task in several ways, highlighting the gendered nature of this romantic story and the male homosexual's access to that story.

Shakespeare's poems are significant for the analysis of Rich's and Hacker's sequences, not only because they constitute the most influential poetic sequence in English literature, but also because they form the most well-known poetic sequence that could be considered homosexual. Of course, naming a person or a work of literature homosexual prior to the recognized institution of the homosexual/heterosexual terminology in the late nineteenth century can be problematic. Eve Sedgwick refuses to identify the sonnets as homosexual, not because the relationship of the two men may not have been sexual, but because the use of the term is anachronistic and because "there is not an equal opposition or a choice" between something related to homosexuality and heterosexuality (*Between* 35). Bruce Smith is less hesitant: "Shakespeare's sonnets address the connection between male bonding and male homosexuality with a candor that most readers, most male readers at least, have not been willing to countenance" (270). Their disagreement about the sexuality involved centers on the structural function of the marginalized Dark Lady. Since Smith is not constrained by Sedgwick's thesis, he sees the constant slippage between the homosexual and homosocial, between the erotic and the Platonic. For him, the Dark Lady functions as no more than a contrasting love, given much less attention because "it was the bond between male and male that seemed the more complicated and problematic" (257). In the core of the sonnet sequence, the first 126 poems, the images are replete with sexuality, Smith argues, from puns to vegetative images, moving the narrative by degrees from homosocial to homosexual desire (248). But for Sedgwick, the Dark Lady is a structurally necessary figure that legitimizes and even cements the male-male relationship through heterosexuality because "to be fully a man requires having obtained the instrumental use of a woman, having *risked* transformation [or feminization] by her" (40).

I would argue, however, that the existence of the Dark Lady is necessary even if—especially if—the poems are called homosexual. I am convinced by Smith's argument that the relationship between the poet and the young man is sexual, and, like Smith, I have no hesitation using the word "homosexual" in this historical context. In this homosexual context, then, the Dark Lady is needed in the narrative structure in order to position the male in the role of the beloved and still avoid the horror of feminizing him. It is not only the woman who threatens to feminize him; it is also the narrative positioning. For that narrative imperative, Shakespeare constructs a woman to take on not only the position of Other, but also the abject of that position. She is, in fact, reduced to the body. While the poem in which the poet mocks the Petrarchan catalogue of physical beauty—"My mistress' eyes are nothing like the sun"—is standard as an example of the fragmented female body, it is also an example of the female body as grotesque, exceeding its boundaries as Renaissance doctrine dictated was the potential of all female bodies (Stallybrass 126). The woman's body and especially her sexuality were always on the verge of exceeding boundaries; thus, for instance, she was more likely to be a witch than was a male. *The Malleus Maleficarum,* the fifteenth-century compendium of witchcraft, states simply if not tautologically, that "the natural reason [a woman is more likely to be a witch than a man] is that she is more carnal than a man, as is clear from her many carnal abominations" (Kramer and Sprenger 44). Shakespeare in the Dark Lady sonnets sarcastically portrays the traditional Petrarchan "cruel" mistress as cruel indeed, not because she refuses him but because she does not try to become the chaste mistress. She is what he wants and therefore she is damned. She is castigated for her deception ("those lips of thine,/That have profan'd their scarlet ornaments,/And seal'd false bonds of love as oft as mine" (142)) and for her active sexuality which throws the poet into uncontrollable lust. She is, in the sonnet that begins "Two loves I have of comfort and despair" (144), the Renaissance epitome of woman as evil. If sexual puns inhabit the sonnets as a whole, these puns become most blatant in the Dark Lady poems. Like Kristeva's abject, she carries the Renaissance culture's and the narrative structure's otherness, the bodily uncleanliness that protects purity and cleanliness of the subject. While one of the most famous poems, "Th' expense of spirit in a waste of shame" (129) is about the speaker's feelings and not a direct description of the Lady, it is a description of the male controlled by his worst feelings, his dark, feminine, changeable side—his sexual side. Once this narrative position is filled by a grotesque version of the idealized beloved of the traditional sonnet sequences, the beloved young man can be construed as other than the feminized object of desire, what would ordinarily be dictated by the romantic narrative inscribed in the Petrarchan sonnets.

The male homosexual story, then, does not drastically realign the narrative patterns; it does not have to. It only has to avoid feminizing the male beloved. That goal is accomplished in part by retaining the female Other in a grotesque, bodily form and in part by transforming the feminized narrative space of the beloved, the narratee. In other words, woman is structurally necessary in the construction of male sameness. In four poems—sonnets 20, 38, 105, and 116—Shakespeare accords subjectivity to the beloved by granting him the one, unique virtue of male-male as opposed to female-male relationships—constancy. Thus, while, as Sedgwick notes, the beloved "represents the masculine as pure object" (44), he also walks a narrative tightrope that ultimately saves him from the feminized objectivity and passivity of the traditional narratee by the speaker's carefully argued transformation of the passive space of the beloved.

The first of these four poems begins "A woman's face with Nature's own hand painted/Hast thou, the master mistress of my passion" (20). The male beloved contains a "woman's gentle heart" but not "false women's fashion," granting him the emotional but not the physical attributes of woman. His physical relationship with women is merely a service while his relationship with the speaker is on a plane of spiritual love. But this constancy and spirituality do not necessarily rule out physical love; such a description is rather part and parcel of the Renaissance description of male love. While Shakespeare appears to create a neat dichotomy of Platonic friendship and erotic love, the images never stay completely in place. This crucial poem, one that Smith argues is the turning point of the sequence (248), claims the young man as "Mine by thy love" by positioning him as a woman who is not a woman, who in fact redeems what is ordinarily defined as female. In sonnet 38, Shakespeare has the same problem. Wanting to use the young man as a muse for his poetry predestines the beloved to the narrativized female space of the narratee, the purely passive space of the Petrarchan mistress. So the speaker identifies two muses, his own "slight Muse" and the "tenth Muse" which he accords to the beloved. Perhaps not wanting to remember that Plato had already accorded this honor to Sappho, the speaker accords the beloved a place above not only the poet's trifling, earthly muse but also the great muses of the classical world, all of whom were women.

The second two poems, which occur late in the homosexual sequence of 126 poems, affirm constancy without the struggle we see in the early poems. In sonnet 105 the beloved is called "Still constant in a wondrous excellence," and, for that reason, the speaker's verse now must fit new categories. Constancy as an attribute of the beloved demands a new language as well as a new narrative positioning, for now the poet can employ the words, "fair," "kind", and "true" for one person. With the Petrarchan lady or the Renaissance woman, poets could never be sure of the connections among these terms. She who was fair physically was never kind sexually, and the proverbial inconstancy of women made her always untrue. Now a beloved can be all three—that is if embodied in the male. The most famous of these four poems, "Let me not to the marriage of true minds" (116), takes the theme of constancy to its narrative conclusion in a transcendent description of spiritualized love. Here love, real love, is "not Time's fool" and is again contrasted to the feminized bodily images of "rosy lips and cheeks." The male has been rescued from a narrative which might have proclaimed him a mistress, and in the process he has redefined if not redeemed the feminized position, if only for men. Not unlike the more recent movie, *Tootsie,* Shakespeare proves that men simply make better women than women ever can.

It is not surprising, then, that when Adrienne Rich writes a series of love poems in a narrative form, she contrasts her effort to traditional patriarchal love stories. Implicitly she recalls the Renaissance sonnets and particularly Shakespeare's homosexual sequence. Recognizing her poems' affinity with this tradition, even though technically they are not sonnets, Hayden Carruth calls them "sonnetlike love poems—no, call them true sonnets" (272). In one of the central poems (XVII), Rich explicitly calls to mind the central narrative antecedent of the sonnets, the story of *Tristan und Isolde.* Through this reference, she also accords us the clearest picture of her awareness of narrative and of the historical codification of love as significant forces in "Twenty-One Love Poems," the central poems from Rich's mid-1970s collection, *The Dream of a Common Language*. In poem XVII she claims that *"Tristan und Isolde* is scarcely the story,/women at least should know the difference/between love and death."* Since she puts the story in its German title, we can assume that she speaks primarily of Wagner's musical interpretation of that old myth, for she also uses other operas as points of contrast: "neither *Rosenkavalier* nor *Götterdämmerung,"* she proclaims in poem XIII, is a woman's love story. While most critiques of these poems respond to Rich's call for a new poetry and a new language, what Joanne Feit Diehl calls "the woman poet's need to find or reinvent a language in which she can seize the power" (91), Rich is also aware of the power of the narrative and is careful to set her love story with its dual narrators against a culturally defined plot that does not include the lesbian subject.

Denis de Rougemont, in his classic and controversial study of *Love in the Western World*, uses the tale of Tristan and Isolde as the West's central love story. He defines Western love both as passionate, self-consuming transcendence and as a self-centered rather than other-centered concern (41–44). The myth that de Rougemont identifies as central for the West's concept of love, Leslie W. Rabine describes as a story which excludes female subjectivity (12). One could say that the violence of this passion exists because it is set up in oppositional terms that must be resolved and because it moves inevitably toward an all-consuming closure. The story Wagner tells of the fated lovers of medieval fame follows this script. As the opera begins, Tristan is bringing Isolde back to marry his uncle King Marke, but because Isolde is a healer who once cured Tristan's wounds and resents being taken as a kind of slave to a new master, she plans to kill Tristan with a cup of poison. But, on the ship, her servant, Brangäne, substitutes a love potion for Isolde's requested cup of poison, and when both Isolde and Tristan drink it, they fall passionately, inevitably, and tragically in love. When they land and Tristan is forced to hand Isolde over to his uncle—in earlier stories, his father—he does so knowing that he will betray him. Tristan and Isolde meet at night in a lover's rendezvous which, after much passionate singing, is broken up by Marke. Tristan dies in exile, waiting for Isolde; Isolde comes too late but still expires on her lover's body after a rapturous aria, the "Liebestod," the love/death. They are, it is presumed by the music, united in transcendent ecstasy. In Wagner's music the sexual tension is played out in chromaticism radical for its time, never resolving itself until Isolde sings the "Liebestod." Finally, after five hours, the entwined erotic and musical tension is relieved and resolved. This story is embedded with a fatalism which moves the narrative inevitably toward tragedy but also toward a satisfying, albeit unconsummated conclusion. As Joseph Allen Boone notes, this story overcomes the division of genders in a narrative closure of mystical oneness (38).

But the tension of the narrative also involves the relationship between two men. Marke is both Tristan's uncle and his feudal lord, and betrayal of these bonds—both feudal and kinship—is a failure of enormous magnitude. In typical romantic and medieval fashion, this is a male story pitting love against honor. In contemporary terms, this story exemplifies the struggle between heterosexual and homosocial bonding. In a telling comment, Wieland Wagner, the great stage director of his grandfather's operas, makes these astonishing pre-Sedgwickian remarks about the relationship between Tristan and Marke: "The eternal strife between father and son—the best known fundamental conflict of mankind since Freud's explanation of the relationships between Oedipus, Jocasta and Laius— . . . appears to me incomparably more tragic (and mythical!) than Tristan's adultery with his uncle's wife" (5). In fact, in his interpretation, Isolde is reduced to a *femme fatale* (5), a German Carmen who is not an equal subject in the love relationship, despite Wagner's vocal demands on her.

In poem XVII, Rich opposes to that paradigmatic Western love story a seemingly disjointed, erratic tale, one that includes "No poison cup,/ no penance." The speaker's story contains neither essential ingredient of *Tristan* because her story is not about causality or inevitability but about "accidents," not about heroes and heroines caught up in transcendent, unearthly experiences, but about dailiness, heroic dailiness, and ordinariness. The stories of women loving one another are compared to "car crashes,/books that change us, neighborhoods/we move into and come to love." Each of these events is noted for its randomness, its surprise, its happenstance. Because the causality and inevitability of the love story are minimized, they are neither determining nor life-threatening. The alternative image of another narrative trajectory is a tape recorder that "should have caught some ghost of us." Tape recorders are able to catch our unedited, ordinary, and daily ramblings, and it is the mythos of ordinariness that the poetic sequence inscribes. What the tape recorder captures is "this we were, this is how we tried to love." Such events need a new story, for, in terms of the speaker's earlier statement—"No one has imagined us" (I)—these counterplots to the *Tristan* story seem to say, "No one has plotted us." Yet the poem ends, curiously, in a nonrandom series of three lines: "and these are the forces they had ranged against us,/and these are the forces we had ranged within us,/within us and against us, against us and within us" (XVII). The rhythmic, inevitable repetitions of lines, syntax, and words (instead of end rhyme, one word is repeated at the end of each line, "us") suggests the impossibility of purely accidental stories, of a writing that is free from formal constraints. The alternative story, then, is not completely random, but one that involves choice and volition. The tension the poetic sequence maintains is between the pull of a system that prescribes a linear, causal narrative of heterosexual tension and complication resolved in a mystical/sexual union and a narrative trajectory of the lesbian lovers as subjects/objects who transform the narrative tension of separateness and difference.

Rich is so aware of the traditional Western narrative that she more than once compares her love story to well-known Western texts, most tellingly to operatic texts. As she does in "Transcendental Etude" published in the same volume, Rich juxtaposes complex musical structures which take a lifetime to learn and perform with the lives of women who learn their music by "simply listening to the simple line/of a woman's voice singing a child/against her heart" (*Dream* 73). In "Twenty-One Love Poems," Rich singles out *Der Rosenkavalier* and *Götterdämmerung* (XIII) as texts of which to be wary. Both are late German Romantic operas, one by Richard Strauss and the other by Wagner. Both are thematically centered on loss and redemption, and both depend on a complex, highly developed musical vocabulary the lushness of which borders on cloying satiety. At the end of Wagner's last opera in the Ring Cycle, the power-crazed gods have lost their home, and as it goes up in flames, the great Valkyrie, Brünnhilde, rides her horse into the flames, sacrificing her life. From her sacrifice a new order is born, one that depends on love instead of power, but like most of Wagner's heroines, Brünnhilde must lose her life in the process. In a less dramatic but more poignant way the older woman in *Der Rosenkavalier*—she is in her mid-thirties—gives up her young lover to a younger woman, acknowledging her new place in the world as one who is no longer a central object of male desire. Not convinced by the gender ambiguity in Strauss's opera or by the Amazonian woman in Wagner's story, Rich dismisses both narratives as inadequate models for a relationship not dominated by gender hierarchies and inequalities. Instead, Rich wants "a woman's voice singing old songs/with new words, with a quiet bass, a flute/plucked and fingered by women outside the law" (XIII). Her desire is for simplicity as well as sameness, for a small ensemble in which all parts are taken by women, but also for old songs with new words. The old songs recall the matriarchies that fascinated Rich at this time and to which she refers in several other poems (VI, XI, XXI). But old songs also infer old literary forms that are needed for comprehension even while tainted with asymmetrical power structures. Sameness as a structural device, as a means of repositioning the narrative characters, she implies, will simplify this overwrought narrative system.

The lesbian subject changes as the sequence progresses, from two women recreating themselves by giving each other primary attention to the poet as an autonomous, creative female agent who writes within the context of the implied reader of the women's community. In fact, these two lesbian subjects exist in two parallel and interrelated narratives. The first part of the sequence emphasizes the primary counterplot, the relationship of the lover and the beloved, the subject and the object of the story; the second part of the narrative picks up the narrator's singular journey as an independent, creative lesbian subject yet one who is not defined solely in isolation. Central to the narrative of the lover and beloved is the reconstruction of the primarily nonsexualized female body. The challenge for the lesbian writer is to construct lesbian subjects who not only defy the traditional objectification of the female beloved but also reconstitute the lesbian body as other than the abject of the female body, unless parodic. Curiously for someone who has been accused of avoiding the body, Rich constructs this lesbian narrative space through the body. In the narrative of the poet/narrator as a single agent, Rich expands the metaphor of the nonbodily lesbian subject as an autonomous female creator.

These depictions of the lesbian body and mind are set over and against male constructions of the female mind and body and therefore become Rich's symbolic means of stretching both gender and narrative categories. Rich indicates this stretching of boundaries in several ways. She refuses to use the word "lesbian" and instead insists on making all of her references to the two lovers through gender. Thus their same-sex love is defined only by the lines "we were two lovers of one gender,/we were two women of one generation" (XII). It is this slippage that has led many to argue that these poems are "universal," that is, inclusive of heterosexuality, a position to which Rich has strenuously objected (Bulkin 270–71). At the same time, the erotically charged "(The Floating Poem, Unnumbered)" proves to others that Rich is addressing only lesbian specificity (Friedman, "Adrienne" 190). But this slippage between woman-identification and a lesbian eroticism is not only a part of her definition of the "lesbian continuum" but also a part of the metaphoric lesbian subject's "double-play."

The first fifteen poems, including "The Floating Poem," reconstitute the female body as an agent over and against male discourse about the female body. It is a body set against both the sexually objectified female body of pornography, the hysterical woman of poem IV, and the male writer's—Swift's in this case—"loathing the woman's flesh while praising her mind" (V). The first poem begins with the awareness of woman as constructed by Western discourses of love, but instead of references to idealized versions of love in a *Tristan* or a *Romeo and Juliet,* Rich epitomizes the traditional love story as pornography. In other words, she begins her poetic sequence with a reference to narratives, to pornography, science fiction, to tabloids, and to the "rancid dreams" which reduce the woman to fragmented and eroticized body parts. Pornography is merely the flip side of *Tristan und Isolde.* It is the underbelly of romantic fiction that captures Rich's attention and that captures and holds the body which once, like "the long-legged young girls playing ball" had other possibilities. In a later poem, this violence against women is equated with political violence against a male hostage whose *"genitals have been the object of such a sadistic display/they keep me constantly awake with the pain"* (IV). The tyranny that subjects woman to the lash also feminizes a male through imprisonment and torture, providing a horrifying parallel image of the daily reality of women's lives. The lesbian subjects who walk these streets, who try to avoid these stories, must reimagine themselves as women, must retell the story.

Rich's immediate answer to the need for a different story projects an idealism and escapism for which she is often criticized. Here she appeals to nature outside the pavements of civilized mayhem: "We want to live like trees" (I), but instead of imagining an Edenic hideaway she speaks of "sycamores" "dappled with scars" yet still able to grow. While Rich is tempted in these poems to provide a purely utopian solution to the dilemma of women controlled by an anti-feminist and homophobic society, while she is tempted to posit her lesbian figures outside of culture and the narrative in an idealized world of nature or in a fantasy of a new story untainted by any previous story, she ultimately refuses to take that easy gambit. Rich's lesbian subjects do not escape the culture or the narrative form by choosing between two opposing arenas; they inhabit both worlds simultaneously. This space of tension resembles Teresa de Lauretis's concept of a " 'view from elsewhere' " which she describes as a "movement from the space represented by/in a representation, by/in a discourse, by/in a sex-gender system, to the space not represented yet implied (unseen) in them" (*Technologies* 26).

Rich, then, does more than expose the workings of the narrative system as Sexton and Atwood do: she uses it against itself. In the first instance, her primary narrative is structured not by traditionally defined, oppositional genders but by sameness between women. Claire Keyes notes of *The Dream of a Common Language* as a whole that it is about "connectiveness" (162)—in poetry, women's relationships, and language. But sameness and connection reposition the lovers as narrator and narratee in a different narrative dynamic because sameness between the crucial lover and beloved roles as well as the marginalization of male figures starkly refigures the confrontive and transcendental aspects of the romantic narrative.

Rich exposes the romantic story as violent from her first mention of pornography and its angry rape of the female body. The second poem is meant as a contrasting narrative possibility to the first and introduces the second narrator, the lesbian as creator. Where patriarchal stories objectify and subdue women, especially their bodies, the speaker's dream is about connection, about reconstruction. Out of the glare of pornography she constructs her own dreams and her own narrative, which will become the two of them: "*I dreamed you were a poem*" but not a work in isolation, instead "*a poem I wanted to show someone*" (II). Their shared room becomes not only an everywhere, but also a new construction of the nature of love for women against "the pull of gravity." Thus, the central way in which this story is reframed is in the relative positions of lover and beloved and of the poet/narrator and reader. It is difficult to put either in that simple place of power and control. For instance, the first act of love, the first mention of a lover's touch, is of the beloved waking the speaker by kissing her hair. Although in the next poem, the narrator/poet does not resist the traditional poetic desire to describe the beauty of the beloved—"Your eyes are everlasting" (III)—the first body we see is the speaker's. While the center of subjectivity is certainly the speaker as it must be in this form, it is a shared subjectivity which will take on a greater life as the sequence moves forward. The lesbian poet/narrator also establishes the creative act as an interrelationship between creator, object/medium, and reader.

With this poem of delicate touching and reimagining, the female body begins to take on different proportions. Thus, when the beloved's body is described, it is not catalogued objectively or voyeuristically; rather, it is most often described nonsexually in order to counter the fragmentation violently forced upon it in the system itself. On one level, this is an attempt to normalize not only the male-defined abject female body but also the grotesque, sexually rampant lesbian body of the nineteenth-century sexologists which still lives on in popular conceptions of the lesbian. In poem VI, Rich characterizes the beloved's hands, "precisely equal to my own," as holding power, the power to birth a child, to use tools, to touch, to steer a "rescue-ship/through icebergs." The variety of activities associated with the hands gives the beloved an agency she rarely receives in this type of romantic narrative. In fact, the beloved in this poem becomes the protagonist and the speaker the receiver of action. But we could go further. Violence itself is mitigated by the theme of the poem, for these hands, if used in "unavoidable violence," would forge a space in which "violence ever after would be obsolete." Violence is also mitigated by the relationship of sameness between the lover and beloved, for as their hands are precisely equal except for the thumb, we may assume that the lover's hands are also capable of changing violence, of piloting ships, of using power tools. The receiver and initiator of action are indistinguishable in this story.

During this phase of her writing, Adrienne Rich often fantasizes a communication untrammeled by language or other systems of meaning deemed patriarchal. Between the late 1960s and the early 1980s, Rich found language itself a burden. In some of the most well-known lines from *The Will to Change*, she cries, "this is the oppressor's language/yet I need it to talk to you" (16), and in the same volume, in "Our Whole Life," she imagines the opposition of words and the self, with the only poem as life itself. In one critical formulation, made at a poetry reading in 1964, Rich states that "instead of poems *about* experiences I am getting poems that *are* experiences" ("Poetry" 89). By the late 1970s, in a despairing poem entitled "The Images," she imagines herself free of the "guilt of words" (*Wild* 4). In "Twenty-One Love Poems," Rich expresses these sentiments through animal imagery. Narratively, these sentiments ask that we forgo system, form, structure for the immediacy of touch or, in literary terms, the immediacy of language or realism. To idealize nature's seeming immediacy is, as noted above, a tendency of feminist writers at this time. But again, while the utopian is a tempting escape, Rich draws back from the total acceptance of human immediacy uncontaminated by language, literary forms, or other systems. As she notes in poem XIX, "(I told you from the first I wanted daily life,/this island of Manhattan was island enough for me)."

The imagery of "animal passion" (I) is underscored in the opening lines of poem VII, "What kind of beast would turn its life into words?" She asks but does not answer whether this writing is "close to the wolverines' howled signals." In the willingness to identify with the animal on a primal level, she refuses the narrative desire to identify the physical with the abject, with the female side of the dualism. If the body is narratively trapped in the female space of otherness, Rich refuses the dualism by claiming an animal sense for her lesbian subjects, not because animals represent baseness or sexuality gone wild, but because they represent the basic and immediate concerns of all creatures—connection—either through touch or sounds. In Poem X, she identifies her "own animal thoughts:/that creatures must find each other for bodily comfort." Ultimately we need both touch and speech because both provide primal, human connections. Thus, the speaker describes the lovers' closest moment not as an intimate embrace but as a connection publicly claimed on a boat where both of them become violently sick. In the midst of "honeymoon couples" (XIV), they touch in public unselfconsciously for what seems to be the first time. At this point they are totally within their bodies:

> I put my hand on your thigh
> to comfort both of us, your hand came over mine,
> we stayed that way, suffering together
> in our bodies, as if all suffering
> were physical. (XIV)

Instead of seeing this imagery as part of Rich's desire to mute the cultural level of human existence or to reduce lesbian sexuality to gentle touch, I believe her larger purpose is to reinvent the female body in love poetry and narrative. To accept the utter animalness of the two women in love is to refuse to condemn it. At the same time it is to take what the symbolic and narrative system has handed out to the constructed female body and to challenge its meaning, to provide a "reverse discourse."

It is not surprising, then, that the poem following the one on seasickness is the only erotic poem in the series. It is unnumbered. In part, the poem is not numbered because it is about outlaw sexuality and must be placed outside the system of meaning that contains the rest of the poems. In the other poems, Rich works to normalize and desexualize the lesbian body. In this poem, sexuality and the poem itself exceed narrative boundaries, floating above the whole sequence and refusing to be controlled by narrative time. The speaker ends the poem with the eternizing phrase, "whatever happens, this is." The poem is not, then, a part of the plot whose trajectory moves from ecstasy to the dénouement of loss. Its lush eroticism, more explicit than in any poem Rich has written, is evocative and lulls one either into an ecological or an orgasmic fantasy, perhaps both. At the same time, the ritual of lesbian lovemaking must be placed outside of the story because it exceeds narrative and symbolic limits. It is Rich's version of the excessive, undomesticated lesbian body, a partial answer to the constructions of the lesbian body by the late nineteenth-century sexologists. This poem can also be seen intertextually as the one poem in which Rich catalogues the beloved's body in a sexual way. The language is lush, the images are of the natural world. Their sexual bodies are compared to the "half-curled frond/of the fiddlehead fern in forests/just washed by sun."

But while the body is excessive and utopian, this poem refuses, despite its tendencies, the transcendental closure of the traditional, heterosexual narrative. First, it counters the traditional position of the woman in the sonnet sequences by putting the speaker's body in the same position as the beloved's. The positionalities in relationship to desire are not asymmetrical but similar. Once again the importance of sameness restructures the narrative positionalities. The beloved's thighs and nipples are met with the lover's "rose-wet cave," leaving each vulnerable and powerless, each controlling and powerful. It is not that they inhabit the same body, but that the oppositional elements that structure the traditional narrative are modified when Rich refuses to objectify the female body. This fact also reconstitutes the poet/narrator as creative agent. By constructing a different dynamic between lover and beloved, the love relationship refuses transcendence, for despite the last line, the lovers are not immolated by their passion as are Tristan and Isolde and the lovers in Laura Esquivel's *Like Water for Chocolate*. Nor is this poem the end of the sequence. Transcendence has often meant the denial of the female and the body, but Rich forgoes these possibilities to remain firmly rooted in the physical, claiming it and transforming it for her narrative.

After the erotic, unnumbered poem, the separation of the lovers begins, and the bodies become less important as the sequence closes with a poem of "Adrienne alone" (XVIII) choosing "to walk here. And to draw this circle" (XXI). The narrative of the lesbian body converts to the narrative of the lesbian mind; the lesbian body as the excessive female body or autonomous female sexuality becomes the lesbian subject as an autonomous female agent, one with "a sense of desiring oneself; above all, of choosing oneself" (*Lies* 200). It is in this second counterplot that the speaker begins overtly to challenge the narrative necessity for causal inevitability. The gradual separation of the lovers turns into a painful separation of their bodies. At various points the speaker sets circumstances against choice. Circumstances, like narrative systems, must be challenged by willfully forging new boundaries. When they are separated into single beds not by choice but by circumstance, the speaker claims that "Only she who says/she did not choose, is the loser in the end" (XV). When the narrator attempts to recreate connection through a sensuous reimagining of the lover's body across town (XVI), the romanticism is cut by the context of the previous poem about choice and responsibility. Narratively, Rich refuses the inevitability of this separation, the assumption that outside forces alone, including the narrative structure, are weighted against them. The outside forces that she often outlines in this sequence are there and are devastating, but they are not, in the end, determining. As we witness their first separation, the narrator declares, "If I cling to circumstances I could feel/not responsible" (XV). This is the fateful story of Tristan and Isolde, despite the overwhelming anti-woman and anti-lesbian forces set against them. To see themselves as victims would be to succumb to the constructed female position in society and in story. When, in other instances, love between women has been successful, the narrator calls it "heroic in its ordinariness" (XIX). Yet narratively, the speaker has not failed, for from the ashes of the lesbian subjects as two desiring and desired figures she chooses the narrative of the lesbian subject as an autonomous creative agent. The poet/lover who remains alone at the end of the story forges a new narrative position for the woman in the love story—alone, hurting, and alive—but she also remains the lesbian subject in connection with others, in community. She is neither bitterly alone nor in relationship.

Gradually the lovers' separation leaves open "a cleft of light" (XVIII) which becomes the space for the speaker to emerge alone, not triumphant or transcendent or even defiant, but as a figure choosing to continue, to save herself, again to be "the mind/casting back to where her solitude,/shared, could be chosen without loneliness" (XXI). If we exclude the erotic transcendence of *Tristan und Isolde* from "The Floating Poem," then we must also, I believe, exclude the spiritual and creative transcendence that many Renaissance poets achieve on the backs of the female Other. We must also exclude the individualism that accompanies the latter form of transcendence. The construction of this persona as a separate figure is not made by gradually pushing the figure of the beloved into an imagistic role. As the "cleft of light" opens up, the figure standing there appears not at the expense of the beloved but in spite of her. Nor does this single lesbian subject remain without connection, without an identifiable narratee. In other words, the agent or protagonist of this set of poems is never the autonomous figure of male narratives, drawing boundaries around his subjectivity in order to assure his independence from otherness and therefore to claim his individuality. The narrator wills another ending. The narratee in this poem is no longer the beloved, the "you" of the previous poems, nor is the narrator drawn into a "we" of the lovers' dyad. The singular pronoun "I" takes over and the reader is more easily equated with the narratee, who is no longer addressed as "you." Addressing the reader more directly, the singular figure of the narrator, described primarily by her autonomy and by her mind in solitude, wills a larger relationship with her readers, a community of women. The speaker connects herself with other women through matriarchal images, a connection that the lesbian subject posits as the source of female creativity and agency. The lesbian subject redraws her world from her connection with the great prehistorical cultures recalled by monuments such as Stonehenge. Recalling the "ecstatic women striding/ to the sibyl's den or the Eleusinian cave" (VI), the narrator's references to the "dark lintels" (XXI), the circles of a Stonehenge, suggest a ritual of renewal. The connection to other women is maintained, therefore, on a larger level, but it is not one that supercedes or is better than that dyad the two lovers tried to create. It is space still full of the pain of loss, "half-blotted by darkness," yet hopeful. She chooses to put herself, then, in another section of the "lesbian continuum," perhaps one could say in another phase of that continuum of women relating to one another. And it is here that the lesbian subject, the poet/narrator, is acknowledged as the female creative agent, for the efforts to draw a circle, to choose life, to reconnect are all aspects of female creativity and agency. The poet who completes the poetic sequence on lost love and the hurt lover are the narrative agents who draw the circle. In fact, only in this "lesbian continuum," whether in a lover's dyad or in a larger communal setting, are women able to be agents or creators.

Rich's multiple lesbian subjects and their narratives are, then, related. Each creates a lesbian narrative space which realigns the categories of subjectivity and proposes themes and values that undercut and decon-struct narrative's power alignments. By emphasizing the lovers' same-ness—Penelope J. Engelbrecht's "a lesbian Subject and a lesbian Other/ self" (86)—instead of difference, Rich mitigates the divisiveness and conflicts that presuppose narrative tension. She also refuses the transcen-dence that is a part of the love narrative, either the ecstasy of togeth-erness or the transcendence of male individuated spiritual redemption. In the process, she is tempted to move in utopian and essentialist direc-tions, but she rarely rests in such a fantasy. The lesbian subject does not constitute a static utopian category of meaning. It moves, struggles with the given nature of narrative, revises that which constricts it, and forges a different set of values that become possible when retelling the romantic story. It does not forgo linearity and yet it firmly rejects some of narra-tive's most elemental themes and structures. Rich's struggle is to stretch and redefine both narrative and gender boundaries through her construc-tion of the lesbian subject.

Marilyn Hacker's book of poems is both more traditional and more radical. Hacker's sequence of poems consciously recalls the sonnet se-quences, especially Shakespeare's, for not only does she quote in its entirety Shakespeare's sonnet 73, "That time of year thou mayst in me behold," but she also directly reminds us of his lines and specific poetic technique. Because she is also enamored of strict poetic forms, most of the poems follow the modified Italian form with tight rhymes and off-rhymes structuring the octets and sestets. To the sonnets, she adds a few other forms such as villanelles and rondeaux. Caroline Halliday believes that while the use of strict poetic forms, created and solidified by male poets, for a story of lesbian sex might be seen as "a form of subversion," it is ultimately too restrictive (100). But Hacker's strategy, I would argue, explodes the regulated forms with colloquial language, with sex-ual explicitness, and, technically, with enjambments which make the poems read at times like breathless prose being spoken outloud. Unlike Rich's somewhat gentle stretching of definitional boundaries, Hacker grabs the tightest of male poetic forms and forces it to accept not just a lesbian subject, but also a rampant, undomesticated lesbian body and lesbian sexuality. As Liana Borghi accurately claims, "Mixing high structures with low form is a deconstructive strategy" (76).

The narrative at first appears to be traditional and unchallenged structurally. Even more than Rich's slow-paced linearity, which is not set out to encourage a breathless, erotic reading experience, Hacker's love story races with the narrative pressure of a Harlequin romance. Instead of beginning with a relationship already established, as Rich does, Hacker begins with unrequited longing. The narrative and sexual tension are intertwined, and the trajectory is unbroken even by a poem that floats above the narrative linearity. The story moves from longing to consummation to loss in a bold effort to set down the normative narrative pattern as the governing trajectory of her story. The speaker of the poems also appears to be the old lover of the Petrarchan sequences who creates her own subjectivity on the body of the beloved, her narratee. For instance, we continually hear of the lover's turbulent passions that the Renaissance poet might describe as a ship tossed at sea. This lesbian subject is lustful, horny, outrageous, wise in turn, impatient, loving and ultimately devastated by a failed affair. She is left alone and longing, utterly despairing in the dark of winter. Hacker's use of traditional poetic and narrative forms could encourage the conclusion that she merely repeats the structures which control and objectify both women and lesbians. But the power of this sonnet sequence belies that easy conclusion; instead, Hacker undermines the very systems of meaning that she employs. Like Diana Fuss's claim about Irigaray's essentialism, Hacker's use of traditional, ideologically constructed literary forms "functions strategically as a reversal and a displacement" (59) of male narrative and poetic centrality. Hacker provides two plots: first a counterplot determined by the parody of the male-dominated love story and a second one centered on the poet, the goddess-like lesbian poet who weaves her life into textuality and thereby claims language, text, and narrative as her own. The boldness of claiming what Wittig would call a universal subjectivity is a means of upsetting the old, controlling categories. These claims are dependent on the repositioning of the relationship of narrators and narratees.

In important ways, Hacker is consummately aware that she is writing narrative as well as poetry. Hacker's awareness of the narrative she is spinning comes from the obvious connection she makes with Shakespeare's sonnet sequence and other poetic sequences that tell stories and with a running image from the Homeric stories of Ulysses and Penelope, of Achilles and Patrocles. Like Rich, Hacker asks whether the lovers can be called heroes. Rich responds with what Olga Broumas calls "a radical redefinition *of* the heroic" (274) in terms of the ordinary and daily lives that women lead. Hacker boldly identifies herself and her lover in some of the old heroic patterns, at one point putting their nascent relationship in "Two thousand years of Western literature:/potions and swords, the quests, the songs, the trysts" (33). More to the point, the speaker sets Achilles up as a mock heroic figure, "Achilles hung out in his tent and pouted/until they made the *Iliad* about it" (123). In the same poem she asks, "Would we be heroes if things came to it?" (123). But heroism in love is deflated by the time it is identified with Achilles' "fit of pique" (128). Perhaps their petty quarrels as well as grand passions fit the heroic molds of what has passed for the definition of heroism in love, but like her other claims to the masculine traditions of Western literature, Hacker assaults the structures and constructions by claiming them outright and forcing them, with irony, humor, and parody, to fit the love affair.

In one important way, Hacker does not repeat the usual literary story. Instead, she creates what I would call a shadow plot, one that is absorbed into the dominant plot structure yet challenges the very structure it inhabits because it refuses to be controlled by the old pattern. Hacker uses the male-dominated structure as the central narrative trajectory, but uses it in order to parody and expose it, and ultimately to claim it. In other words, writers can use a realistic, linear plot and still challenge it by interrupting both traditional structural positions and thematics. In the first place, Hacker challenges the sonnet sequence's love narrative by eliminating men and male homosocial desire. Like Rich, Hacker marginalizes male figures in the extreme, for these are poetic worlds that are of necessity separated from men. For Rich this position is crucial because the male and what he represents—a system of oppression—are dangerous to women and especially to lesbians. Even the male friend of Rich's poem V who speaks of arranging his books so that he will "look at Blake and Kafka while he types" elicits a series of comments about male objectification of women in their art. The male world in Rich's poems is, in fact, palpable, but individual males are exorcised from the narrative until at the end the male world that so threatens the lovers in the first poem is transformed into the female world of the last poem. Hacker is less overtly political, yet males rarely if ever appear in these poems. The largest male role is reserved for some callous remarks about the loss of love that a male friend makes in the penultimate poem. Otherwise, Hacker constructs a rich world of female relationships with friends here and in France, lesbian couples, her daughter, and, centrally, her lover.

Like Rich, Hacker's concentration on sameness without the conflicting elements of sexual difference has structural and thematic implications, but unlike Rich, Hacker alters the gendered narrative structure less than she highlights it, parodies it, and takes it for her own serious purposes. In using it in such a straightforward manner, she intentionally misuses it. The lesbian body and lesbian sexuality are the agents of this approach to deconstructing narrative. They are excessive and outrageous, almost proving the contentions of the current religious political right wing, which seems to believe uncritically the leftover nineteenth-century sexology that excessive sexuality is the defining characteristic of homosexuality. In this view, the lesbian is female sexuality gone wild. In Hacker's strategy, the lesbian body parodies the constrictions imposed on the female body by social and narrative convention. By exceeding these bounds, Hacker's literal lover enters the metaphoric realm of the lesbian which reconstitutes female sexuality. The lover, for instance, imagines the many ways in which she will make love, both in fantasy before the affair begins and later when they are separated by the speaker's frequent trips to France. Unlike Rich's "Floating Poem," these fantasies are not delicately compared to unfurling ferns. Lines such as "Well, damn, it's a relief to be a slut" (11) and "I seem to flirt with everything with tits" (10) take back a language which has been allowed to men even in sonnet sequences. The sexual puns in Shakespeare's sequence are notoriously risqué, unlike the ethereal images in the one significant woman's poetic sequence before the twentieth century, Elizabeth Barrett Browning's *Sonnets from the Portuguese*. Hacker does not rely on puns when she claims "My eyes and groin are permanently swollen" and "I'd cream my jeans touching your breast" (12). In fact, the earlier poems which depict the fantasies of a lover anticipating sexual consummation conjure the sexual tension of the Petrarchan male lover/speaker. Thus, the undomesticated female body takes over as the subject of the otherwise controlling story of Western love. The result is horror or excitement, depending on who reads the sonnets.

The boldness of this excessive sexuality challenges the narrative form at its core as a system set out to objectify and control female and lesbian sexuality. It proves unable to do so as the lovers romp their way through fantasies, lovemaking, and again at the end, more fantasies. Even in a consciously duplicated and parodied linear form, the narrative is unable to contain this sexuality because no one love is narratively positioned solely as the Other, as object of the gaze or desire. Because the lovers' bodies and sexuality are constructed as the same, the narrative positions are less likely to be constructed on the basis of hierarchical power relationships. Hacker tempts the narrative, however, as the speaker takes on a kind of power that makes her able to create and recreate her lover textually: "your body is a text I need/the art to be constructed by" (50). While the textualizing of the lover's body is in one way an objectification of it, more profoundly it is a process of re-membering rather than fragmenting it. The mitigating image that refuses the objectification of the body of the beloved is the home.

Although the body is seen often as an agent of dissolute pleasure, Hacker also subtly associates it with home. While the erotic is on one level undomesticated female sexuality, on another level it is ironically the domesticity of daily life—of home, of food, of shopping. As Halliday notes, eroticism in contemporary lesbian poetry "does not exist by itself, it coexists with the rest of life" (89). Thus despite the outspoken sexual references, the imagery of home refigures the sexuality as common and ordinary, a refiguring which mitigates the power relationship between the speaker and the beloved. "Your breasts, thighs, shoulders, mouth, voice, are the places/I live, whether or not I live with you" (201), says the speaker, and more directly, "I'd like to throw my laundry in with yours./I'd like to put my face between your legs" (178). The latter quote is reminiscent of the imagery in Rich's "The Floating Poem." Rich's reference hinges on a double meaning of the word "come" when she plays upon the reference to orgasm and to coming home: "Your traveled, generous thighs/between which my whole face has come and come—." The lover's sense of coming home in her lover's orgasm is echoed in the reverse when the beloved enters the lover "where I had been waiting years for you/in my rose-wet cave." The imagery of sexuality for Rich is predictably not fire and ice but coming home; less predictably, Hacker's sexuality of fire and ice is also coupled with the domestic. Hacker's speaker associates lesbian sexuality with eating gourmet meals and with shopping as the lover imagines her soon-to-be beloved. The undomesticated body of lesbian sexuality exists in a fantasy of domestic bliss as the older lover dreams wildly of being a homebody with her younger partner, a wish that the reader absorbs apprehensively. The description of the beloved's "breasts, thighs, shoulders, mouth, voice" (201) in the opening poem of the last, tortuous section of loss is not about fragmenting an objectified lover, but about re-membering the beloved's body as home. Hacker challenges the thematics of the love narrative along with its stark gender differences in this characterization of the lesbian body.

The mitigation of stark difference and therefore of the power relationships of the narrative structure also occurs on other levels. Both lovers are poets and, as a result, they are both positioned as desiring and creative subjects. One is not a speaker while the other is mute, for the beloved as the narratee is given a voice. They exchange poems. As the lover lolls in her beloved France, "a six-foot-four Jamaican Heurtebise/ brought me your sonnets, and took mine away" (32). In one instance, she entitles a poem "What You Might Answer" (35). While we are to assume that the composition of the poem is from the speaker's mind— there is an outside chance that it is the beloved's poem—more to the point is the voice the speaker gives to the beloved. The entire poem is in quotes with Rachel's "I" demanding, in ardent youthfulness, the right to her own independence and her own tastes. Hacker also repositions the female creative voice in narrative as an agent through a revision of mythic characters. Early in the narrative, the speaker calls herself Penelope who "weaves sonnets on a barstool among sailors" (48). Penelope becomes the narrator and creator of her own story, for she not only creates words but refuses to undo what she creates. Much later in the sequence, the speaker picks up the image of weaving for the dual creative life of lover and beloved: "While summer stars burn stories on the sky,/ we pick the threads to keep weaving our own/eye-straining daily handiwork" (167). Their lives and their poems are works of art that they weave and tell.

The unwillingness to position lover and beloved as opposites is also tied to the images of gender ambiguity, especially in the beloved who displays a boy/girl ambivalence and whom the speaker at one point calls "*gynandre*" (70). Separating her daughter and herself from the "masculine" ability to throw a baseball and reveling in her beloved's proficiency, the speaker calls the beloved "a Saturday hero" (109). Yet, while the narrator associates herself with the feminine, at other points, especially when she is lusting after her young student, she thinks of herself as a masculinized desiring agent as she does when she describes a haircut which makes her look "like a bad boy" (30). Despite her play with gender indifference, Hacker insists that they are, in fact, two women: " 'Honey, you look like a twelve-year-old boy./But you go down on me the way, God knows,/only a girl goes down!' " (101). Female agency, desire, and creativity are constructed through a positioning of two women who are primarily attentive to one another. That repositioning allows them to occupy gender ambiguous narrative places; in fact, they occupy both active and passive functions alternatively and indifferently without the stark differentiation that is necessary to traditional narrative paradigms.

The second counterplot, however, is more serious and less parodic, but it too encodes what we might term stealing the narrative. Here the narrator as the singular figure is a lesbian who creates, who forms her own plot, and claims authorship. As a woman and a lesbian, the speaker is doubly not an author, a word that Gilbert and Gubar remind us is identified with "writer, deity, and *pater familias*" (*Madwoman* 4). But the narrator of these poems is not only a lover of the beloved Rachel, she is also a lover of poetry, of poems, of her own writing. In fact, Borghi suggests that "these love sonnets look more often like a courtship of poetry than of the beloved" (77). This "courtship of poetry" is well within the Renaissance tradition of the lover/poet who is often more interested in his fame as a poet than in his love for his mistress. The mistress, in fact, functions as an embodiment of poetry itself. While Rich's narrator seems to say, "look who I have become," Hacker's speaker seems to say, "look at what I have created." As a self-conscious narrator who keeps her awareness of poetic forms throughout, she wages a battle and a love affair with constrictive male poetic forms. In fact, she boldly recalls male poets both directly and indirectly and also dares them—the poets and the forms—to usurp her creative work. She subtly imitates Shakespeare in a number of poems, such as one which forces us to think of Shakespeare's sonnet 73 on aging: "While your old one frets over thoughts like these,/my young one's taken somewhat better charge" (190). The poem ends with a Shakespearean play on words. But along with direct references to male poems and poets, the poet as narrator adds female images of creation such as "I'm cooking/a sonnet sequence and a cassoulet" (25). She also, as is more traditional in male language, feminizes the medium when she claims, with pride, in the same poem, "I'll show you these bitch Welsh quatrains I've tried" (25). The poem, then, sets up a relationship of two feminines, the woman who creates/cooks and the language and forms she clearly loves. This lesbian act then establishes female creativity as lesbian with the same audacity as Rich's earlier claim that lesbian is the creativity in all women. Despite the loneliness expressed in the last poems, Hacker's narrator also displays an arrogant joy in the creative process that defines her as first of all a poet, not a lover.

With this bold seizure of what has been defined as male comes the possibility that the narrator as single creator is a mere imitation of the male persona, one who speaks solely from the authority of himself and creates *ex nihilo*. Hacker mitigates this reading of the narrator as poet by the community within which her poems circulate. The narratees of this second plot are the women with whom she shares her life as poet and as frustrated lover. Less identified with the reader than Rich's implied readers as a community of women, this group of Hacker's narratees contains the poet's friends who are a part of her creative process. She writes for and to them. Julie, one of her best friends in France, is a constant recipient of her letters and poems. In one poem, in which the two friends are traveling together in Italy, the narrator sits with Julie in front of a cathedral. Julie reads the lovers' poems: "*She* has my poems in hand, and yours" (46). The narrator's attention is focused both on Julie's response to their love and, almost more intently, on Julie's critical response:

> we've swapped and read
> first drafts where no one for kilometers
> reads English—so I am itching to know what
> hot crit's cooked now behind that frown of hers. (46)

She even addresses to Julie one of the few poems not addressed to the beloved (165). Other women friends become part of her community. All are a part of the narrative of love; they are also a part of the narrative of poetic creation. Like Rich's "lesbian continuum" in her last poem, Hacker maintains a community of women throughout her short-lived love affair; unlike Rich, whose community is the female audience, Hacker addresses a community of friends structured as characters in the poems. Neither poet, then, is singular but part of a community act of creation, an image that undercuts the trope of the self-sufficient, god-like male poet.

It is not surprising to find that Hacker's last poem begins with a play upon a Shakespearean line, "Did you love well what very soon you left?" (212). Closure is on two levels in this sequence, the end of a love affair—"Never so full, I never was bereft/so utterly"—and the completion of a tour-de-force sonnet sequence. The reference to Shakespeare's line, "To love that well which thou must leave ere long" (73), reminds us that this experience has been triumphantly textualized as well. The downward and upward narrative trajectories refuse to forgo male forms and instead take them on, boldly claiming them for the lesbian subject as lover and beloved and as poet. In the process, the forms themselves shift ever so slightly, exhibiting a thematics of sameness and community that have not been part of the tradition of male love poetry. It is the bold seizure of the forms that allows Hacker to challenge their male-dominated characteristics. Hacker also metaphorizes the lesbian in this titanic struggle. The lesbian body becomes the means to revise male and female places in the narrative, and the creative lesbian refuses the place of silence and passivity that proscribes taking the language and narrative as her own. Both of these images are part of the long tradition of metaphorical positionings of the lesbian subject. Hacker's "severely literal" lesbian subjects are quickly caught up in that intertextualization.

These texts, then, posit a linear narrative, but not one that goes unchallenged by Hacker and Rich. The imitation of the linear love story highlights its artificiality because it is countered by a shadow narrative of two women lovers who refuse the dichotomous subject positions that inhere in the traditional trajectory. The lovers as a couple restructure the dichotomous narrative functions of the active and passive narrative spaces; the lovers create together one version of lesbian narrative space, a narrative interaction of passive and active functions. This mitigation of the stark, gender-defined narrative divisions refuses the transcendence associated with the heterosexual love story. Both lovers are positioned as desiring agents and thus transform the narrative possibilities of narrator and narratee. The assumption of a community either at the closure or during the narrative progression also undercuts the singular attention on the lovers that makes the narrative tension of the love story · acute. One could say that readers are responding to two narrative trajectories at the same time, the trajectory inherent in a *Tristan und Isolde* and the revised, less conflictual version of two women giving each other primary, erotic attention without the presence of any male figure. The lesbian body as the female body and sexuality in excess becomes the central trope by which the lovers' relationships are defined. The other identifiable narrative rests with the narrators as poets. The narrators are both

The Heroic Lesbian Narrative: Marion Zimmer Bradley's *The Mists of Avalon* and Gloria Naylor's *The Women of Brewster Place*

> It is the story that makes the difference. It is the story that hid my humanity from me, the story the mammoth hunters told about bashing, thrusting, raping, killing, about the Hero. The wonderful, poisonous story of Botulism. The killer story.　　—Ursula K. Le Guin,
> *Dancing at the Edge of the World*

> In the feminist utopias some of the words that fall into disuse because they no longer signify are "prostitution," "father," "rape," "heroism," "love," "madness," "homosexuality."　　—Fran Bartkowski, *Feminist Utopias*

The heroic lesbian narrative is one of the most popular of contemporary lesbian literary forms, whether in the story of the dashing single heroine of Rita Mae Brown's *Rubyfruit Jungle* or the utopian lesbian community in Katherine V. Forrest's *Daughters of a Coral Dawn*. As a single, "severely literal" heroic figure, the lesbian character in popular lesbian fiction offers a sense of power and possibility to hungry lesbian readers who have encountered little either inside or outside of school which portrays them with anything but disdain. As could be expected, these stories are satisfying because writers assign the active narrative role to a self-conscious lesbian who makes her own decisions and decides her own fate. It is a role that most lesbians see as their chosen or unchosen role in life, and they want it given heroic status. It is satisfying, then, to read Anne Cameron's Western adventure that allows two lesbians to make their journey westward and to defend themselves, guns and all, against the menace not of Indians but of men. In *The Journey*, Anne and Sarah also play out gender roles as they travel through the early West to win a home of their own. Anne hunts; Sarah cooks. Their adventures are replete with the tensions of violence that structure the single narrative trajectory of the heroic story. This novel ends triumphantly, making it what Catharine Stimpson would call a lesbian novel of "enabling escape" ("Zero" 244). It is also satisfying to read about Sandra Scoppettone's lesbian detective, Lauren Laurano, whose easy acceptance of her homosexuality and whose deductive skills lead her through a maze of conflicting evidence in *Everything You Have Is Mine*. Scoppettone minimizes gender stereotypes except to give her heroine typical male detective qualities, fitting her into the recent rash of male-defined women detectives like Sara Paretsky's V. I. Warshawski and Sue Grafton's Kinsey Millhone. The new woman detective is able to go where she pleases, accomplish tasks on her own, and engage in violence when necessary. The detective novel, like the adventure story, relies on the traditional heroic paradigm, filled as it is with the narrative tension which moves the reader to an inevitable and satisfying closure. These lesbian figures are heroic because they overcome the same obstacles that the male hero would encounter and accomplish these tasks by taking on the traditional characteristics of the male hero. Like Ripley in *Aliens*, these heroines, this time lesbian, flourish in a single narrative trajectory, in part being absorbed by its structure and values and, at the same time, sending a ripple of shock, however minor, through its well-codified categories.

The lesbian community as an heroic agent in popular lesbian stories often attains a mythic power that is denied the single lesbian figure. As Bonnie Zimmerman notes, novels of the "lesbian community (whether they belong to the genre of speculative fiction or not) tend to be intensely idealistic and utopian" (*Safe* 121). These communities gain their agency by being separated from the confines of male society and by gaining or maintaining their independence by battling that same male society. Women in the lesbian communities of popular lesbian texts structure their identity in terms of two relationships: against that which is defined as the patriarchy or simply men and toward that which is defined as essentially female. The definitions of what is female, however, can differ radically from text to text. Sally Gearhart's *The Wanderground* is a well-known popular lesbian utopia which idealizes the lesbian community, in this case a group of women existing at one with nature in a territory safe from the male-dominated City. While not popular in a commonplace sense, Monique Wittig's *Les Guérillères* has gained the status of a lesbian literary classic. Like the conjunction of Woolf's transgressive novel, *Orlando*, and Radclyffe Hall's realistic novel, *The Well of Loneliness*, Gearhart's and Wittig's texts can be considered comparable "lesbian novels." Wittig's postmodern story portrays a less overtly lesbian community, the nondifferentiated subject, *"elles,"* but while this community becomes "the absolute subject of the world" (*Straight* 85) in Wittig's symbolic battle with language, on the level of the text images, the community also wages an epic battle with the presumably male social order and army.

Thus the lesbian community as a narrative hero presents the same narrative problems as the single lesbian hero. As the narrative protagonist, it can be both absorbed into the traditional narrative trajectory, and in some texts this is its ultimate fate, and, at other times, challenge its structural categories. Wittig's text is usually considered more transgressive because of its nonlinear trajectory. But traditional heroic narrative tension is mitigated in both texts, in Gearhart's by a set of short stories each delineating a new event and in Wittig's by a series of short poems each giving a vivid though iconoclastic image of the life of this community. At the same time, neither text is without the narrative tension of heroic conflicts. Gearhart depicts the sense of unease that is part of a community that lives on the edge of dangerous male community, and Wittig articulates a paradigm, however circular, of epic conflict and resolution. The nature of heroism, however, differs in each because the community as a lesbian subject in each is unique. Wittig rejects traditional female identification with nature and instead creates an iconoclastic set of characteristics, including violence, which sets her community apart from other women's or lesbian literary communities. Like Charlotte Perkins Gilman's *Herland,* however, Gearhart's text relies on the idealization of traditionally depicted female virtues: communication, nurturance, and sympathy with nature. Wittig's lesbian subject exceeds the narrative categories of gendered subjectivity and her community, and, as a result, assumes a narrative agency for *"elles."* But the difference in these transgressions is a matter of degree not kind.

The problems of defining an heroic lesbian protagonist in the context of a narrative system are bound up with the already problematic notion of female heroism. For some early critical studies, the task was the identification and recognition of female figures, like Joan of Arc, who took on male roles and characteristics. Current psychological studies accomplish a similar goal through simplistic identification of historical or mythological women who can be held up as models of autonomy and action. The alternative is to elevate traditional female characteristics as heroic, making masochistic saints and a self-sacrificing Virgin Mary edifying models. But once a critic identifies the characteristics of heroism as a problem of the internal logic of a system like narrative, the issue is no longer the identification of women who take on male characteristics or who assume traditional female characteristics as heroic.

In this systematic context, woman in an heroic role can be called a contradiction in terms, for the narrative system not only posits agency as male but also demands social integration, often through the hero's marriage, at the closure. No matter how revolutionary or alienated, the male hero moves toward incorporation into dominant society because he is the outsider who ironically represents the culture's highest ideals. The possession of a woman at his story's end is the central way to represent this cultural inclusion, for, as Northrop Frye declares, "the reward of the quest usually is or includes a bride" (193). Because the woman's relationship to cultural values is more problematic, her heroism does not easily incorporate both love and quest. But, while someone like Rachel Blau DuPlessis perceives love and quest as antithetical for the female hero (7), Lee R. Edwards attempts to claim the opposite: that all "heroism, in fact, appeals to love, makes love its end" (13). This dilemma may not be as profound for the lesbian hero, particularly for the literal lesbian figure, but for the nonbodily metaphoric lesbian hero, the subject of this chapter, love represents the danger of being repositioned, in DuPlessis's distinction, as a heroine rather than as hero (7). Critics therefore must negotiate the problematic conjunction of woman and heroism with fine distinctions about the woman's relationship to society. Maureen Fries, for instance, distinguishes between female heroes, heroines, and counterheroes. Each category is defined in relationship to the dominant culture's values; the counter-hero is the most subversive: "the counter-hero possesses the hero's superior power of action without possessing his or her adherence to the dominant culture or capability of renewing its values" (6). Morgaine in The Mists of Avalon, Fries argues, is such a counter-hero (12). The woman's paradoxical relationship to culture's values, a relationship structured into male quest stories by his relationship to a female love object, is the source of her subversive power as well as her potential defeat by the system which decrees her narrative place as either boundary figure or closure.

The crucial battle, then, for the control and definition of heroism is between the marginalized text image and the narrative as a system. Both female and lesbian heroes are subject to being absorbed by the male-defined, heterosexual plot system. In similar but also significantly different ways, each is the outsider that the system wants to erase. As the excess of the category, woman, the lesbian subject in the heroic male space automatically disturbs the narrative in ways that the female hero cannot, for as the ultimate marginal figure, the lesbian subject is potentially disruptive in any guise. Edwards's instructive use of Victor Turner's distinction between marginals and liminars sets out the categories for this argument and, in the process, refuses any easy dismissal of the character level of narrative. As a cultural anthropologist, Turner identifies two types of societal outsiders: those who leave society only to return and those who by definition are outsiders who can never be accommodated by the social system. The traditional hero is a liminar because, as Edwards notes, "ritual liminality is a kind of antisocial state encysted within a durable surrounding structure" (8). The hero's separation from the social system is momentary, but marginal figures, on the other hand, are more profoundly divorced from society: "Their situation is more extreme than the liminar's, their dilemma more profound. Their absorption by society requires fundamental and permanent changes in the definitions of society or self" (8). The traditional hero of narrative is a liminar, one whose "isolation is impermanent" (8). The traditional hero is also male, whose "heroism is contingent upon some factor—circumstantial or psychological—extrinsic to his sex" (8). Edwards also adds that because "maleness is patriarchy's single absolute requisite," the hero remains a liminar even though he "may be poor, inwardly tormented, part of a racial, ethnic, or religious minority" (8). Women, on the other hand, are always already marginal. They cannot occupy the liminal position because "in patriarchy, femaleness is the ultimate and ineradicable sign of marginality" (9). The male hero is ultimately a conservative figure, one whose challenge to the given order only "provides local change and rearrangement at the price of preserving intact the central terms of order" (9). The female hero exists in a different relationship to the system and thus can challenge the system and its implied values.

While this view veers to the other end of the narratological spectrum because it assumes that a heroine by virtue of being female, by being "quintessentially marginal" (8), challenges the male centrality of the heroic system, it contains the advantage of alerting us to the power of the character who occupies the role of narrative agent. If the lesbian subject more than the female hero is the "quintessentially marginal" narrative figure, then the lesbian figure, especially as it taps into the metaphorical constructions of the lesbian subject in the twentieth century, is a text image of disruptive proportions. What Edwards sees as patriarchy's greatest threat—woman as hero—is also often implicated in the binary system which either forces the female hero into the passive role if she is embroiled in a love situation or re-marks her as male if she forges ahead with heroic aspiration. The narrative works to position the lesbian as either male or female, but because the lesbian subject is already erased by narrative's control, it exceeds narrative's categories because it is not functional in or bounded by the constructed woman's relationship to man. The lesbian subject, then, is the ultimate marginal figure because it transgresses the arbitrary boundaries of gender. This metaphoric figure can function in a traditional narrative scheme and at the same time exist in a different relationship than the male hero—straight or gay—or the straight female hero to the active heroic space. It is this lesbian subject that profoundly disturbs patriarchal notions of heroism because by definition it gains its identity in relation and not by separative dynamics. Thus it attempts, not always successfully because the narrative system has its own power, to alter the gender alignment and the values inherent in that story we call the hero's. It is the lesbian subject that can divorce the active narrative position from its ideologically inscribed gender and therefore infiltrate the narrative system's male and heterosexual designs on the reader.

If the romantic story, then, allows the construction of the couple as a unique lesbian subject who together realign the traditionally dichotomous narrative spaces, the heroic story fosters two narrative subjects, the single and the communal heroine, who restructure the agency of the mobile narrative space by relating differently to the narrative boundary space and closure and by breaking up male bonding. The result is a redefinition of heroism. This heroic figure must, as the romantic lesbian subjects did, exceed the narrative boundaries allotted to the female, refuse the posture demanded of the male hero, and reposition the function of narrative agency. This repositioning happens because, in this case, the movement of the heroic identity and action is more dependent upon sameness rather than difference, on relation rather than separation; but because heroism as culturally defined is formulated by a movement against an enemy through which the community or single figure is identified, the heroic lesbian subject must reposition itself in a system of meaning that depends on oppositional positioning. In popular fictive forms, this battle is less often won, even though the mere appearance of a lesbian figure unsettles some of the traditional narrative mechanics. It is less often won because most popular stories limit the connection of the lesbian subject with the metaphorical antecedents constructed by twentieth-century lesbian theory and thus its ability to realign narrative structure. The metaphoric potential of the lesbian subject refuses the narrative's desire to codify the figure as either male or female. Often the singular lesbian subject as narrative agent—as protagonist and/or narrator—is too easily codified as male and controlled by the characteristics assigned to the mobile narrative space.

In other texts, the metaphoric lesbian subject is a nonbodily figure that often defies identification, but as an heroic agent is directly or indirectly associated with the positionality of the lesbian as woman who defies traditional gender categories. The metaphoric lesbian subject identified in the third chapter is already an heroic figure of cultural movements—of lesbian-feminism, modernism, and postmodernism. This figure is always already in a narrative of liberation, a narrative that moves from the constriction of culturally defined gender boundaries and heterosexuality to a utopian space which, as Ellen G. Friedman notes of some women's texts, evokes the "unpresentable as the not yet presented" (242) and as deconstructive of the previous restrictive boundaries of woman and lesbian. This figure, then, is a natural for the heroic plot because it is already structured as excessively female, not simply a redesigned man, nor simply a female passive, nurturing figure. Neither gender definition will do for the transgressive, heroic lesbian subject. At the same time, this heroic lesbian subject must also wage a battle with the traditional plot line and plot space, what Margaret Atwood calls the "white plot."

But traditional heroic narrative values and structures, as we have seen, resist the lesbian subject because these values and structures depend upon a strict gender dichotomy and on male bonding. Well-honed themes of honor and conquest are structurally dependent upon male bonding and the female as Other. Because heroism needs the Other, the woman, against which to measure itself, what Josette Féral calls the West's "Savage" (88), the ultimate demand of heroism is the control and conquest of whatever is defined as female, whether Circe, the medieval dragon, or the Wicked Witch of the West. Catherine Keller concludes from her analysis of myth that "misogyny and heroic masculinity are indistinguishable" (86). From this perspective it is easy to see why psychological feminist critics equate the stories and culture of heroism with the male maturation process. Dana Heller clearly summarizes the process and its values: "To kill and to restore: the cycle of the quest equates an antagonistic process of individuation with maintaining the universal order. Competition guides the dialectic structure of the quest and defines male heroism as an aggressive destiny achieved through exercise of physical strength. The world provides the necessary stage, a place where one may attain the ultimate boon: manhood" (3).

This individualism, however, is predicated on a tribal bonding. Honor is one of the key values that heroism demands, and it is often set against love; Tristan, for instance, loses his honor because he chooses love over loyalty to his kinsman and liege lord. Honor is dependent on a psychic as well as narrative individuation that bonds one man to another, even if in antagonism. Carol Gilligan's description of the different ethics of men and women allows insight into the nature of the heroic value system, for, in effect, she describes the difference between love and honor. Based on the male maturation process of individuation, male ethical choices, she argues, value adherence to an abstract principle at the cost of human connection. Women's ethical decisions are based on the mitigating circumstances of relationships with other people. Bonding for men, then, comes in the agreed-upon adherence to larger, shared goals rather than intimate relationships. This code of honor often appears in a choice between obedience or loyalty to a male ruler, group, or friend and the love of a woman.

Two of the most revolutionary constructions of classical Western heroism, Milton's *Paradise Lost* and Joseph Conrad's *Heart of Darkness,* do no more than reinstate male centrality by affirming male bonding: bonding at a distance, refusing female bonding, bonding in male communal relation, and controlling the symbolic female who is present. Milton sets out consciously to revise the heroism of the classical epics with the Christian heroism of Adam. Satan is the example of the old, violent heroic paradigm; Christ the exemplum of the new, "the better fortitude/Of Patience and Heroic Martyrdom/Unsung" (IX, 31–33). Adam is to imitate Christ, yet he needs the figure of Eve in order to distinguish mature from immature and even dangerous heroism. More than merely needing Eve as the Other, the narrative also needs to refuse the potential for primary female bonding. In an early scene in which Eve recalls her awakening to life, she looks into a pool and sees her own image. She is attracted to it: "Bending to look on me, I started back,/It started back, but pleas'd I soon return'd,/Pleas'd it return'd as soon with answering looks/Of sympathy and love" (IV, 462–65). In fact, she "pin'd with vain desire" (IV, 466). Her attraction to herself, often identified as narcissism, is quickly foiled by the intervention of a voice— God's—which leads her to Adam.

But James Holstun claims that this scene can be examined in terms of lesbianism, an all but erased phenomenon in early modern Europe. For Holstun, this dramatic episode invites the reader to imagine lesbian desire, but the scene also "defuses it and makes it invisible in order to master Eve (and woman) more thoroughly" (855). With that refusal the text creates Eve as the mirror for Adam, for as Virgina Woolf notes, "mirrors are essential to all violent and heroic action" (*Room* 36) be- cause they contain "the magic and delicious power of reflecting the figure of man at twice its natural size" (35). As Milton states it, "Hee for God only, shee for God in him" (IV, 299). While Milton cuts off Eve's potential for female bonding, for there are no other women in Paradise, Adam is allowed several choices for bonding: primarily Eve or God, male or female. In this veiled clash between love and honor, Adam makes the wrong choice when he chooses to accept Eve's offer of the apple and with that her love and companionship. The choice of what to do when Eve offers Adam the opportunity to disobey God is a much- discussed crux in this complicated poem. Is it a simple either/or, either God or Eve? Or should Adam ask God for another chance for both of them? Raphael has already warned Adam of the danger of loving Eve too much, but when the crucial decision confronts him, Adam decides that he cannot live without Eve. C. S. Lewis expresses the issue harshly yet squarely in terms of a heroism that is familiar to us:

> If conjugal love were the highest value in Adam's world, then of course his resolve would have been the correct one. But if there are things that have an even higher claim on a man, if the universe is imagined to be such that, when the pinch comes, a man ought to reject wife and mother and his own life also, then the case is altered. (123)

While Milton wishes to emphasize "A paradise within thee, happier far" (XII, 587) and the virtues of patience and fortitude, the structural ele- ments of the heroic narrative remain the same in *Paradise Lost*: individu- ation based on the separation of the male from the female, an objectification of what is female, the refusal of female bonding, and the concomitant idealization of honor based on individuation and male bonding.

Conrad comes at the time when writers are questioning the absurdity and cost of the heroic colonial adventure. But the sense of an uneasiness about heroic quests and heroic ideals, even an interrogation of Europe's imperialist agendas, does not necessarily mitigate the text's structural investment in those same agendas. Sedgwick's triangular model of narrative structure exposes the system that implicitly reaffirms heroism while overtly denying it. In this reaffirmation, female bonding is not a possibility because the few women in this story are minor, far removed from one another, and exist as traditional symbols of otherness. The most obvious example is the "wild and gorgeous apparition of a woman" (76) who appears as Kurtz is carried to the ship. She is the mysteriousness of the jungle, that part of Marlowe and of Europe with which Marlowe tries to come to terms. This sexually available femininity is predictably set against the purified ideal of womanhood, Kurtz's long-suffering Intended, who is described as having "fair hair, this pale visage, this pure brow, [which] seemed surrounded by an ashy halo" (90). But the energy between Kurtz and Marlowe is the source of the novel's power. Marlowe is both attracted to and repelled by the text that has been created around Kurtz. If Kurtz represents imperialism at its worst and best, intent both on killing and rescuing the jungle's inhabitants, Marlowe represents a cynicism about either project and yet an intense attraction to it. The bond they forge, which sets them up not as antagonists but as the same, as brothers, is consummated when Marlowe goes to the Intended and lies to her, a lie that allows Marlowe to keep Kurtz to himself. If this homosocial bond were read metaphorically, one could argue that there is a sexual tension between the narrator, Marlowe, and the object of both his scorn and his desire, Kurtz.

In the context of the West's powerful heroic system of structural alignment and accompanying values, the problem for the heroic lesbian subject is how, in refusing the oppositional gender alignment in the narrative pattern and in the concomitant value system, to create narrative interest and viability as well as a new set of values. When contemporary women authors write the lesbian subject into their narratives, they do so with an awareness of narrative's recuperative powers and with a similar awareness of the lesbian's uniqueness as a marginal figure. In the 1970s and 1980s, this figure, both as a literal figure and as a nonbodily subject, appears in countless stories embodying women in communities or woman as single and autonomous narrative agents. These women writers often choose the heroic story as a model because the alternative, the love story, too often forces woman to be a part of his story, not the subject of her own. The heroic woman's story of these decades often includes women relating to one another, either in a dyad or in a larger community, structuring, in many cases, the nonbodily lesbian subject as an heroic narrative protagonist. In choosing two seemingly unrelated texts in which neither text nor author draws attention to lesbianism, one book by an African-American woman and the other by a Euro-American woman, I am addressing the problems of the nonbodily lesbian subject as protagonist and narrator. Marion Zimmer Bradley explores the single heroic figure in a complex relationship of narrator and protagonist, and Gloria Naylor creates a intricate community of protagonists who meld into a single unit in the primary focalizer's vision at the end of the story. The racial difference, I believe, also creates two separate although related definitions of the lesbian subject. Only in acknowledging this difference can we begin to posit an inclusive definition of the lesbian narrative.

Nearly two-thirds of the way into Marion Zimmer Bradley's *The Mists of Avalon*, the central character, Morgaine of the Fairies, now an old woman, returns to her home in Avalon after years of exile. She brings with her a younger self, Lancelet and Elaine's child, Nimue, to become a priestess of the goddess. At home at last, Morgaine encounters a former self in Raven, the woman sworn to serve the goddess with her silence. In the dark of the night, Raven enters Morgaine's sleeping quarters and awakens her. With a religious fervor that borders on the sexual, Raven removes her own cloak, takes Morgaine in her arms and touches "her slowly, with ritual silence and significance" (639). Raven quietly gives Morgaine the silver crescent, the ritual ornament of the priestess, and Viviane's ritual knife, items that Morgaine left behind when she flew in anger from Avalon and her Aunt Viviane's control. Then, in an act of bonding, each pierces herself: "from the breastbone she [Raven] pricked a single drop of blood, and Morgaine, bowing her head, took the knife and made a slight cut over her heart" (639). In an already sexually charged scene, the tension becomes stronger in their next exchange: "Raven bent to her and licked the blood away from the small cut; Morgaine bent and touched her lips to the small, welling stain at Raven's breast, knowing that this was a sealing long past the vows she had taken when she came to womanhood. Then Raven drew her again into her arms" (639–40). In the italicized words in this passage, which indicate her inner thoughts, Morgaine recounts her heterosexual passions—Lancelet and Accolon—"*Yet Never*," she says of this reunion with Raven, "*have I known what it was to be received simply in love*" (640).

Two other scenes confirm the erotic energy between the two women, energy not translated into sexual contact, but exuding the kind of spiritual erotic energy in Audre Lorde's definition of the erotic as power. Earlier in their lives, when Raven and Morgaine were being initiated into the rites of the Goddess, the connection of their bodies was a part of Morgaine's awareness of religious ritual. In that context, Viviane is a bodiless figure in the ritual in which "shining hands laid something in Morgaine's hands, then in Raven's" (166). Morgaine feels the power of the moment "as if she were standing among multitudes beyond multitudes thronging the top of the Tor" (166). But the immediacy of the body is felt only with Raven: "She could feel the warmth of Raven's body near hers, though they nowhere touched one another" (166). Alone this passage would mean little, but combined with the highly charged passage above and another section preceding the great moment in which the Goddess's Holy Regalia—spear, cup and dish—are misappropriated in the Christian ritual of the Mass, these descriptions, full of potential lesbian energy, constitute a pattern of placing women in primary relationship with one another at crucial events in the story. In the third instance, Raven and Morgaine have traveled to Camelot to repossess the Holy Regalia. The day prior to Pentecost, they stop to rest, leaving an hour to travel to Camelot the next day. Raven is frightened and exhausted, but insists on being part of this quest. When they lie down to sleep, Raven asks Morgaine to hold her, and in a scene both motherly and erotic, "Morgaine clasped her close and kissed her, rocking her like a child" (765). Then, Morgaine "held Raven against her, touching her, caressing her, their bodies clinging together in something like frenzy" (765). Morgaine feels the world responding to their closeness, "trembling in a strange and sacramental rhythm around them" (765). The images of the world shaking imitate an orgiastic frenzy as "woman to woman" (765) they "together call on the life of the Goddess" (766). The movement of erotic images ends with the world lovers "at last quiet in each other's arms" (766).

The simulated lovemaking of this section is blatant and not out of context. Depictions of women loving women in Avalon are made without negative comment, as if this were as natural as heterosexual love. Only in the Christian world is there any tension or shame about homoerotic desires. In the fairy world, where Morgaine resides for a while in dream time, she, "to her surprise, . . . found the maiden—yes, she looked somewhat like Raven—twining her arms round her neck and kissing her, and she returned the kisses without surprise or shame" (405). It is Lancelet who is tormented by his relationship and attraction to Arthur and whose potential homosexuality is scorned. Mordred recounts a story about Lancelet to the court: " 'something of a ballad made when they thrust a harp into his hand and bade him play, and he sang some lay of Rome or the days of Alexander, I know not what, of the love of knightly companions, and they jeered at him for it. Since then, his songs are all of the beauty of our queen, or knightly tales of adventure and dragons' " (713). The only hint of homosexuality in the Christian world that is free from this pain occurs, first, between Raven and Morgaine the night before they enter Camelot for the great feast and, second, at the final parting of Lancelet and Gwenhwyfar when she is willing to admit that " 'Your heart was always with Arthur, my dearest. I often think the only sin we did was not that we loved, but that I came between the love you had for each other' " (864).

While the short scenes I have described, amounting to only several pages in a book of 876 pages, do not contain the romantic tension that Bradley lavishes on the great heterosexual affairs of the book—Igraine and Uther Pendragon, Morgaine and Lancelet, Morgaine and Accolon— they are scenes charged with unmistakable lesbian energy. Each scene, particularly the two lengthy scenes between Raven and Morgaine, is a short interlude in the text's heterosexual thematics. Together these scenes form the radical core of a book that Lee Ann Tobin argues embodies a "simultaneous conservatism and subversion" (154). The two fully developed homoerotic scenes happen at crucial times in the movement of the narrative. They represent Morgaine's return to her self and to her calling as a priestess of the Goddess, her acceptance of the quest that Viviane gave her before Morgaine left Avalon in anger. It is a quest to keep Avalon alive, and it involves danger in a world now occupied by alien Christians and a God that demands that only He be worshipped. In other words, these are pivotal scenes. From these powerful connections with Raven, Morgaine gains the strength and courage to attempt her difficult mission. How, then, in a basically heterosexual text are we to read these short but erotic and undeniably lesbian sections? They could be viewed as innocent but intense religious rituals devoid of real sexuality or as curiosities in a long book that might need curiosities to sustain itself. In fact, it is the religious nature of each scene which might lead us to dismiss the eroticism as "only" spiritualized energy. Instead we need to ask why this spirituality is eroticized in such obvious ways and why these erotic scenes occur at crucial junctures in the text and in Morgaine's journey.

On the surface, Bradley's narrative neatly bifurcates the world between two geographical areas that symbolically and stereotypically represent male and female principles. Structurally this bifurcation encompasses two narratives struggling for ascendancy. The male Christian world of Britain is in the process of insuring the sexual dichotomization of a world that had once been ruled by women and had existed without hierarchy and binary opposites. Arthur's search for peace, necessitating numerous battles, forms the hegemonic narrative against which Avalon must intervene, for Arthur not only must wage wars against potential male usurpers but he must also choose between the Christian world of his wife and the pagan world in which he was raised and to which his sister Morgaine nominally adheres. Morgaine is pitted against Gwenhwyfar—as she is in most accounts of the Arthurian tales—as a structural opposite. Arthur must choose between them. But while that reenactment of the Arthurian narrative continues in this mammoth text, the central journey, Morgaine's, is a counterplot dependent for its disruptive potential on the lesbian scenes I have outlined. Morgaine's journey is an attempt to intervene in the headlong, linear projection of Christianity's triumph; she fails to rout this story and its anti-feminism from the shores of Britain, but she does attain a peace in the sustained ability of her story to intervene in what will be the future narrative paradigm. Those interventions depend upon repositioning women in primary relationships with one another. Thus the counterstory to Christianity's single trajectory of good (male) triumphing over evil (female) is a lesbian story which repositions women as autonomous and desiring agents *because* they are in primary relationship with one another.

Women occupy radically different positions in the narratives of Avalon and Camelot. In a world gradually becoming Christian, as if in punishment for woman's previous ascendancy, the priests and especially the vicious St. Patrick, insist that women are sinful, weak, unreasonable and, at best, passive helpmates to their husbands. As women have done throughout history, Arthur's wife, Gwenhwyfar, becomes the patriarchal enforcer of Christianity's negative view of women. The women of Camelot dutifully fulfill the roles of giddy onlookers, gossiping while they spin, and ignoring the greater political issues and moral questions of their day. On the other hand, while Avalon is slowly fading into the mists because people no longer believe in its values, it still remains a sanctuary for alternative values. It worships the goddess along with the gods, its religious island is peopled by priestesses who guard and develop the powers of the Sight, and ultimate authority is vested in a woman, the Lady of the Lake. In one way, Avalon is like the Forest of Arden in Shakespeare's *As You Like It*, full of possibility, intuition, the Sight, and a magic beyond empiricism and beyond what Lancelet calls the place where "the real struggles of life are taking place" (146). It does not lack the power and willingness to be violent when necessary—in other words it does not simply represent the other side of the binary code—but its narrative trajectory lacks the single-mindedness of the male-identified pattern.

While heterosexuality is a central part of its concerns, Avalon refuses to dichotomize the sexes as does the Christian world. Its great religious festival is the marriage of the King Stag to the Goddess to ensure the fertility of the land. "What of the flow of life between their two bodies, male and female, the tides of the Goddess rising and compelling them?" Morgaine seems to ask when the much-desired Lancelet retreats from making love to her (324). Morgaine enacts this ceremony twice in her life, once with Arthur, her brother, and once with Accolon, her lover in old age. Because of her upbringing in Avalon, Morgaine firmly believes that a woman's body is her own to give to whomever she wishes. She accepts none of the Christian-imposed values of the sinfulness of sex, especially for women outside of marriage. The ritual marriages are ceremonial and nonbinding as are the number of affairs that Morgaine has, one with Kevin the Harper and another, under the nose of her husband, Uriens, with Accolon. This sexual autonomy is, in one way, a new positioning of female desire, for while in the Christian world dualisms imply hierarchy, in Avalon they do not. The short passages on homoeroticism also restructure the neat dependence on dualism that orders the Christian narrative. Instead of positioning female desire within the dualistic system which fosters the world of Camelot, the lesbian scenes realign female desire, giving Morgaine the power as a narrative agent at crucial junctures in her journey. Only when her energy has been directed toward women as represented by Raven can she perform the next step in her journey. It is not heterosexual desire which narratively moves the protagonist or which gives to the narrator the power of speech; it is the momentary lesbian erotic scenes which break up male bonding, realign the gender boundaries, and claim for the female a subjectivity not allotted in the Christian dualistic system. Morgaine has become the lesbian heroic subject.

Morgaine as narrator also repositions her as a lesbian heroic subject, although her situation as narrator is not straightforward. From one perspective, all the story elements could be considered the province of an omniscient, third-person narrator. But Bradley complicates this easy solution because she first signals the division of narratives into a text of facts and conversations—summary and scene—and the italics of inner thoughts, suggesting a dialectic of first- and third-person narration. Second, while the prologue begins with a simple statement, "MORGAINE SPEAKS" (ix), Morgaine announces, in italics, that the following tale is her story *"But this is my truth; I who am Morgaine tell you these things, Morgaine who was in later days called Morgan le Fay"* (xi). Thus, Carrol L. Fry identifies her as "the central character, the narrator, and the moral center of the book" (337). As the story proper begins, we are invited to think of the passages spoken by Morgaine as the omniscient narrator telling her tale while the passages in italics reflect her inner, first-person thoughts. These multiple narrative voices, contained in one name, also complicate the narrative structure which on the surface appears to be an old-fashioned adventure story. Morgaine's narrative positioning recalls the shape shifting that has been associated throughout history with her character. In legend she is both good and evil, both Arthur's nemesis throughout his reign and his loving sister when he is dying. Historically this can be accounted for as part of the many texts from which her character is pulled, from her likely origin as the Celtic Triple Goddess, Morrigan, to the gradual whittling away of her power in the French romances, and finally, for English audiences, to her negative representation in their key text, Thomas Malory's *Le Morte D'Arthur*. In Bradley's version, Morgaine explains these ambivalences psychologically; she has been both *"Arthur's greatest friend"* and *"his darkest enemy"* (x) not because of whimsy or inconsistency but because of her loyalty to the Goddess, whom Arthur gradually abandons. The enigmatic scenes in Malory in which Morgan le Fay attempts to kill her brother, such as her attempt to slay Arthur using Accolon and switching

Excalibur for another, but innocuous, sword, are in Bradley's text given explanations that place Morgaine as the defender of the Goddess religion and as an advocate of its return to Britain at any cost. Morgaine in *The Mists of Avalon* is a figure who loses her way, loses her primary mission, and spends the rest of the book finding again that old path. She is not blameless even in this feminist text, but neither is she the enigmatic figure of Malory's text who hates Arthur without cause, as Accolon declares, "ye shall understand King Arthur is the man in the world that she most hateth, because he is most of worship and of prowess of any of her blood" (I, 134). The ambivalence about Morgaine's role in Bradley's text is not about an enigmatic necromancer or witch but about a shape-shifting narrator.

This problematic narrator is further complicated because the italics can also represent the silent thoughts of other women characters. The "I" narrator is not solely Morgaine, but Morgause, Igraine, or whatever woman is the chief focalizer at the time. Charlotte Spivack identifies this shifting narrative point of view through first Igraine, then Viviane, and finally Morgaine (150). If these focalizers are all narrated through Morgaine's voice, then the narrator's voice becomes voices as Morgaine gathers together the primary women characters—who could also be called aspects of the Goddess—to occupy the narrative function of narrator. One explanation of this confusion of point of view is that Morgaine has the "gift of the Sight" (x) and therefore has the omniscient narrator's power to read other characters' minds. The other women characters could also be considered aspects of Morgaine, the representative of the Goddess. But the structural implications are also important: in allowing a confusion of first- and third-person narrators and of different characters to occupy the first-person role, Bradley refuses to define the narrator and the protagonist as simply a single individual who is Morgaine and instead allows Morgaine to be the center of a community of women claiming the narrative positions of power. Like her position as protagonist of an adventure story, Morgaine's power as narrator exists because its position is primarily defined in relationship to other women. In taking on narrative roles in which her power is determined by her primary relationship to women, she continually undercuts the male bonding of Thomas Malory's originary text that highlights the relationships between men, the erotic triangle of Lancelet, Gwenhwyfar and Arthur, and the warrior brotherhood of the Round Table. Heroism, even in a single individual, is redefined through relationship to sameness.

Agency in the narrative is a function of women coming together on a narratological level as protagonists of their own story and as narrators of their own inner thoughts. This otherwise confusing set of narrators sets in motion a number of separate narratives, a narrative of facts in each woman's life and an inner, psychological narrative explaining her motives and justifying her actions. In Morgaine's double narrative, the latter is a drama of inner awareness in which the "I" narrator learns to accept the will of the Goddess and the former a story of her journey through several worlds: the facticity of Camelot, the receding and ever-changing world of Avalon, and the dream world of the fairies. The narrative trajectory is never singular nor is the narrative agent contained in a literal figure. This is a text in which agency is structured in terms of Morgaine relating primarily to other women, either as a protagonist or as a narrator. In that guise she becomes the nonbodily metaphorical lesbian subject as narrator as well as protagonist.

The closure of this story reflects these several narrative trajectories and their concomitant narrative problems. As a lesbian subject, even as a nonbodily, metaphoric one, Morgaine does not close her story with a heterosexual union. Love is central to the conclusion of her quest, but it is formulated on the basis of two distinct narratives, the Christian story, based on the traditional Arthuriad, and Avalon's story, predicated on narrative intervention. For instance, as part of the traditional Arthurian adventure story, Morgaine's quest seems to end in failure. While she lovingly tells the dying Arthur, in order to comfort him, that he did not fail in his mission, she feels that she failed in her own mission to keep Avalon and the Christian world in touch with one another. But what fails in Arthur's story, in the penultimate section that recounts Arthur's death and Morgaine's taking him to Avalon, does not fail in her own story. In the epilogue, she returns to the world to visit Viviane's grave near a Christian convent. She recognizes there that the goddess is present in the female saints and, in particular, in Mary. She realizes that Avalon's narrative will continue to intervene in the usurping Christian narrative. The narrators of these last sections are also multiple—an omniscient narrator telling of Gwenhwyfar entering a convent and leaving her one-time love, Lancelet; a penultimate section which begins, "MORGAINE SPEAKS" (865), followed by the italics of Morgaine's story of the last days of Arthur; and finally the epilogue, told in third-person narrative with Morgaine's intervening thoughts in italics. Real closure, then, comes not with the death of Arthur but with Morgaine's return to a woman's religious community, a community that reminds her of the priestesses of Avalon. Her ability to include the nuns in her vision and to love them allows her to see how thin the mist is between these two worlds and how possible it will be to intervene in the narrative paradigm that the world recognizes. Female bonding is, then, always on the verge of breaking up the male bonding on which the Christian world and its stories depend.

Bradley, like Rich and Hacker, lesbianizes the woman's narrative position by putting a female character in primary relationship with other women or a women's community. The positioning can, under certain circumstances, lesbianize the women's community as well as the single protagonist. This effect occurs when the women's larger community rather than a single individual becomes the protagonist of a narrative and maintains its cohesion and identity in terms of lesbian figures in its midst. A number of important literary scholars have resisted this connection, pointedly denying any metaphoric connection between lesbians and a larger, straight female community. Nina Auerbach bases her distinction between the two groups on a positional distinction. Using the work of psychiatrist Charlotte Wolff, Auerbach assumes that lesbians in a group function as men because they exercise independent power: "for Wolff only a lesbian community has the integrity of 'a group of men alone': by herself, a heterosexual woman can constitute only a sexual plea" (7). If the lesbian is not the same as other women, then she must be defined as male or as an imitative male; if she is the same as other women, then she is (mis)constituted as a sexual plea, that is, as a passive instead of an active figure. Male bonding, in other words, is heroic; as Auerbach puts it, "The immediate authority generated by literary communities of men comes not merely from their possession of universal symbols of power, . . . it springs too from the powerful motion of the quest which so often gives them their structure" (7–8). Female bonding, exclusive of lesbians, is a "furtive, unofficial, often underground entity" (11), distinctly unheroic. Joseph Allen Boone's separation of lesbians from his consideration of women's communities in literature depends in part on the era he is studying and in part on an unwillingness to see a homoerotic element in female plots which he recognizes in male communities. Like Auerbach, he argues that women's communities are marginal in which the very "marginality of the female community becomes a metaphoric center" (280) that constitutes a counterplot to what he defines elsewhere as the ubiquitous marriage plot. While it is not clear in his analysis whether a lesbian narrative would be similarly structured, he does makes it clear that in an era later than his historically determined area of study, empirically defined lesbian plots would constitute a counterplot.

It is African-American women writers of the 1970s and 1980s who play the most crucial role in the construction of women's communities as active narrative agents. The connection between the individual and the community constitutes Jewelle Gomez's definition of black women's heroism (126–27). Some of the most important African-American texts of the 1980s, particularly Alice Walker's *The Color Purple* and Gloria Naylor's *The Women of Brewster Place,* also explore the connection between these communities and central lesbian characters, providing a lesbian metaphoric center for female narrative agency. But to term these African-American literary communities "lesbian" is to run counter not only to Auerbach and Boone, but also to a number of African-American feminist critics who, as Jewelle Gomez notes, resist the lesbian implications of popular African-American women's writing (134). Along with this theoretical issue is the real difficulty of discussing the topic of lesbianism in a community whose survival depends on racial cohesion. African-American women critics describe being caught between theories of the lesbian which bibliographer JR Roberts claims "has connoted 'white, middle class lesbian' " (xi) and what Ann Allen Shockley calls the "overall homophobic attitude of the black community" (134). This later issue, she claims, places the writer in an impossible dilemma: "Black women writers *live* in the black community and *need* the closeness of family, friends, neighbors, and co-workers to share in the commonality of ethnicity for surviving in a blatantly racist society" (134–35).

The problem of using the term "lesbian" as a metaphor is a crucial one for African-American critics. Barbara Smith is one of the first African-American literary critics to call a nonsexual relationship between two women in an African-American woman's novel lesbian; in this 1979 definition she echoed many of the then current theories of the lesbian as a metaphor for women's primary relationships with one another. In her classic essay, "Toward a Black Feminist Criticism," Smith refers to Toni Morrison's *Sula* as a lesbian novel, not because the central characters are lesbian, which they are not, but because the novel offers a critique of "heterosexual institutions of male/female relationships, marriage and the family" (189). The metaphoric connection of straight women and lesbians became for the African-American women's community as problematic as it did for the white, feminist community. Deborah E. McDowell disagrees with Smith's metaphoric definition of lesbian for the same reasons many disagreed with Adrienne Rich's notion of a "lesbian continuum": "Smith has simultaneously oversimplified and obscured the issue of lesbianism" (190). Barbara Christian, who reserves a chapter in her book, *Black Feminist Criticism,* for the theme of lesbianism, resists the metaphoric connection between the African-American women's community and African-American lesbians. In another essay she concludes that while the novels of women of color in the 1980s begin to explore lesbian relationships, "This exploration is not, I believe, to be confused with the emphasis on friendship among black women that is a major theme in earlier literature" ("Trajectories" 246). Smith herself seems to retract her earlier metaphoric impulse in a later essay in which she demands "verisimilitude and authenticity" instead of "emotional primacy" as the conditions for "Black Lesbian characters" ("Truth" 224–25).

As problematic as this connection is, these texts of the 1980s that portray women in dyads or communities of "primary intensity" must be examined within the context of the controversy over the metaphoric lesbian, for at the least, as Adrienne Rich noted, no reader can "fully comprehend female struggle and woman-to-woman bonding without the work of these [black women] writers" ("Wholeness" 10). Nor can any critic fully comprehend the lesbian narrative without an analysis of Walker's and Naylor's texts, both of which include prominent if not central lesbian characters that structurally determine the narrative positioning of the larger women's communities. Whether portrayed negatively or positively, these lesbians are the metaphoric center of their communities and enable the community to become the texts' narrative agents. At the same time, these novels significantly reconstruct this metaphoric lesbian community to include men because of the dual allegiance of the African-American woman to her sex and her race. Current critical circles, in fact, often replace the more separatist word "lesbian" with an Afro-centric term "womanist," a term that Alice Walker coined to include, among many other things, women's primary relationships with one another. At the beginning of *In Search of Our Mother's Gardens,* Walker includes four definitions of "womanist" in a mock dictionary format. The first and the third definitions refer to the joy and to the independence of being an African-American woman, the latter suggesting the refusal to be defined by a woman's relationship to a man. But in her second definition of womanist, Walker claims that it is "a woman who loves other women, sexually and/or nonsexually" and, at the same time, "sometimes loves individual men, sexually and/or nonsexually" (xi). Walker's ultimate concern is that this figure be "committed to survival and wholeness of entire people, male *and* female" (xi). The inclusion of the black male in female communities transforms the metaphoric lesbian subject and the narrative structure in Gloria Naylor's and Alice Walker's novels, for in a narrative sense, it is easier to revise narrative space without the pressure of male presence than it is to create female agency, either communally or singly, that includes the male. This perspective challenges a separatist definition of the lesbian narrative.

Because Alice Walker's novel *The Color Purple* has been the focus of numerous analyses, I will address it only briefly, but because it is the paradigmatic African-American text to connect lesbians to a larger community, one which ultimately includes men as well as women, I must not ignore it. I will reserve most of my analytic effort for a more problematic novel, *The Women of Brewster Place,* in which Naylor depicts two lesbians who are shunned by the women's community. Walker's narrative strategy is to redirect the attention of her female characters, particularly the lamentable Celie whom we find in a horribly abusive situation at the beginning of the novel. Celie is repositioned as a lesbian subject through images of sight, which reinforce her power as the novel's primary narrator and focalizer. Celie's first step toward agency happens when she sees Shug's picture, which she uses to find solace and support before she meets her. Shug also initiates Celie into sexuality, by guiding her to see herself: "inside look like a wet rose" (69), Celie announces. As Celie comes alive through her repositioning toward Shug instead of Albert, their sight of one another allows other women to join their point of view. When Celie tells Albert that she is leaving with Shug, the two men—Albert and Grady—offer angry and yet pious declarations of the duties and needs of a woman. Shug, of course, overtly refuses these pronouncements, and begins to laugh: "Shug look at me and us giggle. Then us laugh sure nuff. Then Squeak start to laugh. Then Sophia. All us laugh and laugh" (171). As Linda Abbandonato notes, "the eroticism of women's love for women is at once centralized and incorporated into a more diffuse model of woman-identifying women" (1108). As they reposition themselves, the men also shift their point of perception to view the world through the eyes of the women. Albert repeats Shug's philosophy; Harpo, who has been struggling unsuccessfully to make Sophia mind, finally gives up: "I ast Harpo do he mind if Sophia work. What I'm gon mind for? he say. It seem to make her happy" (237). The men, then, shift their focus and are included in the harmonious family that makes possible the text's closure. As Molly Hite claims in her insightful analysis of this novel as a romance in the tradition of Shakespeare's plays, Walker makes marginal figures and couples central to the novel's project (103–26). By bringing everyone together in an improbable happy ending—as the genre of romance implies—the community and closure are given a lesbian status.

By including men in this community anchored by the lesbian relationship and positioning of Shug and Celie, Walker implicitly includes men as part of a lesbian subjectivity as I have defined it. If men can occupy this space, are we still to claim that the lesbian subject is constructed in relationship to woman even though it disturbs and destabilizes gender boundaries? Because I have defined the lesbian subject first of all as a positionality, it must also be available to male characters, but because men and women—textually constructed or otherwise—are differently positioned in any given system of meaning, each gender informs that lesbian space differently because each functions differently in relationship to desire and agency. The lesbian subject and the concomitant lesbian narrative space, then, are not neutralized as a space of undecidability. As expansions and disturbances of the spaces usually allowed to the textually constructed woman, the lesbian subject and its parallel narrative function are spaces of freedom and redefinition for woman. Male characters function differently in this space. Thus, in one of the most satisfying scenes in Walker's book, Albert and Celie sit on the porch sewing together. By repeating Shug's religious philosophy, he repositions himself as more passive than active: "I think us here to wonder, myself. To wonder. To ast. . . . The more I wonder, he say, the more I love" (239). Male figures in this space are repositioned by losing absolute agency and assuming redefined heroic qualities.

Like Walker, Gloria Naylor questions the boundary often drawn between lesbian communities, lesbians, and heterosexual women's communities. Two of the women who are part of the title, *The Women of Brewster Place*, are lesbians, but they are often seen as pitiable or victimized characters, certainly not the basis for community cohesion. In describing her negative reaction to the book because "Naylor's depiction of our lives [is] so completely demoralizing and not particularly realistic" ("Truth" 230), Barbara Smith concludes that "both Lesbian characters are ultimately victims" (225). To Barbara Christian these women are sympathetic outcasts; in fact, the larger women's community is complicit in the death of one of the lesbians because it refuses to nurture these "different" women (*Black* 196). Christian contends that the survival of this heterosexual women's community depends not on a metaphoric lesbian cohesion but on "Women mothering other women" ("Gloria" 358). I intend to suggest an alternative approach: the lesbians in this book are not primarily victims or outsiders; instead, they form the metaphoric center of the female bonding that becomes a powerful narrative agent by the end of the text.

Mothering indeed is one of the strongest images of women's bonding in this community. In this sense, the lesbians represent the outcasts and antithesis of the women's community, women who are not perceived as nurturers and who are not in turn nurtured. But Naylor also suggests that the lesbians are the mirror of the heterosexual women's community, as Mattie, the central figure in the novel, suggests. In fact, the argument about whether "The Two" are the same as or different from the larger women's community is an argument at the core of the text, one that Mattie and her friend Etta Mae explore at length and one that the two lesbians, Lorraine and Theresa, also explore between themselves. Lorraine and Theresa's arguments, which are frequent, are about their place in the community. Lorraine longs for inclusion in the larger community and is on the alert for slights which might identify her as different. Their argument has apparently raged for years. Just before Lorraine leaves their home for the last time, they clash again on this issue. Lorraine explains her new friendship with the wine-besotted Ben as a safe haven: "When I'm with Ben, I don't feel any different from anybody else in the world" (165). Theresa insists that Lorraine's desire not to feel different is also a refusal to accept her homosexuality. But Theresa's last words emphasize that to be a lesbian in a homophobic world constitutes an eternal conflict between "them and us": "And as long as they own the whole damn world, it's them and us, Sister—them and us. And that spells different!" (166).

Naylor uses the possibility of similarity between the lesbians and the straight women as a means to transform female narrative passivity into narrative agency. The novel's narrative trajectory includes a series of independent, separate stories that coalesce as a cohesive narrative only when the lesbians enter the picture in the penultimate chapter. Only then do the independent stories come together in Mattie's dream, a narrative shift that also requires a change of narrator.

The women's community is divided by the entry of the lesbians into its life. For the most part, the women of Brewster Place define reality in terms of their relationship to men. Each of the early vignettes begins with a woman seeing the world through men's eyes and ends with a powerful female relationship redefining that reality. This relationship is often in terms of an older woman nurturing a younger woman. Mattie accomplishes this task more than once, just as she was mothered by Miss Eva when she had no place to go after being forced from her parents' home. Mattie returns the favor by refusing to let Miss Eva's grandchild, Ciel, die at one point in the story. Ciel's husband has left, she has been forced to have an abortion, and the only "thing [she had] ever loved without pain" (93), her daughter, has died of an electrical shock. After the funeral, Mattie observes that Ciel is about to let go of life. Mattie steps in to save her, and in one of the powerful and lyrical sequences in the book, Mattie rebirths her. She rocks her, she bathes her, she holds her, she puts her to bed. The metaphors range from birthing to baptism to gently making love. When Mattie's longtime friend, Etta Mae, is in need of Mattie's acceptance, Mattie also offers unconditional love in the form of unconditional acceptance. When what Etta Mae calls one of her *"business opportunities"* (61) fails, Mattie stays up late at night to pick up the pieces. Etta Mae's hope that she will find a man to take care of her leads her to flirt with the guest preacher, but it is he who eventually controls the assignation. Etta Mae returns to Mattie's apartment, where she is staying, to find Mattie waiting up for her, and "she climbed the steps toward the light and the love and the comfort that awaited her" (74).

Mattie is the focal point of an unofficial women's community held together by nurturing; she is also the person who points out the continuity between the lesbians and the heterosexual women's relationships with one another. It is not that the lesbians do not fit at Brewster Place; they fit so well that they are threatening. Mattie's shy recognition of this fact in her conversation with Etta Mae allows the reader to see the lesbians as metaphors for the power the community can and, in Mattie's dream, does achieve. In their conversation, Etta Mae desperately attempts to make a distinction between the women lovers and women friends, but Mattie keeps probing the similarities. She knows that she has loved women and some more deeply, she says, than any man, and "there been some women who loved me more and did more for me than any man ever did" (141). In fact, Mattie muses, after Etta Mae tries to articulate the difference between the two loves, " 'Maybe it's not so different, . . . Maybe that's why some women get so riled up about it, 'cause they know deep down it's not so different after all' " (141). That sameness is underscored a few pages later when Lorraine nurtures Theresa in the same way Mattie has nurtured the others. In frustration with the harassing slights she and her lover have experienced, Theresa hurls the ingredients of her meat loaf at their main nemesis's window. In the midst of Theresa's laughter, which ultimately turns to tears, Lorraine cradles and comforts her lover. The lesbians are included by implication in the larger community's ideal of women nurturing one another. Like Mattie's description of the lesbians as the mirror of women's love of one another, this scene underscores the ways in which the lesbians reinscribe in their own relationship the characteristic most often associated with heterosexual women and their relationships, that is, mothering.

Mattie's sense of the continuity between these two types of relationships is not shared by the community at large, whether male or female. When "The Two" move into Brewster Place, the other women are at first relieved that these new women do not take any interest in their men, but this fact also gradually insults them. In fact, it is "their friendly indifference to the men on the street" that constitutes "a brazen flaunting of unnatural ways" (131). Sophie is the mouthpiece for the view that these women are fundamentally different and must be excised from the community. Significantly, the culmination of the tension occurs at the block association meeting which Kiswana arranges and hosts in her own apartment. Sophie brings up the topic in moral terms: " 'What they doin'—livin' there like that—is wrong, and you know it' . . . The Good Book say that them things is an abomination against the Lord" (140). Etta Mae, whose outspokenness allows her to meet Sophie head on, tells Sophie to mind her own business, appealing to privacy and the right to live one's life as one sees fit, even though Etta Mae is not totally comfortable with the implications of a lesbian relationship. Etta Mae relies on her own right to lead her life as she chooses, and she cautiously is willing to give the same right to a relationship that she does not understand. Sophie speaks for the community's desire to define itself through the Other, an element against which their identity is secure. Sophie, in other words, is shoring up the system that depends on male centrality, displacing her own fear of deviance onto the sexual relationship of Lorraine and Theresa. The struggle for female narrative agency is the struggle between male power and bonding and what the male system identifies as deviance. It is the system that C. C. Baker and his cohorts assert when they rape Lorraine and, as a result, rid the community of the other deviant, Ben.

When Lorraine innocently enters Kiswana's apartment during this divisive argument, she "went over and stood by Ben" (143) in a move that unites the two outcasts. Their connection with one another is structurally significant because it represents the conjunction of nurturing and deviance, of sameness and difference, and the difficulty of maintaining that connection in a world or a narrative structure that depends on male agency and male bonding. Both Lorraine and Ben are problematically related to the larger community, and the text's struggle is to resolve or at least define that relationship. On the most obvious level, each is ostracized from the center of the community's definition of itself, one a lesbian, the other a drunk, yet they find in one another a source of love that each needs. They replicate the nurturing that is at the center of the women's community. In Ben's "damp ugly basement" (165) Lorraine feels that she is not different from others. Ben gives to her not only an accepting love but a bond with a male who has a necessary although tangential relationship to the larger community. Ben finds his lost daughter in Lorraine, and Lorraine finds a loving parent and therefore acceptance in Ben. Ben, for instance, is the only man in the novel who is treated sympathetically, and as a result he symbolically becomes part of the women's community. But the consequence of Ben's repositioning is the loss of the male agency that C. C. Baker jealously guards.

The two people who clearly accept Lorraine are Mattie and Ben. Ben is a significant, opposite-gendered, parallel to Mattie. Naylor gives both of them a story that allows us to understand the reasons for their present condition. No other figure is allotted detailed stories of a previous life. Both have been disappointed by their former lovers or spouses, and both inordinately loved a child who hurt them. That parallel status, another means by which Ben is accorded a symbolic inclusion in the women's community, also makes him vulnerable to the destructive impulses that depend on male agency asserted through male bonding. This system needs to rid itself of the potential that a male can be feminized. When C. C. Baker, a young punk on the block, is confused by the lesbians and his inability to control them, he unleashes his and his followers' rage against Lorraine. Naylor provides an understanding but power-laden description of his wild hostility: "Before he had learned exactly how women gave birth, he knew how to please or punish or extract favors from them by the execution of what lay curled behind his fly. . . . And the thought of any woman who lay beyond the length of its power was a threat" (161–62). The text punctuates the heroic expectations of C. C.'s gang when Naylor calls them "dwarfed warrior-kings" (169). In the ripple effect of the rape, the crazed Lorraine kills Ben, believing him to be one of her rapists. It is as if the male narrative system in the guise of C. C. Baker exerts its power by ridding itself first of the ultimate threat to male power, the lesbian, and second of the threat of a feminized male.

Naylor does not end the novel in such destruction. In Mattie's dream, which constitutes the bulk of the last chapter and is the most challenging section on a narrative level, the women's community is constituted as a narrative agent, a narrative agent forged in a dream world rather than the primary, realistic world of the text. The omniscient narrator who has confidently introduced us to the different women characters of Brewster Place forgoes its power to allow Mattie as a focalizer/narrator to present her dream/story more directly than any character has been allowed so far. The narrative within a narrative begins: "Even Mattie's sleep was fitful, her dreams troubling" (176). At the same time, the narrator announces that all the women of Brewster Place had dreamed that week, allowing the possibility that Mattie's is a collective dream. The block party, then, happens as Mattie's dream, and when the narrator takes over at the end, the day is dawning, supposedly to be repeated as Mattie dreamed it. As this dream story continues, the text becomes centralized and its direction profoundly linear. The various women characters come together to party with each other and with the men of the community and finally to tear down the wall that has limited both their movement and agency.

Up to that point, the women's community is indeed what Nina Auerbach terms the "furtive, unofficial, often an underground entity" (11) of many heterosexual women's narratives. The various narratives of Mattie, Etta Mae, Ciel, Kiswana, and Cora Lee are separate stories that intersect only when one character appears in another's story. Each figure becomes the narrative center of her own story, although the feeling that each is in some way a victim of the oppressive system makes it easy to determine that the character is also the victim of a narrative system.

Each figure, narrated by an omniscient narrator, could be viewed as a passive space through which the male agents, although tangential, pass, making the community even more furtive and unofficial. The power of nurturing is both the power of survival and, because it is so furtive and unofficial, a defensive posture. The power to survive is in this instance a passive power; narratively it takes on the passive space.

But once the lesbians are introduced and the text argues about their position vis-à-vis the larger women's community, that same community begins to change. With the interposition of "The Two" in the penultimate chapter, the women's community that takes down the wall becomes the metaphoric lesbian subject that claims narrative agency. In the dream, the remaining lesbian, Theresa, joins the group in its rage against the wall and all it represents. As Theresa comes out of her apartment with her suitcase to hail a cab in order to leave the community, she realizes that the block party, like so many other parts of the community, did not initially include her: " 'Dumb bastard, they're only having a lousy block party. And they didn't invite me' " (187). But Cora Lee's words, " 'Please. Please' " (187), the only words Lorraine could utter after being brutally raped, spur Theresa to join what the cab driver describes as a riot. "She grabbed the bricks from Cora and threw one into the avenue, and it burst into a cloud of green smoke" (187–88). She asks Cora Lee for more. But this newly powerful position is not absolute, for it is narratively enacted only in a plot within a plot, with an ambiguously defined narrator—the dreaming Mattie—making the power assumed by this community ambiguous.

The structural position occupied by men in this novel is also indecisive, but what is clear is that Naylor refuses a separatist position. C. C. and his gang's violation of Lorraine signals the attempt of male bonding to take over narrative agency. In one sense, the text works out a struggle between male and female bonding as the source of narrative agency. The male bonding that rapes Lorraine is destructive, depends on an heroic, territorial ideal, and upon the control of women, particularly on the control of female bonding. Mattie's dream, the dream of all of the women, in the last chapter is the feminist text's attempt to rewrite the breakup of female bonding. In order to accomplish this, Naylor must portray the women's community as stronger than it normally is, and she does this through the connections she forges between Mattie and the lesbians, making the community that is dreamed of a metaphorical lesbian subject and therefore a more powerful female narrative agent than is possible with heterosexual female communities in literature. In this dream, female bonding replaces male bonding as the mover of the text, but, at the same time, men are not entirely absent from the final community. Nor are they constructed as the women's or the lesbians' Other. The gender of the real enemy, who is not C. C., is never clearly revealed. Although included more problematically than in Walker's text, the men are present even though peripheral. Despite the fact that Ben has been killed, he remains the ideal figure of the male who could be included in this larger community. When the women begin to pull apart the wall, brick by brick, "All of the men and children now stood huddled in the doorways" (185). This situation leaves them out of narrative agency but includes them in the group for whom the women tear down the wall. The agency claimed by this community is now more than furtive because it refuses to stand in relationship to male domination; it breaks up male bonding, and yet includes males along its reconstituted gender and sexual lines.

Both novels, then, conclude with an affirmation of identity through relationship with other women, affirming a concept of heroism that refuses the separative, individualistic heroism of the traditional male quest story. Both novels also end with visions or dreams. Morgaine experiences both the Sight and a dream, each leading her to the different closures of her two different narratives. Mattie dreams the triumphant end of Naylor's story, although we do not see whether she lives the dream, while the framing narrator concludes her elegy to the death of Brewster Place with the flickering dreams of the "colored daughters of Brewster" (192) who keep the street on the edge of survival. Both visionary ends indicate the desire to incorporate the "to be presented" into a realistic narrative along with the tyranny of the real that declares the impossibility of the utopian future. The positioning of these lesbian subjects in this final space indicates a narrative desire to reposition heroism itself. The quests end not in transcendence nor in the separative identity of the traditional hero nor in the alienation of the modern hero. It is not the goal of these heroic acts to separate, to divide, or to conquer, but to connect. Nor is the enemy against which the heroic subjects fight clearly gendered. The lesbian subjects repositioned in terms of sameness and relationship devise a different narrative strategy as well as different heroic virtues.

Unlike Adrienne Rich and Marilyn Hacker, whose open lesbianism and literal lesbian figures provide a context through which to claim that their poetic sequences are lesbian narratives, neither Bradley nor Naylor allows such access to a critic bent on including their novels as lesbian narratives. But like Rich's and Hacker's stories, their novels construct lesbian subjects. They do this through textual means alone—lesbian characters, lesbian erotic tension—which then allows the critic to interpret the female bonding in terms of the twentieth-century construction of the lesbian subject. It is not, then, the lesbian themes or even the literal lesbian characters that connect these texts under the umbrella of a lesbian narrative. The connection can be made, instead, through the complexly formulated lesbian subject, in its bodily and, in these novels in particular, its nonbodily guises.

The Postmodern Lesbian Text:
Jeanette Winterson's *Sexing the Cherry*
and *Written on the Body*

We can and should be critical of narrative structuration,
but I doubt if even the most devoted practitioner of
anti-narrativity can do without it.   —Robert Scholes,
    "Language, Narrative, and Anti-Narrative"

But the truth is other as truth always is.
    —Jeanette Winterson, "The Poetics of Sex"

Following on the late nineteenth-century's depiction of the lesbian as
a monstrous creature whose body exceeds all cultural—or what the
sexologists would call "natural"—boundaries, the postmodern lesbian
subject is a figure of bodily and sexual monstrosity intent on shocking a
complacent society. It is also natural that the generation of lesbian
theorists following the lesbian-feminists should reinstate the body, desire, and sexuality as central to lesbian identity. But by constructing
images of a grotesque and excessive body and clothing, these contemporary lesbian theorists defy both the nineteenth-century medical and literary communities of heterosexual males and the lesbian writers of the
1970s who aligned themselves with heterosexual feminists. Images of
the postmodern lesbian subject's sexuality—this time a celebrated monstrosity—include the butch-femme couple and, more shocking, the vampire. Sue-Ellen Case writes that the "vampire is the queer in its lesbian
mode" ("Tracking" 9), and, like its imagistic counterpart, the vampire
challenges definitional boundaries of gender and sexuality. Representing
the extreme of postmodern configurations of the lesbian, the vampire's
strengths are, Case continues, her inability to "see herself in the mirror,"
leaving her "outside that door into the symbolic;" her bite which
"pierces platonic metaphysics and subject/object positions;" and her

168

kiss which "brings her the chosen one, trembling with the ontological, orgasmic shifts, into the state of the undead" (15). The queer vampire "becomes an activism in representation" (15). Like Case's construction of the butch-femme couple, the vampire trades on an image of female monstrosity determined by the refusal to maintain culture's boundaries for the female body and behavior.

Postmodern lesbian writers like Kathy Acker seem to agree, representing the lesbian in bodily terms that shock or disgust the reader. In her short story, "The Language of the Body," Acker describes the lesbian body and lesbian desire in ghoulish terms. The narrator/protagonist, who at the beginning of the story is ambivalently involved in a heterosexual marriage, records a crude and violent conversation between her husband and an aristocratic lesbian. In the conversation, the heterosexual man and lesbian imagine, in choral terms, the murders of many young women by a woman known as "The Scarlet Witch" who "kidnapped young girls in order to get their blood" (405). As the conversation continues, the two become sexually aroused as they imagine more sexually sadistic scenes. The narrator/protagonist leaves, disgusted. Later, when she is involved in her own lesbian relationship, her lesbian body, while not vampirish, is described through unpleasant bodily, female bodily, imagery: "Suddenly, I had my period. This blood was brown and smelly. Actually it looked like shit" (410). Like the nineteenth-century sexologists' worst nightmares of the lesbian body, the postmodern lesbian body can be excessively and cruelly sexual and therefore explode "natural" gender boundaries; unlike those male imaginings, the postmodern lesbian body is more about language and textuality than about the length of a lesbian's arms or a lesbian's propensity for criminal activity.

The lesbian subject as the grotesque female body is, in these writers' imaginings, a retextualizing of the female body and desire, a re-presentation of the female body on which Western culture has written its narrative codes and patterns. Monique Wittig's classic book, *The Lesbian Body*, refuses any image that traditional textuality reserves for the female body, either negative or positive. In her series of poems, the female body becomes unrecognizable because it is lesbianized, because it is repositioned as both subject and object in the narrative system. To accomplish this repositioning, Wittig minutely anatomizes and tears apart the female body, organ by organ, cell by cell, orifice by orifice. This body is ultimately the body of language and narrative, and when, nearly two-thirds of the way into the book, the lesbian body is scattered in pieces, it begins to utter a new language: "Your lip your tongue modulate the new language in gutteral sounds" (103). The grotesque lesbian body has for its counterpart in postmodern lesbian theory the butch-femme couple that, through a comparable excess, refuses not only the categories of the female body but also the boundaries which distinguish male and female bodies. Through clothing, the butch-femme couple parodies heterosexual roles as well as heterosexually constructed bodies. To use Carolyn J. Allen's terms for Djuna Barnes's *Nightwood,* these images of the postmodern lesbian subject "become examinations of dichotomous difference" ("Sexual" 185). Because narrative depends on "dichotomous difference," the bodily grotesque lesbian subject subverts or, according to some, undoes the narrative system. The postmodern lesbian subject, then, is a consciously textualized construct that refutes the dominant images of woman as body—as beauty, as object of desire, as textually controlled Other—and establishes the grotesque female body/sexuality as the means to gain control over representation.

Because the topic of much postmodern lesbian writing is language and the body, it follows that the horrid smells, the violence, and the sexual sadism as well as the sexual confusion of cross-dressing in those texts are, in effect, metafictional discussions about lesbian and female representation in language and narrative. The three short stories that conclude the intelligent collection of lesbian short fiction, *The Penguin Book of Lesbian Short Stories,* demonstrate the centrality of this issue for contemporary lesbian writing. In each short story, the undomesticated or grotesque lesbian body struggles to find a linguistic and narrative space while the text exposes the difficulty of joining together the traditional coded system of meaning and the lesbian body. For some writers, especially Acker and the postmodern purists we have already examined, neither the narrative system nor the individual character survives this scrutiny, for to represent the unrepresentable—the lesbian— demands a radically open text, refusing narrative and ontological definitions. But while narrative as a system can be questioned, as it has been since the advent of modernism, it cannot be destroyed, even in the most radical of stories. These writers, in fact, use the traditional narrative system not as an envelope in which to drop characters but as a paradigm which must be questioned and manipulated for their own purposes. Each writer—Acker, Jeanette Winterson, and Emma Donoghue—recog-

nizes the paradox of an ideologically biased narrative system and, especially for Winterson, its utilitarian necessity and flexibility.

Kathy Acker's short story, discussed above, is an example of the
radical disruption of narrative linearity, of subject position, and of closure that would earn it the imprimatur of postmodernism. Like the
theorist Judith Butler, Acker refuses to "name names" (Phelan 779) and
therefore leaves no categories unquestioned. From the beginning of this
story, dream and reality are so mixed that the reader is left to wonder
when each occurs or, more accurately, how the events reported in each
state are different from one another. As statement of reality, a sentence
such as "We returned to the hotel at the end of the world" (405) makes
the reader question the neat boundaries of narrative as well as any of the
tidy boundaries of Western dichotomous thinking. The narrator/subject
of the story represents postmodernism's mantra that "identities are flexible, contradictory products of multiple intersecting conditions" (Roof
158). After the dialogue between the husband and the aristocratic lesbian, the narrator runs away "to find the relation between language and
the body rather than this sexuality that's presented by society as diseased" (407). She discovers this new language in a section called the
"*Masturbation Journal*" (407), and in the most linear part of the story,
she strips away the contours of society's language to discover her body
outside of any relationship. In three days she finds the possibility for
linguistic representation. But she discovers this language—and the
places where language and the body are not possible—alone. If we read
linear progression as cause-and-effect, we could conclude that as a result
of this discovery she begins to sleep with women. While the text does
not make her newfound lesbianism the direct result of her insight into
the relationship of language and the body, it does imply a connection,
although a connection more dream-like than rational. The story ends
appropriately with the narrator planning to go to a "drag-queen ball"
(410). It is then that she experiences herself as grotesque, her menstrual
fluid ugly and unregulated. As if struggling with an image of narrative
closure, the female narrator at first experiences an unregulated and
offensive menstrual flow which she checks "by plugging the hole up with
a clean Tampax" (411). The closure teeters between the undomesticated—smelly and grotesque—female body and the controlled, closed
female body of male expectation. At the same time the closure teeters
between gender and sexual identifications. She is lesbian, her body

waxes with uncontrollable reproductive urgency, she is going to a ball with a drag-queen, and she daringly decides "to dress in full formal" (410). It is as if the closure cannot contain the multiple gender and sexual possibilities that it normally wishes to settle with finality.

Like its male counterpart, this privileged lesbian postmodern narrative is considered experimental writing that depends on a nonlinearity that decenters its subject, the notion of truth, and the closure of the protagonist's journey. The truth is always other in postmodernism. The subject is intentionally fragmented, like the lesbian's dismembered body, along a plotline whose trajectory turns upon itself and refuses closure. The lesbian narrative idealized by queer theory exhibits the playfulness, the disruptiveness, and the undecidability that the narrative system struggles in vain to control. Lesbian stories like Acker's parody naïve genres like the heroic quest or romance, for both represent the closed system that subjugates through gender and sexual otherness as well as racial, ethnic, and class otherness. Structurally, as Mária Minich Brewer explains, this disjuncture in modern narratives "may be seen to stem from a discontinuity created between essential terms: process without assigned Finality; multiple textual effects without an identifiable Cause; writing that possesses neither a simple Origin nor End; signifiers without immediate access to a privileged Signified" (1141). Closure is of particular ideological concern in those theories that view the narrative as a trajectory that parallels "completion to heterosexual intercourse" (Roof 18). In Judith Roof's theory, "narrative mastery" *is* "privileging the end" (34). Narrative openness, then, is proffered as the antithesis to traditional narrative order and closure; the subject follows suit as a figure whose "identity" is deferred along a plane of dispersed meaning.

As narratives of utopian freedom, these postmodern dreams of total openness are problematic. As Linda Hutcheon notes in *The Politics of Postmodernism,* contemporary thinking and narrative often exhibit "a paradoxical desire for and suspicion of totalization" (63). The desire for totalization is already obvious in the utopian gestures of the postmodern construction of the lesbian subject; it is also apparent in postmodernism's use of narrative linearity and closure. Its deconstructive impulse is comprehensible only in relationship to the utopic gesture; the suspicion of totalization exists only within the desire for the same. Postmodern fiction, then, is not diametrically opposed to the traditional narrative system because it can only exist, as is often remarked, within the context of the reader's—and the writer's—traditional expectations which constitute or are constituted by narratives codes. These expectations consist of a beginning and an end. For instance, in Frank Kermode's study of closure, modern distaste for an ending merely places the narrative accent on the middle rather than "tonic-and-dominant finality"; as he puts it, "we think in terms of crisis rather than temporal ends; and make much of subtle disconfirmation and elaborate peripeteia" (30). Modern and postmodern narratives seem plotless and lyrical, more anti-plot than rounded whole. Their goal appears not to find out something because, they assume, there is nothing to discover; rather the goal is to delay closure endlessly. But closure, whether a part of the text or the reader, always happens because it is always projected. Marianna Torgovnick places current thinking in this context: "Endings, we are told, both 'ravel' and 'unravel' the text, with interpretation a constant and constantly self-canceling act. Such ideas have a tantalizing newness and a certain abstract validity. But they violate what common sense and practical experience tell us: novels do have forms and meanings, and endings are crucial in achieving them" (4). While "common sense and practical experience" may be vague terms, they do indicate the expectations under which readers and writers operate. Disruptions of these expectations have meaning only because of the expectations themselves. Total narrative openness is, then, fictitious. Linearity and closure are expected aspects of narrative, and while they have been used to patriarchal effect, they can also be used or misused strategically for other purposes. Linearity, like essentialism, is not "essentially" a male domain, and postmodernism's dramatic and strategic use of narrative totalization—from linearity to closure—is one of its most powerful tools.

On another level, the theory of subject undecidability is also problematic, especially for women. In her reading of the impossible conjuncture of postmodernism and feminism, Patricia Waugh claims that the "postmodern deconstruction of subjectivity is as problematic for women as the liberal construction of self"(16). Just as Sandra Gilbert and Susan Gubar detail the different way in which male and female writers reacted to World War I (*No Man* 258–323), men and women today are related differently to the breakdown of Western metaphysics. Alice Jardine's influential analysis of this current metaphysical crisis, *Gynesis,* reveals the problematic relationship of women to the "new kind of *querelle des femmes*" which posits "woman" but not women as a privileged space (102). Both analyses suggest that when men are displaced from their position as the center of the world, they declare the world meaningless and idealize unstable identity. Women and people of color, on the other hand, have always existed in the marginal place of incoherence and otherness; they know its costs. Barbara Christian, in her well-known essay "The Race for Theory," bemoans the co-optation of "our most daring and potentially radical critics (and by *our* I mean black, women, Third world)" in terms "alien to and opposed to our needs and orientation" (68).

Men and women, whether gay or straight, are as differently related to the decentered subject as they are to narrative disruption. Perhaps that is why we have different, gender-related, postmodern constructions of queer identity in two recent books. Already discussed above in some detail, the important critical texts by Wayne Koestenbaum and Elizabeth Meese both entertain the postmodern refusal of boundaries between imaginative and critical literature, but they also highlight the difference between the lesbian and gay male postmodern writing subject. Koestenbaum's subject is constructed as a separate textual figure with his only point of reference and identity the distant operatic diva such as Maria Callas. This identity is always shifting, never stable, and never defined by gender: "I dream of an undivided space, no W, no M , the M an upside-down W" (176). That undivided space is found in opera because it is a form which continually crosses and challenges boundary lines such as music and words. This identity position is also constructed in the closet, for Koestenbaum makes much of the solitariness and even loneliness of the "shut-in" opera fan listening to records. Meese's persona is constructed in a wholly different fashion. In her lengthy letter to her beloved, her rhetorical position is constructed not in isolation or alienation, but in relationship. Koestenbaum's constructed identity fits perfectly into postmodernism's notion of a destablized but individualistic subject; and while Meese is also an advocate of postmodernism, her rhetorical posture refuses the isolation and alienation of Koestenbaum's persona. In letters from "L" to "L," Meese positions her text in relationship to other lesbian love letters, the ones to and from Vita and Virginia, Gertrude and Alice; at the same time, she addresses, in the form of letters, writers like Nicole Brossard and Olga Broumas whom she also analyzes in the more scholarly portion of her text. Her position is then woven in relationship to other lesbian lovers, to lesbian writers whom she loves, to her own lesbian lover. The lesbian as a postmodern writer is a shifting identity but one always taken in relation to another who is curiously the same.

Thus, the writers of these short stories, including Kathy Acker, work within and against the traditional narrative categories. Challenging these categories is not to refuse them but to restructure their relationship. Closure is a crucial place for this paradox. In Acker's story, while the gaps between cause/effect and dream/reality make the projected space of closure for either the sequence of events or for the narrator/subject problematic, other signals reaffirm the finality of this narrative category. The narrator, for instance, maintains a generalized linearity and even a causal relationship among events. In the last paragraph, the tenses of the story change, often a technical signal for closure. This signal affords the reader a sense of an ending that aligns the sequence of events and also puts into perspective the multiple positions taken, at the end, by the narrator/subject. Thus, while the reader cannot recuperate the lesbian subject as a stable identity at closure, its various disruptive positionings are comprehensible through the story's shift from the differential hetero-sexual relationship of the husband and wife to the problematic sameness posited among the narrator and first, her lesbian lover, and second, the drag-queen with whom she will go to the ball. Instead, then, of refusing closure, this story's ending structures the character's multiple gender and sexual positionalities as a utopian place of freedom from gender constrictions. Two other short stories in the above collection, one by the subject of this chapter, illustrate a postmodern mode of lesbian writing that is identified by its concern for the relationship of the lesbian body to language and yet uses, strategically, linearity, identity, and closure.

Winterson's humorous short story, "The Poetics of Sex," posits a series of familiar, typically condescending heterosexual questions which lesbians often hear: "*Why Do You Sleep with Girls?*" "*Which One of You is the Man?*" "*What Do Lesbians Do in Bed?*" etc. The narrator answers each one of these questions by telling a nontraditional but still linear love story of her lover, Picasso, and herself; at the same time, the answer to each question refuses the terms of the question, thus un-dermining the system of meaning which on one level it adopts. The answers are poetic *non sequiturs*. To the first question, the narrator responds not with a theory of the origin of homosexuality but with a poetic description of the sexual satisfaction she enjoys with her lover: "She plumps me, pats me, squeezes and feeds me" (412). In effect, the speaker refuses the question's gambit by refusing the subject positions that the question demands. To the question, twice repeated, "*Were You Born a Lesbian?*" the narrator answers, again metaphorically, that

Picasso birthed her and named her Sappho. In the second response to this same question, the narrator sets up a dialogue between her lover as Mary and the angel, Gabriel, mimicking the Annunciation. In this answer, birth becomes falling in love and making love becomes a metaphoric feeding: "Feed me, Feed me now" (417). The story humorously refuses to reduce the answers to the same literal level on which the questions are posited. The seemingly linear story, which gains narrative tension near the end when the lovers are separated and then reunited, claims its revised narrative ordering by refusing the system of meaning delineated in the questions. It denies narrative's positioning not by a denial of linearity but by a refusal of the subject positions demanded in each question. Thus, the lovers, too, refuse traditional oppositional positioning.

Another of these stories, Emma Donoghue's "Words for Things," presents an historical story of an Irish girl growing up in the eighteenth century and attempting to understand her lesbian feelings when there are no words for them. The protagonist's love and hoarding of words— "Words were a treasure to be hoarded and never shared" (391)—are stymied at various junctures, when, for instance, her mother burns a manuscript containing her imaginative writings. But she is taught the crucial "words for things" (393) when her governess makes sure that she knows about sex. The most prominent sexual word for a thing is the euphemistic "bit" for penis (393). But there are no words for her "thing," which, because she has different feelings, she can only imagine in grotesque terms that would qualify her as a freak. She is left to imagine running away to a Galway fair as a freak to show her "thing" when it grew (398). But she only imagines this end; instead the story as narrated by a third-person voice ends in two sentences which project the future. She will become a rebel who "would spit at bailiffs" and become an "adulteress in Italy" (398). In the final comment, she "would meet the governess's daughter, who never knew her mother, and would tell her, I knew your mother" (398). The projected future allows the closure to be considered typical and ordinary. Yet the disjuncture between language and the body is not resolved by a conclusion in which Margaret, the protagonist, reconciles her feelings to the world or language. The resolution evokes "this unpresentable as the not yet presented" (E. Friedman 242). The subject has been repositioned as neither male nor female but partaking of both in the context of a female homosocial conversation with the daughter of her first female love, her governess.

All of these stories problematize closure, that point in the narrative where the reader expects to have the subjects and identities settled. In fact, postmodernism intends to defy meaning on a variety of fronts, but its particular aversion to closure functions as its most disturbing as well as powerful characteristic. Closure is the final positioning of the figures that move through the text. In relying on plot movement for this deconstruction, the modern subject is dispersed by nonlinearity and therefore cannot be maintained. Thus nonlinearity in the modernist guise of lyricism is the perfect element for the alienated, nonessentialist modern subject, and the denial of closure is the ironic affirmation of the alienated and dispersed subject. Without closure there is no fixed identity. Whether set out in Lacanian terms of psychological alienation or the linguistic terms of Derrida's deconstruction, the alienation of the subject from itself has been the crucial way to tell modernism and postmodernism from the liberal enlightenment subject that dominates nineteenth-century realism. Jeanette Winterson is a postmodernist writer who tests the precepts of postmodernism, and in the process she can also be defined differently from the male or the gay male postmodern writer. I would argue that she is more closely affiliated with the lesbian writing tradition which includes the lesbian-feminists than with male postmodernism.

Jeanette Winterson's *Sexing the Cherry* and *Written on the Body* interrogate the narrative system by positioning the metaphoric lesbian body as an excessive female body in both the heroic and romantic plots' categories of agent and narrator. Yet while each text disrupts the narrative's expected binary system as well as, at times, its linearity, closure is surprisingly totalizing. While these novels call attention to and challenge the narrative form, they both desire and suspect totalization. Winterson is a postmodern writer, one whom Susan Rubin Suleiman calls a "feminist postmodernist" (248n23), who is willing to "name names" and risk closure. In a previous novel, *Oranges Are Not the Only Fruit*, Winterson portrays a young lesbian growing to sexual awareness in a fundamentalist religious community. The two books under consideration in this chapter, however, do not trade directly on lesbian images and themes. In fact, they seem to avoid making lesbianism a narrative concern. *Sexing the Cherry* contains a number of minor lesbian characters, but the primary female character, Dog-Woman, is heterosexual, although only in a technical sense because her fantastical size defeats her few attempted sexual liaisons. This fantasy of an impossibly huge woman in seventeenth-century England and her son, Jordan, whose journeys defy time and space, leaves little obvious room for lesbian interpretation. The second book entices the critic of lesbian fiction but remains problematically aloof. In *Written on the Body,* Winterson depicts a love relationship in which the beloved, Louise, is identifiably female, but the lover, the first-person narrator, exhibits no corresponding gendered markings, and in fact displays an ambiguous variety of stereotypical markings.

Readers and reviewers respond differently to the two novels. *Sexing the Cherry* is perceived as experimental and unconventional (Krist 691, 694) while *Written on the Body* as a story is "minimal and not altogether original" (Hoffert 195), albeit with Winterson's trademark elegant writing. Like my students who think the ungendered narrator is a gimmick, reviewers like Winterson's fellow writer Sarah Schulman claim that the "plot hovers dangerously on the precipice of device" (20). The collective question seems to be: how important or trivial is the ungendered status of narrator and what effect does it have on the potential postmodern designation for a rather ordinary love story? But more problematic is the designation of either novel as lesbian. One reviewer, Charlotte Innes, discusses at length the new kind of lesbian writing that *Sexing the Cherry* exhibits. This new writing by lesbians—"writers who are lesbian whose work is obviously informed by their lesbianism"— represents a complex "new phase in lesbian fiction" (64). In this novel, Winterson as one of these writers "takes the lesbian experience, presses it through a sieve of history, fairy tales, myth and literary allusion, mixes in a little social criticism, and a lot of humor, and then shakes it to a froth on some other level of time and space" (64). These claims are all introductory to the discussion of the novel, but once into the specifics of *Sexing the Cherry,* Innes drops the word "lesbian," leaving the reader with no knowledge of what constitutes the "lesbian" in this new world of supposedly lesbian fiction. Laura Doan, on the other hand, idealizes this text as the essence of the postmodern lesbian—all undecidability— and as the fictional embodiment of Judith Butler's *Gender Trouble* (152–53). Perhaps because *Written on the Body* is a romantic story, readers find it easier to identify the narrator as lesbian and, as a result, conclude that while the language is always stunning, the story is commonplace. As one reviewer writes, "I make my assumption because, though Winterson, a lesbian novelist, gives no specific clues, her book is clearly propaganda for the idea that gender has no significance to lovers"

(Koenig 61). The reader's dilemma is captured by the argument that erupted over the book's consideration for a 1993 Lambda Literary Award, awards given for the year's best gay and lesbian writing. As reported in a local gay newspaper, the selection committee could not decide whether or not Winterson's novel was, in fact, lesbian fiction. One faction believed that it should be disqualified, and the other faction claimed that the book could only be understood as lesbian fiction ("Lammys" 19). But although Winterson makes neither text overtly lesbian, both books can be read as lesbian narratives when analyzed from the perspective of the metaphoric lesbian subject. These novels may illustrate the critical importance of the metaphoric lesbian subject to a theory of lesbian narrative that would include Winterson as one of its modern practitioners.

Sexing the Cherry displays postmodernism's "desire for and the suspicion of totalization." The novel juxtaposes two primary narrators whose bodily representations function as challenges to the narrative categories of agent and narrator. One narrator, the young man Jordan, espouses the philosophical musings of a postmodernist questioning the stability of time and space. He travels in worlds of fairy-tale characters and houses without floors. The other narrator, Dog-Woman, is stolidly anchored in the flesh and in the historical time of the English Civil War, but her impossibly immense size—she is literally compared to an elephant and a mountain range—also posit her story as anti-realistic. Each narrator has a twentieth-century, realistic counterpart who philosophically and psychologically enacts the bodily determinations of the seventeenth-century characters. But what is at stake in these wonderful flights of fantasy is not psychology or philosophy, in spite of the lengthy mid-novel philosophical discussion of time and space, but the narrative. The juxtaposition of alternative narratives underscores the artificiality of the narrative system, especially the male heroic story. Although, on the surface, Jordan is the proponent of traditional heroic values through his narrative trajectory and stated desires, both narrators explode that system. It is Dog-Woman as the lesbian body who engenders a firm alternative story and who eventually encompasses Jordan in her narrative rather than she by his.

In the harshest and simplest form, this battle between a male and a female story is set forth in a tale Jordan tells but that in reality has been told to him. Jordan's desire for heroism includes the novel-long search for his ideal beloved, Fortunata. It is a search that goes for naught because when he finds her, she refuses to go with him. In effect, she refuses to be the closure of his story. Rejecting him, Fortunata tells this story as the reason for her refusal, and Jordan, in turn, tells his mother the tale that Fortunata, "a woman who does not exist" (*Sexing* 149) told him, a "story of Artemis and why she was in her service" (149). The story recounts a fierce battle between two mythological figures, Artemis and Orion, and a fiercer battle between two narratives that contest each other for the definition of heroism. Orion claims his traditional narrative prerogative by raping Artemis, and she, in return, refuses her positioning in his story by killing Orion. Prior to this encounter, Artemis chooses to live alone and to hunt for herself. She knows about "heroes and the home-makers" (150), but while not rejecting the dichotomous differences "that made life possible" (150), she prefers the "freedoms of the other side" (150). Orion comes to her camp one day, "bellowing like a bad actor" (151). He eats her goat, belches, and assumes that she will not talk because "he knew about her already" (151). He then suggests marriage. Artemis chooses to talk. "Orion raped Artemis and fell asleep" (151). She revenges herself: "She killed him with a scorpion" (152). Like all heroes, such as Margaret Atwood's Ulysses, Orion wants the woman to be a part of his story. As in Atwood's metafictional tale, that patriarchal requirement is symbolically rape. But unlike Atwood's poetic narrative, Artemis has a distinctly different narrative to tell and, instead of imagining an Edenic setting with her redeemed Orion, her story must rid itself of the hero. While starkly displaying the antagonism between male and female agency in this story, Winterson engages her two primary narrators, Jordan and Dog-Woman, in a more subtle and complex battle.

Jordan's first-person story is heroic but not violent; more accurately it is mock-heroic. He directly declares his narrative intentions midway through the book: "I want to be brave and admired and have a beautiful wife and a fine house. I want to be a hero" (114). In fact, he is so obsessed with being a hero that he wants to be grafted onto his friend and mentor, Tradescant "so that [he] could be a hero like him" (85). Tradescant is the king's gardener who has traveled to the new world to bring back exotic plants. With this identification comes the mock-heroic goal of Jordan's quest, a pineapple. But like all other heroic stories, Jordan also searches for Fortunata, the woman who should play her proper role in his story as the point of its closure. Jordan as narrator and protagonist fashions an adventure story with fantastic journeys through space and time, and yet he looks for a very traditional ending, Fortunata, the dancing princess. She refuses and instead urges him "to be complete" (166) on his own. Neither his mother nor Fortunata will provide this space of closure for him: "I wanted her to ask me to stay, just as I now want Fortunata to ask me to stay. Why do they not?" (114).

The parodic *coitus interruptus* of Jordan's journey signals postmodern issues. His narrative appears to interrogate the concerns of Winterson herself, who at the beginning of the book poses two modern conundrums. What is reality when one language we know—the Hopi Indian language—has no tenses for past, present, and future and when one scientific definition of matter is empty space and points of light. If the logical and chronological relationship of events embedded in language is artificial and matter is a mental construct, then the narrative on which Western minds depend for meaning is also an artificial construction that may be no more than empty space and points of light. These questions about time, matter, and space are posed most profoundly in Jordan's narration. But while Jordan flies through space as a part of his quest, the narrative structure of his journey is fairly ordinary. Like the Twelve Dancing Princesses, whose revised stories make up the center section of the novel, Jordan's travels defy gravity and time, allowing him to see other sides of reality and to hear other stories. For instance, he first encounters a fantasy "city of words" that forms a word-filled canopy over the earthly place of utterance; soon after he sees Fortunata, "a woman whose face was a sea voyage I had not the courage to attempt" (15), in the house with no floors. Recalling the role of Helen as the face which launched a thousand ships in the ur-heroic story, Fortunata becomes the fixed point for his heroic adventures. Although the narrator's voice displays ambiguity, it is also in Jordan's narration that the text directly addresses philosophical issues of time and space.

These philosophical questions reflect on our culture's closely guarded gender boundaries, including the boundaries needed to maintain the heroic narrative. Jordan traverses vast spaces, asks philosophical questions, and cross-dresses, all suggesting his narrative as the center of questions about dichotomous difference. At the same time, his narrative journey is structurally familiar. Because Jordan's journey is both traditional and disruptive, he learns to become a different narrative agent, eventually positioning himself as part of Dog-Woman's story rather than his own. In searching for his beloved Fortunata, he must pass through a number of boundary spaces, all identified as female. Instead of helping him or even providing him with an obstacle to conquer, the women who occupy these spaces have repositioned themselves in relationship to one another and do not function as they should in an heroic story. In one instance, in order to talk to some women about Fortunata, Jordan dresses as a woman, one of several sexually ambiguous positions he takes, and enters a "pen of prostitutes kept by a rich man for his friends" (26–27). Rather than being confined by walls, these women come and go at night as they please via a stream underneath the house. The stream passes by a convent, and every night the nuns fish out the prostitutes to free them to search out their own lives and pleasures. Some stay at the convent to meet their lovers, others go elsewhere. These two women's communities, acknowledging none of the dichotomies with which the patriarchal world identifies women, are allies. Jordan's contact with these women while dressed as one of them opens him to women's "private language" (29). He learns, in fact, that women loathe men and know how to manipulate them: "I never guessed how much they hate us or how deeply they pity us" (29). Instead of raping the women in order to contain them in his story, Jordan positions himself, over the course of the novel, as a different kind of hero, one who accepts Fortunata's rejection and returns to his mother to become part of her story.

The most significant boundary space that Jordan crosses is the home of the Twelve Dancing Princesses. These are the folk figures who, in the original story, escape every night from their locked room and return, exhausted, to their home in the morning. Finally, one prince refuses their sleeping draught and discovers their secret. Their father's reward is the dispersal of his daughters to the prince and his eleven brothers. But this is not the story Winterson tells. In this distinctly marked section, Jordan becomes the assumed narratee for the princesses' stories. Told in short, one-page sequences, these stories recount the time after the marriage of each princess to a prince. Traditionally, this is the point of narrative quiescence because the situation after marriage is unnarratable. But for these twelve princesses, marriage becomes the boundary space that they cross on their way to their home together. Each, in fact, claims to be the subject of her own story. The story-telling reversals are punctuated with literary reversals: "That's my last husband painted on the wall" (49) and "He walked in beauty" (50). The princesses refuse to be the closure of any prince's story just as they refuse to be Jordan's boundary space. Some kill their husbands after neglect or abuse, some fall in love with women; in fact, one husband happily turns out to be a woman. Rapunzel's story returns in a violent fashion. It is told not through an "I" narrator but as a folk tale of which the speaker may or may not be a part. The prince who rescues Rapunzel blinds her lover. The identity of the "I" is with the blinded lover who finds her sisters again and reserves a few lines for her own marriage to one of the princes. She immobilizes him with a kiss, turning him into a frog (52). Jordan listens to their stories, but when he asks about the missing sister, Fortunata, they only marvel at her lightness and reveal her name. No one gives him directions.

These narrative refusals indicate the text's interrogation of gendered categories. Jordan resists and cooperates with this blurring of sexual and gender boundaries in his story of his desire to become a hero. Jordan's airy body, in fact, contradicts the women's list of rules to understand men: "Men deem themselves weighty and women light" (30). These boundary crossings in Jordan's story are fraught with homosexual implications that Dog-Woman's story outwardly resists. Both Jordan and Tradescant cross-dress in Dog-Woman's narration in order to attend the trial of Charles I, a crucial event in Dog-Woman's story: "Tradescant and Jordan dressed themselves as drabs, with painted faces and scarlet lips and dresses that looked as though they'd been pawed over by every infantryman in the capital" (71). Jordan, she adds, has a "fine mincing step and a leer" (71) that seem to invite a number of offers. But if Winterson had wanted to revise narrative through a postmodern critique of its binary system, she could have stopped right there. Instead, Dog-Woman as narrator and protagonist of her own story appears to offer a conservative and humorous resistance to Jordan's story; but the conservatism is a ruse for a bodily female subject that reorders the narrative gender positionings.

Dog-Woman wants the most traditional of stories for her son, not a story in which he runs away and loses his heart, but one in which he becomes the hero he wants to be. When Dog-Woman, at the beginning of her story, encounters her neighbor's negative prediction for Jordan, she responds, "I should have killed her and found us a different story" (7). She wants to be the mother of a hero, she says, as she waits for him to return from his voyage: "When I got news of Jordan's return I knew he would be returning as a hero and that I had to meet him as a hero's mother" (122). Because she is solicitous of Jordan's story, she seems to undo Jordan's discovery that time and matter are relative. On the contrary, she appears to be invested in keeping the boundaries intact. In the crucial scene from which the title of the book comes, Jordan tells her about the art of grafting the cherry. Dog-Woman, in the conservative voice that marks her philosophy, asks "Of what sex is that monster you are making?" (85). He explains that it would still be female, but she responds that monsters like that, hybrids, have no gender and "were a confusion to themselves" (85). The humor of her position rests partly in her depiction as an older person—everyone's mother—who resists change and demands the best, that is, the most traditional, for her child.

But the meaning of her size cannot be encompassed by the monstrous, all-engulfing mother. Dog-Woman is the exaggeration of everything earthly; she is the grotesque personification of culture's symbolic connection of nature and woman. Her body weight is also a constant reminder of her static place in an historical narrative, although Jordan does take her on one memorable trip outside of time and space. But her size functions as the text's refusal to acquiesce to culture's attempt to control the woman's body. The grotesque female body positions Dog-Woman as the narrator and agent of her own story, a story which gradually absorbs Jordan into it, repositioning him at the closure of her narrative. Her size, then, functions on a narrative level as a source of power and agency. Because, through her body, she escapes the patriarchal constructions of woman, her mythical size, rather than being a source of embarrassment, works to accomplish her moral and political agenda in one of the most dangerous times in English history, the seventeenth-century English Civil War. Violence is the most common image associated with her body. For instance, she threatens to smother in her breasts one man who resists a request (5); as a child, she breaks her father's legs when she sits on them to hear his stories (20–21); and later she kills her father when he tries to sell her as a freak. That, she says, "was my first murder" (122). After the execution of Charles I, to whom she is strongly loyal, she seeks revenge by following strictly the preacher's injunction to gouge out enemy eyes and teeth (92). Dog-Woman chalks up 119 eyeballs and 2,000 teeth (93). This violence is also associated with her attempted sexual contacts. Unlike Jordan, she is not ambiguous sexually, but her size renders her sexual encounters fraught with danger—at least for her paramours. In one instance, she is repelled by the fellatio she is asked to perform and, disgusted, "spat out what I had not eaten and gave it to one of my dogs" (41). In another attempt, her would-be lover becomes stuck and must be pulled out of her. None of this activity fazes or interests her, for as she notes, "there's no man who's a match for me" (4). To tell her own tale and to occupy the usually male-defined position of agency, the character must be an exaggerated and physically grotesque figure who threatens everyone, from Jordan to the Puritans who hypocritically denigrate the body and then engage in perverse sexual practices. Her violence is primarily a textual violence.

This interpretation could be accomplished, and indeed has been, without the mention of a lesbian subject. But Dog-Woman, I contend, is such a figure, not because she attempts sex with women as well as men, which she does not, nor because she makes close relationships and a community with other women or even one other woman, which she shuns, but because her size constitutes the disruptive agency that is only possible with a lesbian subject. She is the grotesque and exaggerated female body that conditions postmodernism's metaphoric construction of the lesbian body, and she functions primarily as a disrupter of textuality and its positioning of woman. Her sexual encounters, rather than indicating heterosexuality, imply the impossibility of heterosexuality in a woman who creates her own narrative and claims her own agency. Dog-Woman's miserable failure as a heterosexual women is a refusal of the male stories for which she has been intended, whether her father's, the Puritans', her supposed lovers', or even Jordan's. Her modern counterpart only reinforces this positioning. As a chemist, the twentieth-century Dog-Woman takes on the problem of industrial pollution and is, in the story, presently "camping by a river and going mad" (143). As a child, her body was fat, but now in adulthood, it is normal but remains in her mind as an *alter ego* "huge and powerful, a woman whose only morality was her own and whose loyalties were fierce and few" (142). The power that swells in rage over the usurping and destructive tactics of industry defines a position the subject takes and sets her up as an actor in the text. The rage and power associated with size are reminiscent of the most well-known metaphoric definitions of lesbian. "What is a lesbian?" asked the Radicalesbians in 1970; they answered, "A lesbian is the rage of all women condensed to the point of explosion" (240). It is not, in a reverse logic, that size alone constructs the lesbian subject, but that her size constitutes her refusal of the male story with its positions of subjectivity and its inevitable heterosexuality.

While the excessive body, whether operating "realistically" or mentally in the narrative, points to a lesbian subject, Dog-Woman's character goes out of her way to reinforce the binaries that Jordan, with a deft touch, undoes. Dog-Woman is always careful to remark upon her ladylike appearance as if to insist on gender distinctions when her bodily proportions and her violence defy them. In contrasting her eating of a peach with Tradescant's, she insists that "I bit into mine, but in a more ladylike fashion" (17). The point, I believe, is not to see Jordan's and Dog-Woman's dichotomous potential as postmodern theorists, but to affirm the gender difference that must underlie even a deconstructionist's effort. This position allows Winterson to maintain the importance of gender while deconstructing it. The lesbian body of Dog-Woman is, indeed, a woman's body, constructed as it is. This subjectivity is neither trapped in male characteristics or space nor repositioned as a traditional female. This lesbian body is the repositioned female body in the mobile narrative space, and it accomplishes in a more dramatic way the lesbian act of stealing the narrative.

Both characters, Jordan (and his modern counterpart, Nicholas Jordan) and Dog-Woman (and her counterpart, the chemist), are repositioned in their respective narratives. Jordan is refused his heroic agency, and Dog-Woman attains her agency in a different narrative form. At the closure, their stories come together, and instead of being positioned as either the boundary or the closure of his story, Dog-Woman takes Jordan into hers. He consents to her agenda when, as Nicholas Jordan, he asks—"Surely this woman was a hero?" (159) and joins her at her river camp. Even then his desire for rest is shunted aside as she proclaims, in her last statement, "Let's burn down the factory" (165). This follows shortly upon the seventeenth-century Dog-Woman's complaint about London, "This city should be burned down" (164). Closure happens as all the narratives coincide in the purgation through fire of a perverse social order. In fact, the ending neatly brings together the two historical strains as well as all four narrative voices in an event that would befit the closure of any linear story. The novel closes with a great cataclysmic event—the Great Fire of London in 1666.

This text is alive on a metafictional level. It observes the clash of narratives as structuring devices and continually remarks on and remakes itself. While positing a myriad of postmodern positions, Winterson closes her novel by totalizing the preceding events and subjects/ characters. The Great Fire of London of 1666 sweeps away the rubble as Jordan and his mother leave on his boat in the Thames. The fire is her revenge on the male narrative. Jordan, however, appears to be the last speaker, although it is he who has joined his mother in her story. Yet the last speaker/narrator is inconclusive. Most logically, it is Jordan because it begins "As I drew my ship out of London" (167), the statement we expect from him after the end of Dog-Woman's story. Yet the narrator is just as likely to be the twentieth-century counterpart of Dog-Woman, whose "rowing boat" is tied up at the river bank. The single voice incorporates both male and female in a futuristic, utopian dream of possibility. It is she and Jordan who have the last word and posit a future together, as a single narrative voice, beyond the stasis of this sin-infested world. It is a lesbian future, empty space and points of light, reached only with the revaluation of narrative space by the lesbian subject as Dog-Woman.

Written on the Body is both an easier and a more difficult story to name as lesbian. It is easier because the novel contains a central love story that can, with little ingenuity, be imagined as lesbian. In fact, if Winterson had resolved the gender of the narrator/lover, her story and its linear narrative tension could have been, as it has been already, called a rather ordinary romantic tale. It is, at the same time, more difficult to call this novel lesbian because the reader's task is not primarily to identify the gender of the narrator, as tempting as that is. It does not work for the reader to search for gender clues—the mention of a shirt, a nipple, a motorcycle—for none of these provides conclusive evidence. The task, instead, is to analyze the reconfiguration of lover and beloved deter-mined by the repositioned and redefined female body of the beloved, Louise. Like *Sexing the Cherry* and Wittig's *The Lesbian Body*, this text depends on a repositioning of the female body through its representation as excessive; and like these two other narratives, the excessive female body is a challenge to the traditional Western textualization of the female body. In this context, it is more important to determine the narrative positions of the lovers than the gender of the narrator. In fact, I would argue that the traditional romantic story is reclaimed as a lesbian story *because* the gender of the narrator remains unclear.

But the narrator cannot be ignored; rather, s/he must be approached with other questions in mind. The narrator of this story contrasts the story s/he is telling about the beloved Louise with other, past affairs, always aware that s/he is describing love through a set of phrases and a narrative system which have the power to trivialize her/his feelings. Throughout the early sections of the novel, the narrator tells the hilari-ous because predictable stories of past love affairs with women—with the "anarcha-feminist" (21), Inge, with Bathsheba, the dentist, and with the staid, homebody Jacqueline who works at the zoo with "small furry things that wouldn't be nice to visitors" (25). The narrator, in fact, positions itself as a very traditional male lover who seeks as a relationship goal "Ecstasy without end" (21) and calls him/herself a "Lothario" (20). Under some critical inquiries, these descriptions could render the narrator as either male or as a butch to Louise's femme. The latter possibility would bring into play Sue-Ellen Case's analysis of the gender disruption of the butch-femme couple. But later in the novel, the narrator also tells the reader about boyfriends with similar outlandish characteristics, perhaps repositioning the butch as a femme. None of these assumptions, however, furthers an analysis of the novel, for the narrator's primary characteristic is not gender but her/his recognition that s/he is trapped within a story which is fraught with clichés, including, we may assume, the gender resolution that our readerly and social expectations demand. The narrator is constantly aware of his/her entrapment in and desire for distance from culture's love stories such as Bacall and Bogart films (41). In fact, early in his/her relationship with Louise, s/he tells us that Louise is more like a Victorian or Gothic heroine than a modern woman (49). The narrator only knows love—as it has been told and as we relive it by reliving stories—as a cliché. When Louise comes along, s/he is caught trying to escape these truisms while being bound to repeat many of the same words and story lines. The question becomes how to love without being trite, without repeating the same story.

The irresolvability of the narrator's gender may be mirrored in Winterson's refusal to assign her/him a consistent narrative voice or narratee. Most of the story is told in an intimate, ardent first-person voice, but near the middle of the text this voice abruptly shifts to an omniscient third-person to narrate the story of Louise's husband's—Elgin's—parents. S/he also moves back and forth from addressing Louise as a narratee to speaking to the reader as an embedded "you," changing focus to declare incantatory love poetry to Louise and to justify her/his difficult choices in love to what is assumed to be a wary reader. For instance, in arguing for his need to leave Jacqueline, whom s/he chose, not for sexual attraction, but in order to settle down, s/he addresses the reader: "Contentment is a feeling you say? Are you sure it's not an absence of feeling?" (76). At other times Louise is directly addressed: "You are still the colour of my blood. You are my blood" (99). This haphazard shift between what Robyn R. Warhol calls an "engaging narrator" who "encourages identification" with the reader and a "distancing narrator" who discourages it (812) reflects other shifts. The narrator also makes contradictory claims to the truth or fictionality of this love story. In one significant comment, the narrator anticipates the reader's incredulity by acknowledging that "I can tell by now that you are wondering whether I can be trusted as a narrator" (24). A more direct statement of trustworthiness—"you are wondering whether I can be trusted"—would not invoke so starkly the fictional position of the narrator and thus the artificiality of the story. Later, the same narrator, opposes her/his "real" story to fiction, insisting that while artificiality is a part of the narrative system, the present story exceeds that system. When s/he finally confronts Elgin, for example, the narrator explains, "He spun round. I didn't think people did that in real life, only in kooky crime thrillers" (169). Near the end of the story, opera (187) and Russian novels (160) are both invoked as elaborate fictional trajectories that significantly skew the meaning and potential of "real" life.

These shifts of narrative level and voice highlight the metafictional nature of this novel. It is a story about story, about the possibility of telling the same story in a different form but not in an unrecognizable form. The revised story must begin not with the refusal of trite phrases like "I love you" or melodramatic tragic endings nor with the narrator, but with Louise. At one point, when Louise states her unequivocal decision to leave Elgin, the narrator claims, "This is the wrong script. This is the moment where I'm supposed to be self-righteous and angry" (18). The right script must start with the reconfigured female body of Louise, for it is the female body which has been the basis for the clichéd Western romantic story against which the narrator struggles. Only when the beloved is retextualized can the narrator be repositioned and a different story told.

From the beginning of their relationship, the narrator maps his/her story on the body of the beloved. In the early stages it is mapped out in traditional, almost Petrarchan, imagery that reminds the reader of English literature of John Donne and William Shakespeare, among others. Winterson describes the lovers making love as a means to encompass the whole world, as a way to make "a little room an everywhere." These descriptions indicate both the impossibility of avoiding romantic clichés and their power when revised: "I will explore you and mine you and you will redraw me according to your will. We shall cross one another's boundaries and make ourselves one nation" (20). The beloved is also compared to nature (29), one of the most disabling positions for the woman because of the muteness of nature and therefore of the beloved.

But at the midpoint of the novel, the female body is radically remapped not by a slight transformation of the traditional imagery but by an almost impossible conjunction between cancer and love. The conflict which creates a powerful narrative tension because it delays resolution of the story is Louise's cancer. When the narrator learns of Louise's disease, s/he ironically decides to leave her because it is the only condition on which her husband, a noted cancer specialist, will treat his wife. In a desire to merge with the beloved on another level, even from the distance of Yorkshire where s/he has gone in self-exile, the narrator spends time studying the disease in minute detail. Only the imagery of this merger differs from our expected forms. In this "sucking, sweating, greedy, defecating self" (111), s/he finds a love poem to the beloved. Like Wittig's violent anatomizing of the female body in order to retextualize it, Winterson's narrator anatomizes the female body that is out to destroy itself, a body that duplicates itself outside of the rules (115). This excessive female body is imagined through a disease that reproduces itself wildly at a cellular level. In effect, the disease remaps the body and changes the narrator to the bones of her/his own body. Like the romantic narrative which provides both the grid and the opposition for the narrator's story, Louise's diseased body represents both the traditionally negative and disruptively positive descriptions of the female body as excessive. Once restructured as excessive, the love relationship and the lovers become lesbian.

The central section of the novel sets aside narrative movement and instead juxtaposes medical and poetic descriptions of parts of the human anatomy. While the linear movement of the story slows down—in fact, this section delays the resolution of a tense narrative situation—the female body is reconstructed. On a narrative level, this section can be read as the boundary space which the lover must cross in order to know her/himself. As a poetic description of the female body, it is reminiscent of the Petrarchan catalogues—or more accurately, fragmentation—of the beloved's body. As another in a series of narrative shifts, then, this change of narrative level catalogues details rather than events. It is significant that this section, which could be called an elaborate descriptive passage, set in the mind of the narrator, necessitates the disruption of narrative time in order to reposition the female body. But once repositioned, the female body does not call for a completely different narrative trajectory. If anything, the return to the linear narrative heightens the tension as the conflict between Elgin and the narrator for Louise comes to a conclusion. This conflict demands that we also apply Sedgwick's erotic triangle as well as the narrative functions or spaces for the beloved and the lover in order to understand Winterson's struggle with narrative order.

In the middle section of the novel, separated by chapter headings that recall a medical text's discussion of various elements of the body, Louise's body is reinscribed. But different from the traditional paradigms of the beloved as a fragmented body and a boundary space, this section reinscribes Louise's body as excessive and grotesque while it also writes the narrator's body as the same. It is this mutuality of bodies—the title, for instance, leaves the subject of the phrase "written on the body" undetermined—that creates a new love narrative. The narrator describes wanting to enter the beloved's body, to "crawl inside you" (115) in order to protect her body from the encroaching disease. This penetration is not sexual as is the predictable imagery of eating that fills the love story prior to the narrator's knowledge of Louise's disease. Instead of traditional and trite statements of the love-besotted narrator—"Let me be diced carrot, vermicelli, just so that you will take me in your mouth" (36)—the images of bodily union in this section are constructed as poetic transformations of medical facts. As in the short story discussed above, Winterson takes a predictable, in this case medical, vocabulary, and refuses its terms; instead, she writes her own medical description of the body as a poetic amalgam of reversals, puns, and metaphors. For instance, because on a literal level cells on the surface of the skin are dead, the narrator imagines "The dead you is constantly being rubbed away by the dead me" (123). This transformation of both bodies and of the nature of love refuses and yet uses the medical language. As she does with narrative as a whole, Winterson uses the form but restructures the basic relationships. In this case, she revises imagery of the female body in order to restructure the relationship of lover and beloved. Thus, for instance, by learning every cell of the body, and transforming these cells into a poetic imagery which violates romantic expectations, the narrator becomes Louise's body rather than controls or possesses it: "Myself in your skin, myself lodged in your bones" (120). It is this mutuality, this sameness rather than heterosexual romantic difference, which constitutes the narrator and Louise as the lesbian subject.

Neither the images nor the lover's exploration of the beloved's anatomical body is romanticized. In fact, as with Wittig's retextualization of the lesbian body, violence is a necessary part of Winterson's project of renarrativizing the female body because the power embedded in the traditional textual system resists another paradigm of subjectivity. But, if as I have noted above, violence is also inherent in the traditional narrative system, both in the struggles and values of the heroic story and in the romantic story of love as death—or marriage—and transcendence, Winterson's images of violence demand explanation. How do they revise the violence already embedded in the system? In *Sexing the Cherry*, Dog-Woman unleashes an unrealistic but intense violence—she crushes men against her gigantic body and murders countless Puritans. The surrealistic quality of the character mitigates the gruesomeness of the violence, but the text still highlights violence in the images of eyes and teeth being torn from Puritans' skulls. In the central section of *Written on the Body*, Winterson appears to answer directly Wittig's violent imagery in *The Lesbian Body*. Winterson's images are less alienating as a description of love than Wittig's lovers tearing apart each others' flesh. In fact, while violence is referred to, it is the violence of a former injury that is matched on the lover's body by a love bite (118) or the refusal of the lover to be cut by the diseased body's projected angles (131). In a section reminiscent of Wittig's writing, the lover imagines exploring the cavities of the beloved's body, "hook[ing] out your brain through your accommodating orifices" (119). Winterson, however, refuses to present these imaginings directly, as an extended description, but rather quickly poeticizes these images. The potential injury to the hand, the possible stigmata, is transformed immediately into a metaphor: "Nail me to you. I will ride you like a nightmare. You are the winged horse Pegasus" (131). Death and disease become the imagistic entry into the beloved's body. Winterson's primary image of retextualization is remapping or remarking the body, transforming violence into images of knowledge and love. If we consider this medical section of Winterson's novel the boundary space of the female body which the lover must traverse, a space comparable to the Petrarchan poet's anatomizing of the female body and the hero's journey through a female-defined natural world, then this static section is the core of Winterson's effort to reposition the lovers in relationship to one another. The medical discourse is a means to an intimate form of knowledge which transforms the lover into a figure positioned as the same.

A narrative and ontological pattern of sameness is the result of this retextualization. The narrator directly refers to this surprising situation, for s/he remarks that while sexual attraction is usually based on differ-ence, in their case "there are so many things about us that are the same" (129). Later, the narrator calls Louise "my twin" (163). The narrator, even earlier, becomes Louise's body and her text: "She has translated me to her own book" (89). What is written on the beloved's body is also written on the narrator's body, and the reconstitution of the love rela-tionship is accomplished by repositioning the lovers as the same. Thus it is that the "L" which begins as part of the lover's early infatuation with Louise (40) returns as an emblem for both Love and Louise when the narrator reads an elaborately decorated "L" in an illuminated manu-script; finally it is written on the narrator's body as an internal tattoo inscribed in the same section which anatomizes the beloved's body. It does not take much intuitive grasp of literature to imagine that this "L" is also written as Lesbian, for to write the female body outside of male homosocial and heterosexual desire is to write Lesbian or, in the terms of my argument, to write the lesbian subject into lesbian narrative space. This revision takes seriously what I believe exists only as a narrative possibility—Mieke Bal's argument that the power of the subject and object is "equally divided over the two actors" (29). The object has the power to grant or deny the subject's desire, and the "he" must wait for "her" response (29). Louise is given agency in this section, and both become, interchangeably, the desiring figure and the desired one. They have become the lesbian subject without ever definitively resolving the gender issue of the narrator.

But Winterson does not fix these positions as utopian absolutes; instead she returns them to the trajectory of the love narrative. She enters the reinscribed bodies and the realigned positionalities of the lovers into a linear plot which highlights narrative tension and seems to intensify an erotic triangle which is played out in a predictably dramatic physical confrontation with Louise's husband, Elgin. If anything, the traditional narrative tension and its gender implications become stronger. Louise is not present as a character throughout the telling of this last section of the novel until the problematic closure. Having been a central presence prior to Elgin's ultimatum to the narrator, she is now a phantom in his/her imagination. In fact, it is her absence that begins to negate the potential power of the erotic triangle that Eve Sedgwick proposes as the paradigm for so much of English narrative. Opposed to her somatic absence is the stolid new lover, Gail Right, a humorous counterpart to Dog-Woman. And once again, the narrator highlights the opposition between fictionality and reality, as if the narrator is attempting to avoid the expected plot movement and closure of opera and Russian novels. But the question recurs: how does one avoid clichés—including the clichéd positions, movement, and closure of the love narrative—when one has only clichés as linguistic potential? The last paragraphs posit two clichéd possibilities: Louise's physical return or the narrator's false image of her return which only heightens his/her loss. Both resolutions are trite, and yet, Winterson seems to say, we have to use the clichés while we at the same time liberate them for innovative functions.

The renewed predictability of the romantic story is, therefore, not an indication that the lovers are forever stuck in the same story of Western romance. By structurally repositioning the lovers, the story can be repeated but on a different level. Thus, the novel's closure is both a set of clichéd possibilities, and, with the repositioned lovers, a projection of new possibilities. Winterson, therefore, writes the first sentence of the last paragraph with "This is where the story starts" (190). The room that imagistically becomes an everywhere in clichéd Petrarchan terms now repeats itself with the repositioned lovers. The story ends with multiple narrative possibilities, what the narrator claims is not necessarily "a happy ending but here we are let loose in open fields" (190), what in critical terms might be called the "not yet presented."

In another context, Winterson has said that "Freedom has a price. Form is by definition shape and choice. The form you choose has its own restrictions, its own rules, however innovatively someone uses it" ("Outrageous" 27). What I find most interesting about Jeanette Winterson is her combination of conventional narrative form and postmodern dissonance. She is considered one of the most innovative writers of this era, and her book jackets are covered with tributes in this tone from fellow writers like Gore Vidal and Muriel Spark. Yet she accomplishes this innovation within the elastic boundaries of the narrative system, using it against itself by repositioning the categories of narrator, agent, and object. Specifically in these two novels, the disruption that Winterson's texts enact is not through a twentieth-century nonlinearity or lack of closure, so much as through a reconstruction of the female body as an excessive, even grotesque figure, a figure in its new structural alignment which becomes the lesbian body, and that in turn redefines the boundaries of gender and therefore of conventional narrativity.

SEVEN

Conclusion

What we are about is re-metaphoring the world.
— Marilyn Frye, *Willful Virgin*

Narrative is, as Roland Barthes has said, everywhere (*Image* 79), and as such, it is or should be a recognizable part of our theoretical projects as well as our fiction. Nowhere is this structure more apparent than in the generational antagonism that pits one theory or "ism" against another. Relying on problematic assumptions of better insight or a different context, a younger generation claims to surpass its elders in vision and in truth. In the clash with the evil predecessor, the monster Error, the more theoretically sophisticated, usually younger writers supplant and conquer their adversary, setting up a simple linear narrative trajectory in which truth triumphs over error and naïveté. Lesbian-feminism stands accused of both faults. But the problem with lesbian postmodernism's claim is not its arrogance but its narrativity. When this new theory condemns a dangerous ideological model, the master narrative, and proposes, instead, anti-narrative as an ideal, the irony is thick. Lesbian postmodernism, I would contend, has set up such an ironic paradigm, in the process maligning the very theoretical shoulders on which it stands.

By refusing to acknowledge its own complicity in the master narrative and its concomitant gender ideology, lesbian postmodernism is doomed to repeat the same fallacies. Thus, in a Foucauldian sense, lesbian post-modernism acts as an instrument of ideological containment as much as a tool of subversion. It functions as a means of ideological containment not only in its reliance on an implied narrative but also in its acceptance of notions such as gender undecidability and indeterminancy. Rather than acting as a displacement of the gender binary, especially as it exists in the narrative system, gender indeterminancy maintains the center/margin pattern of Western culture. It reinstitutes the gender neutralism of liberal enlightment philosophy, leaving us once again blind to the gender structure underlying terms such as "objectivity" and "the queer subject." Lesbian postmodernism, in accepting gender neutrality, reinvents the hidden gender dichotomy that allows the male to occupy the structural center and female to forage on the margins. I would suggest instead that shifts in theory need to be recognized as part of a different narrative movement, one that complicates rather than destroys what has preceded it and one that acknowledges the flexibility as well as the power embedded in the Western narrative system. In this way, not only will current theory restructure its theoretical narrative in complex interaction with its predecessor, but it may also acknowledge the elusiveness, complexity, and diversity of the lesbian narrative.

My intention has been to outline a structural way to describe diverse stories of the last twenty-five years under the rubric of the lesbian narrative. This approach depends on expanded and, I realize, controversial definitions of both lesbian and narrative. I have argued that twentieth-century women writers have developed two expanded, nonclinical meanings for lesbian, both of which depend on a tangential connection to gender. The bodily and the nonbodily lesbian subjects have been used by women writers to put into crisis the controlling gender structure of narrative and at the same time to forge an expanded definition of woman. Narrative as a system of meaning has been challenged and changed by this intervention. But my attempt to answer two large critical and theoretical questions—what is the lesbian in a lesbian narrative and what is the narrative structure that accommodates, contains, or repels this lesbian—inevitably leaves certain problems unresolved.

They came to the fore near the end of my writing, while taking a walk with a friend. I explained to her the various problems I was having trying to define a lesbian narrative, as if talking would free my head of its intellectual chatter. I had just introduced her to Isak Dinesen's "The Blank Page," which Margaret Reynolds includes in her collection of short lesbian fiction. I had never before considered that story as lesbian, but within the parameters I had been setting out in my argument I had to allow its possibility. As I noted in the first chapter, Reynolds claims that lesbianism is "the real unwritten history" (xx) of Dinesen's story but offers no concrete evidence or theory for her interpretation. She says about this story what she says about Woolf's *A Room of One's Own*, the lesbianism is "not explicit. But it's there" (xxii). What I have proposed in this book is a way to define the "it" that is "there." My friend instead gave me an enticing formula that called into question my own answer. First, she said, you declare that the work is lesbian and then you (will) read it that way. While this suggestion posits the "it" in the reader instead of in the text, I was intrigued both by the simplicity and profundity of this formula. For a formalist who cut her literary teeth on New Criticism, I have always found myself squeamish about approaches to literature that rely on the reader, although as a contemporary formalist, I accept that narrative structures condition both the textual system and the reader's expectations. But her formula for deciding what literary works are lesbian and what are not challenged me on other levels and encouraged me to shore up my own definition.

Lesbian narratives are unique because of the difficulty of finding the "it" in either the text or the reader. My theory is an attempt to define an "it": the twentieth-century lesbian subject. Because I insist that this figure has been and is currently constructed in relation to gender, I have described this figure broadly. The danger is always that such a definition is too broad; as a result I have attempted to draw some boundaries. Judith Fetterley, in describing her approach to Sarah Orne Jewett's *Deephaven*, uses not only Jewett's life-long relationship with a woman but also her own experience to justify seeing this text as lesbian. She concludes, "Predisposed for the reasons expressed above to read *Deephaven* as a lesbian text, I find it responsive to such a reading" (165). In this suggestion, what is lesbian migrates from writer and reader through the text. In contrast, my attempt has been to name the "lesbian" in a text; first to identify it and then, unless lesbian is "severely literal," to draw boundaries around a definition which could become too vague and therefore meaningless. I am also aware, however, of the broad strokes I have used to sketch the lesbian subject, leaving the possibility that too many texts, perhaps including Faulkner's, might be included. My definition is intended to eliminate that chance. Fetterley, for instance, does not accept that "any nineteenth-century text dealing with the friendship of two women should be read as a lesbian text" (164). In the essay that precedes Fetterley's in the same collectin, Diana L. Swanson, while refusing the anachronistic use of the term "lesbian," suggests the opposite: "The presence of female friends works in many eighteenth- and nineteenth-century novels as a force subversive of the compulsory heterosexuality inherent in the novel's controlling conventions and formal closure" (155).

What these diverse opinions suggest is that to name a text "lesbian" is not an easy task. My purpose has been to discover an independent construct which I call the lesbian subject, a broad construct that I suggest is already a part of the language and literary system of this century. In reading lesbian texts, then, I would insist, like Fetterley, on some context to justify that reading—a context I locate more in the text or the writer than in the reader. Locating that which is lesbian in the reader might lead to a solipsism I am reluctant to endorse. The reader is constructed and reconstructed by the various discursive uses of lesbian in this century, and the positive depictions by women writers in these last twenty-five years have reconfigured for us as readers the discursive patterns of both lesbian and woman. This effort by women writers is part of a goal that Marilyn Frye described recently: "What we are about is re-metaphoring the world" (*Willful* 70).

In her book *Sexual Anarchy,* Elaine Showalter compares the disturbance of gender and sexual boundaries at the ends of two centuries, the nineteenth and the twentieth. What I have identified as the lesbian subject of the last twenty-five years has to be put in this historical context, for the last quarter century has seen a heightened exploration of the metaphoric lesbian as part of and perhaps the central part of a larger sexual anarchy. What remains after this study is the need for the development of a more thoroughgoing historical context. In setting out the last twenty-five years—roughly from the beginning of the current feminist movement—I have identified in broad and sweeping terms an historical period of great complexity. Much more research is needed to relate the development of theories of lesbian to various social and political phenomena: racial and ethnic movements, the lesbian and gay movements, feminism, the New Right, and the basically conservative politics of this era, especially in the 1980s, with Margaret Thatcher in England and Ronald Reagan and George Bush in America.

But in recalling Reynolds's phrase again—the "it" that is "there"—I have also posited the importance of a "there" in my definition of the lesbian narrative, for I have made much of the need to acknowledge the system of meaning any writer or reader engages while positing or encountering the lesbian subject. While I accept current feminist and lesbian analyses that the narrative is an ideological system which inscribes male centrality, female marginality, and lesbian absence, in my view narrative is more flexible than is allowed by current postmodern theorists. Rather than seeing the narrative subject caught irreversibly in the political cogs of narrative, leaving nonlinearity as the only means of ideological disruption, I insist that narrative's positions of subjectivity—

narrator, agent, focalizer, closure—also can be instruments that disturb and reconfigure narrative's agenda. The lesbian subject of this century restructures the traditional narrative system rather than stands as a point of undecidability in a monolithic system of "narrative mastery" (Roof 34). The binary structure of theories that pit narrative against anti-narrative or traditional linear story against experimental writing is self-destructive. The lesbian narrative that I envision, then, is a revised story but one that allows for the possibility of a linear trajectory and a somewhat normal closure as well as for experimental writing. Without such a possibility, the definition of a lesbian narrative remains elitist and exclusionary. To argue, for instance, that lesbian must only be a point of confusion in the master narrative's project of control and mastery is to eliminate the stories that lesbians tell one another, that we write for one another, that we read when we retire from our lives in the nonlesbian world. While we must acknowledge the centrality of textuality in any analysis of lesbian fiction, experimental writing cannot be our litmus test, nor should we condemn it in a fit of reactionary conservatism. The same must be said of more accessible fiction; it does not hold the key to what can be called lesbian fiction. The different works, then, that Bonnie Zimmerman, Elizabeth Meese, and Judith Roof consider in their readings of lesbian fiction should all be included under the umbrella of the phrase "lesbian narrative." This genre is too interesting, complex, and challenging to do otherwise.

Works Cited

Abbandonato, Linda. " 'A View from Elsewhere' ": Subversive Sexuality and the Rewriting of the Heroine's Story in *The Color Purple*." *PMLA* 106.5 (1991): 1106–15.

Acker, Kathy. "The Language of the Body." In *The Penguin Book of Lesbian Short Stories*. Ed. Margaret Reynolds, 399–411. New York: Viking, 1993.

Alcoff, Linda. "Cultural Feminism versus Post-Structuralism: The Identity Crisis in Feminist Theory." *Signs* 13.3 (1988): 405–36.

Allen, Carolyn. "Review." *Signs* 17.1 (1991): 233–36.

———. "Sexual Narrative in the Fiction of Djuna Barnes." In *Sexual Practice, Textual Theory: Lesbian Cultural Criticism*. Ed. Susan J. Wolfe and Julia Penelope, 184–98. Cambridge, MA: Blackwell, 1993.

Allison, Dorothy. *Bastard out of Carolina*. New York: Dutton, 1992.

Andreadis, Harriette. "The Sapphic-Platonics of Katherine Philips, 1632–1664." *Signs* 15.1 (1989): 34–61.

Anzaldúa, Gloria. *Borderlands/La Frontera: The New Mestiza*. San Francisco: Aunt Lute Books, 1987.

Atwood, Margaret. "Circe/Mud Poems." *Selected Poems: 1965–1975*. Boston: Houghton Mifflin, 1976.

———. *Surfacing*. Toronto: McClelland & Stewart, 1972.

Auerbach, Nina. *Communities of Women: An Idea in Fiction*. Cambridge, MA: Harvard University Press, 1978.

Bakhtin, Mikhail. *Rabelais and His World*. Trans. Helen Iswolsky. Cambridge, MA: MIT Press, 1968.

Bal, Mieke. *Narratology: Introduction to the Theory of Narrative*. Trans. Christine van Boheemen. Toronto: University of Toronto Press, 1985.

———. "The Point of Narratology." *Poetics Today* 11.4 (1990): 727–53.

Barale, Michèle Aina. "When Jack Blinks: Si(gh)ting Gay Desire in Ann Bannon's *Beebo Brinker*." *Feminist Studies* 18.3 (1992): 533–49.

Barnes, Djuna. *Nightwood*. New York: New Directions, 1946.

Barnfield, Richard. *The Complete Poems*. Ed. George Klawitter. Selinsgrove, PA: Susquehanna University Press, 1990.

Barthes, Roland. *Image, Music, Text*. Trans. Stephen Heath. Glasgow: Fontana, 1977.

———. *Writing Degree Zero and Elements of Semiology*. Trans. Annette Lavers and Colin Smith. Boston: Beacon Press, 1970.

Bartkowski, Frances. *Feminist Utopias*. Lincoln: University of Nebraska Press, 1989.

Baudelaire, Charles. *One Hundred Poems from "Les Fleurs du Mal."* Trans. C. F. MacIntyre. Berkeley: University of California Press, 1947.

Benjamin, Walter. *Charles Baudelaire: A Lyric Poet in the Era of High Capitalism*. Trans. Harry Zohn. London: NLB, 1973.

Benstock, Shari. *Women of the Left Bank: Paris, 1900–1940*. Austin: University of Texas Press, 1986.

Benveniste, Emile. *Problems in General Linguistics*. Trans. Mary Elizabeth Meek. Coral Gables, FL: University of Miami Press, 1971.

Berger, John. *Ways of Seeing*. New York: Penguin, 1977.

Bogin, Meg. *The Women Troubadours*. New York: Paddington Press, 1976.

Boone, Joseph Allen. *Tradition Counter Tradition: Love and the Form of Fiction*. Chicago: University of Chicago Press, 1987.

Booth, Alison. "Introduction: The Sense of Few Endings." In *Famous Last Words: Changes in Gender and Narrative Closure*. Ed. Alison Booth, 1–32. Charlottesville: University Press of Virginia, 1993.

Bordo, Susan. "Feminism, Postmodernism, and Gender-Scepticism." In *Feminism/Postmodernism*. Ed. Linda J. Nicholson, 133–56. New York: Routledge, 1990.

Borghi, Liana. "Between Essence and Presence: Politics, Self, and Symbols in Contemporary American Lesbian Poetry." In *Homosexuality, Which Homosexuality?* Ed. Dennis Altman et al., 61–81. London: GMP Publishers, 1989.

Boswell, John. *Christianity, Social Tolerance, and Homosexuality: Gay People in Western Europe from the Beginning of the Christian Era to the Fourteenth Century*. Chicago: The University of Chicago Press, 1980.

Bradley, Marion Zimmer. *The Mists of Avalon*. New York: Ballantine Books, 1982.

Bredbeck, Gregory W. "B/O–Barthes's Text/O'Hara's Trick." *PMLA* 108.2 (1993): 268–82.

Brewer, Mária Minich. "A Loosening of Tongues: From Narrative Economy to Women Writing." *Modern Language Notes* 99 (1984): 1141–61.

Brooke-Rose, Christine. "Whatever Happened to Narratology?" *Poetics Today* 11.2 (1990): 283–93.

Brooks, Peter. *Reading for the Plot: Design and Intention in Narrative*. New York: Alfred A. Knopf, 1984.

Brossard, Nicole. *The Aerial Letter*. Trans. Marlene Wildeman. Toronto: The Women's Press, 1988.

Broumas, Olga. "Review of *The Dream of a Common Language*." In *Reading Adrienne Rich: Reviews and Re-Visions, 1951–81*. Ed. Jane Roberta Cooper, 274–86. Ann Arbor: The University of Michigan Press, 1984.

Brown, Judith C. *Immodest Acts: The Life of a Lesbian Nun in Renaissance Italy*. New York: Oxford University Press, 1986.

Brown, Rita Mae. *Rubyfruit Jungle*. New York: Bantam Books, 1973.

Bulkin, Elly. "Lesbian Poetry in the Classroom." In *Lesbian Poetry: An Anthology.* Ed. Elly Bulkin and Joan Larkin, 265–78. Watertown, MA: Persephone Press, 1981.

Butler, Judith. *Gender Trouble: Feminism and the Subversion of Identity.* New York: Routledge, 1990.

———. "Imitation and Gender Insubordination." In *Inside/Out: Lesbian Theories, Gay Theories.* Ed. Diana Fuss, 13–31. New York: Routledge, 1991.

Byatt, A. S. *Possession: A Romance.* New York: Vintage, 1990.

Cameron, Anne. *The Journey.* San Francisco: Spinsters/Aunt Lute, 1986.

Carlston, Erin G. "*Zami* and the Politics of Plural Identity." In *Sexual Practice, Textual Theory: Lesbian Cultural Criticism.* Ed. Susan J. Wolfe and Julia Penelope, 226–36. Cambridge, MA: Blackwell, 1993.

Carpenter, Edward. *Love's Coming-of-Age: A Series of Papers on the Relations of the Sexes.* New York and London: Mitchell Kennerly, 1922.

Carruth, Hayden. "Excellence in Poetry." In *Reading Adrienne Rich: Reviews and Re-Visions, 1951–81.* Ed. Jane Roberta Cooper, 271–73. Ann Arbor: The University of Michigan Press, 1984.

Carruthers, Mary J. "The Re-Vision of the Muse: Adrienne Rich, Audre Lorde, Judy Grahn, Olga Broumas." *Hudson Review* 36 (1983): 293–327.

Case, Sue-Ellen. "Toward a Butch-Femme Aesthetic." In *Making a Spectacle: Feminist Essays on Contemporary Women's Theatre.* Ed. Lynda Hart, 282–99. Ann Arbor: University of Michigan Press, 1989.

———. "Tracking the Vampire." *differences* 3.2 (1991): 1–20.

Castle, Terry. *The Apparitional Lesbian: Female Homosexuality and Modern Culture.* New York: Columbia University Press, 1993.

Chatman, Seymour. *Story and Discourse: Narrative Structure in Fiction and Film.* Ithaca, NY: Cornell University Press, 1978.

Chauncey, George, Jr. "From Sexual Inversion to Homosexuality: Medicine and the Changing Conceptualization of Female Deviance." *Salmagundi* 58–59 (Fall 1982–Winter 1983): 114–46.

Chopin, Kate. *The Awakening and Selected Stories of Kate Chopin.* Ed. Barbara H. Solomon. New York: New American Library, 1976.

Christian, Barbara. *Black Feminist Criticism: Perspectives on Black Women Writers.* New York: Pergamon Press, 1985.

———. "Gloria Naylor's Geography: Community, Class, and Patriarchy in *The Women of Brewster Place* and *Linden Hills.*" In *Reading Black, Reading Feminist: A Critical Anthology.* Ed. Henry Louis Gates, Jr., 348–73. New York: Penguin, 1990.

———. "The Race for Theory." *Feminist Studies* 14.1 (1988): 67–79.

———. "Trajectories of Self-Definition: Placing Contemporary Afro-American Women's Fiction." In *Conjuring: Black Women, Fiction, and Literary Tradition.* Ed. Marjorie Pryse and Hortense J. Spillers, 233–48. Bloomington: Indiana University Press, 1985.

Cixous, Hélène. "The Laugh of the Medusa." In *New French Feminisms: An Anthology.* Trans. Keith Cohen and Paula Cohen. Ed. Elaine Marks and Isabelle de Courtivron, 245–64. New York: Schocken Books, 1980.

Clément, Catherine. *Opera, or the Undoing of Women.* Trans. Betsy Wing. Minneapolis: University of Minnesota Press, 1988.

Cohen, Ed. "Who Are 'We'? Gay 'Identity' as Political (E)motion: (A Theoretical Rumination)." In *Inside/Out: Lesbian Theories, Gay Theories.* Ed. Diana Fuss, 71–92. New York: Routledge, 1991.

Colette. *The Pure and the Impure.* Trans. Herma Briffault. New York: Farrar, Straus & Giroux, 1967.

Collecott, Diana. "What is not said: a study in textual inversion." In *Sexual Sameness: Textual Differences in Lesbian and Gay Writing.* Ed. Joseph Bristow, 91–110. London: Routledge, 1992.

Conrad, Joseph. *Heart of Darkness: A Case Study in Contemporary Criticism.* Ed. Ross C. Murfin. New York: St. Martin's Press, 1989.

Crecy, Susan. "Ivy Compton-Burnett: Family as Nightmare." In *Lesbian and Gay Writing: An Anthology of Critical Essays.* Ed. Mark Lilly, 13–22. Philadelphia: Temple University Press, 1990.

Creed, Barbara. *The Monstrous-Feminine: Film, Feminism, Psychoanalysis.* London and New York: Routledge, 1993.

Culler, Jonathan. *Structuralist Poetics: Structuralism, Linguistics, and the Study of Literature.* Ithaca, NY: Cornell University Press, 1975.

de Beauvoir, Simone. *The Second Sex.* Trans. H. M. Parshley. New York: Bantam, 1961.

DeJean, Joan. *Fictions of Sappho: 1546–1937.* Chicago: The University of Chicago Press, 1989.

de Lauretis, Teresa. *Alice Doesn't: Feminism, Semiotics, Cinema.* Bloomington: Indiana University Press, 1984.

———. "The Essence of the Triangle or, Taking the Risk of Essentialism Seriously: Feminist Theory in Italy, the U.S., and Britain," *differences* 1.2 (1989): 3–37.

———. "Feminist Studies/Critical Studies: Issues, Terms, and Contexts." In *Feminist Studies/Critical Studies.* Ed. Teresa de Lauretis, 1–19. Bloomington: Indiana University Press, 1986.

———. *The Practice of Love: Lesbian Sexuality and Perverse Desire.* Bloomington and Indianapolis: Indiana University Press, 1994.

———. "Queer Theory: Lesbian and Gay Sexualities: *An Introduction.*" *differences* 3.2 (1991): iii–xviii.

———. "Sexual Indifference and Lesbian Representation," *The Theatre Journal* 40 (1988): 155–77.

———. *Technologies of Gender: Essays on Theory, Film, and Fiction.* Bloomington: Indiana University Press, 1987.

de Rougemont, Denis. *Love in the Western World.* Garden City, NY: Doubleday, 1957.

DeShazer, Mary K. *Inspiring Women: Reimagining the Muse.* New York: Pergamon Press, 1986.

Diehl, Joanne Feit. " 'Cartographies of Silence': Rich's *Common Language* and the Woman Poet." In *Reading Adrienne Rich: Reviews and Re-Visions, 1951–1981.* Ed. Jane Roberta Cooper, 91–110. Ann Arbor: The University of Michigan Press, 1984.

Doan, Laura. "Jeanette Winterson's Sexing the Postmodern." In *The Lesbian Postmodern*. Ed. Laura Doan, 139–55. New York: Columbia University Press, 1994.

Dollimore, Jonathan. *Sexual Dissidence: Augustine to Wilde, Freud to Foucault.* Oxford: Clarendon Press, 1991.

Donoghue, Emma. "Words for Things." In *The Penguin Book of Lesbian Short Stories*. Ed. Margaret Reynolds, 387–98. New York: Viking, 1993.

DuPlessis, Rachel Blau. *Writing Beyond the Ending: Narrative Strategies of Twentieth-Century Women Writers.* Bloomington: Indiana University Press, 1985.

Edwards, Lee R. *Psyche as Hero: Female Heroism and Fictional Form.* Middletown, CT: Wesleyan University Press, 1984.

Ellis, Havelock. *Studies in the Psychology of Sex*, Vol. 1. New York: Random House, 1940.

Engelbrecht, Penelope J. " 'Lifting Belly Is a Language': The Postmodern Lesbian Subject." *Feminist Studies* 16.1 (1990): 85–114.

Esquivel, Laura. *Like Water for Chocolate.* Trans. Carol Christensen and Thomas Christensen. New York: Doubleday, 1989.

Evans, Martha Noel. *Masks of Tradition: Women and the Politics of Writing in Twentieth-Century France.* Ithaca, NY: Cornell University Press, 1987.

Faderman, Lillian, ed. *Chloe Plus Olivia: An Anthology of Lesbian Literature from the Seventeenth Century to the Present.* New York: Viking/Penguin, 1994.

———. *Surpassing the Love of Men: Romantic Friendship and Love between Women from the Renaissance to the Present.* New York: William Morrow, 1981.

Farwell, Marilyn R. "Toward a Definition of the Lesbian Literary Imagination," *Signs* 14.1 (1988): 100–18.

———. "Virginia Woolf and Androgyny." *Contemporary Literature* 16.4 (1975): 433–51.

Fassler, Barbara. "Theories of Homosexuality as Sources of Bloomsbury's Androgyny." *Signs* 5.2 (1979): 237–51.

Féral, Josette. "The Powers of Difference." In *The Future of Difference*. Ed. Hester Eisenstein and Alice Jardine, 88–94. New Brunswick, NJ: Rutgers University Press, 1985.

Fetterley, Judith. "Reading *Deephaven* as a Lesbian Text." In *Sexual Practice, Textual Theory: Lesbian Cultural Criticism*. Ed. Susan J. Wolfe and Julia Penelope, 164–83. Cambridge, MA: Blackwell, 1993.

Forrest, Katherine V. *Daughters of a Coral Dawn.* Tallahassee, FL: Naiad Press, 1984.

Foster, Jeannette H. *Sex Variant Women in Literature.* Tallahassee, FL: Naiad Press, 1985.

Foucault, Michel. *The History of Sexuality, Volume I: An Introduction.* Trans. Robert Hurley. New York: Pantheon Books, 1978.

Friedman, Ellen G. "Where Are the Missing Contents?: (Post)Modernism, Gender, and the Canon." *PMLA* 108.2 (1993): 240–52.

Friedman, Susan Stanford. "Adrienne Rich and H.D.: An Intertextual Study." In

Reading Adrienne Rich: Reviews and Re-Visions, 1951–81. Ed. Jane Roberta Cooper, 171–206. Ann Arbor: The University of Michigan Press, 1984.

———. "Lyric Subversion of Narrative in Women's Writing: Virginia Woolf and the Tyranny of Plot." In *Reading Narrative.* Ed. James Phelan, 162–85. Columbus: Ohio State University Press, 1989.

Fries, Maureen. "Female Heroes, Heroines and Counter-Heroes: Images of Women in Arthurian Legend." In *Popular Arthurian Traditions.* Ed. Sally K. Slocum, 5–17. Bowling Green, OH: Bowling Green State University Popular Press, 1992.

Fry, Carrol L. " 'What God Doth the Wizard Pray To': Neo-Pagan Witchcraft and Fantasy Fiction." *Extrapolation* 31.4 (1990): 333–46.

Frye, Marilyn. *The Politics of Reality: Essays in Feminist Theory.* Trumansburg, NY: The Crossing Press, 1983.

———. *Willful Virgin: Essays in Feminism, 1976–1992.* Freedom, CA: The Crossing Press, 1992.

Frye, Northrop. *Anatomy of Criticism: Four Essays.* Princeton, NJ: Princeton University Press, 1957.

Fuss, Diana. *Essentially Speaking: Feminism, Nature and Difference.* New York: Routledge, 1989.

Gamman, Lorraine, and Margaret Marshment. *The Female Gaze: Women as Viewers of Popular Culture.* Seattle: The Real Comet Press, 1989.

Garber, Marjorie. *Vested Interests: Cross-Dressing and Cultural Anxiety.* New York: Routledge, 1992.

Gearhart, Sally Miller. *The Wanderground: Stories of the Hill Women.* Boston: Alyson Publications, 1984.

Genette, Gérard. *Narrative Discourse: An Essay in Method.* Trans. Jane E. Lewin. Ithaca, NY: Cornell University Press, 1980.

———. "Time and Narrative in *A la recherche du temps perdu.*" Trans. Paul De Man. In *Aspects of Narrative: Selected Papers from the English Institute.* Ed. J. Hillis Miller, 93–118. New York and London: Columbia University Press, 1971.

Gilbert, Sandra M., and Susan Gubar. *The Madwoman in the Attic: The Woman Writer and the Nineteenth-Century Literary Imagination.* New Haven: Yale University Press, 1979.

———. *No Man's Land: The Place of the Woman Writer in the Twentieth Century,* Vol. 2: *Sexchanges.* New Haven: Yale University Press, 1989.

Gilligan, Carol. *In a Different Voice: Psychological Theory and Women's Development.* Cambridge, MA: Harvard University Press, 1982.

Gilman, Charlotte Perkins. *Herland.* New York: Pantheon Books, 1979.

Golden, Carla. "Diversity and Variability in Women's Sexual Identities." In *Lesbian Psychologies: Explorations and Challenges.* Ed. Boston Lesbian Psychologies Collective, 19–34. Urbana and Chicago: University of Illinois Press, 1987.

Gomez, Jewelle. *Forty-Three Septembers: Essays by Jewelle Gomez.* Ithaca, NY: Firebrand Books, 1993.

Grahn, Judy. *Another Mother Tongue: Gay Words, Gay Worlds.* Boston: Beacon Press, 1984.

———. *The Highest Apple: Sappho and the Lesbian Poetic Tradition*. San Francisco: Spinsters Ink, 1985.

Greene, Gayle. *Changing the Story: Feminist Fiction and the Tradition*. Bloomington: Indiana University Press, 1991.

Gubar, Susan. "Sapphistries." *Signs* 10.1 (1984): 43–62.

Hacker, Marilyn. *Love, Death, and the Changing of the Seasons*. New York: Arbor House, 1986.

Hall, Radclyffe. *The Well of Loneliness*. New York: Pocket Books, 1950.

Halliday, Caroline. " 'The Naked Majesty of God': Contemporary Lesbian Erotic Poetry." In *Lesbian and Gay Writing: An Anthology of Critical Essays*. Ed. Mark Lilly, 76–108. Philadelphia: Temple University Press, 1990.

Halperin, David M. *One Hundred Years of Homosexuality and Other Essays on Greek Love*. New York: Routledge, 1990.

Haraway, Donna. "A Manifesto for Cyborgs: Science, Technology, and Socialist Feminism in the 1980s." *Socialist Review* 15.2 (1985): 65–107.

Hart, Lynda. *Fatal Women: Lesbian Sexuality and the Mark of Aggression*. Princeton, NJ: Princeton University Press, 1994.

Heilbrun, Carolyn G. *Toward a Recognition of Androgyny*. New York: Harper Colophon Books, 1973.

Heller, Dana A. *The Feminization of Quest-Romance: Radical Departures*. Austin: University of Texas Press, 1990.

Hite, Molly. *The Other Side of the Story: Structures and Strategies of Contemporary Feminist Narration*. Ithaca, NY: Cornell University Press, 1989.

Hoagland, Sarah Lucia. *Lesbian Ethics: Toward New Value*. Palo Alto, CA: Institute of Lesbian Studies, 1988.

Hoffert, Barbara. "Review [of *Written on the Body*]." *Library Journal* 118.3 (February 15, 1993): 195.

Holstun, James. " 'Will You Rent Our Ancient Love Asunder?': Lesbian Elegy in Donne, Marvell, and Milton." *ELH* 54.4 (1987): 835–67.

Homans, Margaret. *Women Writers and Poetic Identity: Dorothy Wordsworth, Emily Brontë, and Emily Dickinson*. Princeton, NJ: Princeton University Press, 1980.

Hutcheon, Linda. *The Politics of Postmodernism*. London: Routledge, 1989.

Innes, Charlotte. "Rich Imaginings [A Review of *Sexing the Cherry*]." *Nation* 251.2 (July 9, 1990): 64–65.

Irigaray, Luce. *Speculum of the Other Woman*. Trans. Gillian C. Gill. Ithaca, NY: Cornell University Press, 1974, 1985.

———. *This Sex Which Is Not One*. Trans. Catherine Porter with Carolyn Burke. Ithaca, NY: Cornell University Press, 1985.

Jagose, Annamarie. *Lesbian Utopics*. New York and London: Routledge, 1994.

Jardine, Alice A. *Gynesis: Configurations of Woman and Modernity*. Ithaca, NY: Cornell University Press, 1985.

———. "Opaque Texts and Transparent Contexts: The Political Difference of Julia Kristeva." In *The Poetics of Gender*. Ed. Nancy K. Miller, 96–116. New York: Columbia University Press, 1986.

Jay, Karla. *The Amazon and the Page: Natalie Clifford Barney and Renée Vivien*. Bloomington: Indiana University Press, 1988.

Jonnes, Denis. *The Matrix of Narrative: Family Systems and the Semiotics of Story.* Berlin: Mouton de Gruyter, 1990.

Jung, Carl. *Two Essays on Analytical Psychology.* Trans. R. F. C. Hull. New York: Meridian, 1956.

Kaplan, E. Ann. "Is the Gaze Male?" In *Powers of Desire: The Politics of Sexuality.* Ed. Ann Snitow, Christine Stansell, and Sharon Thompson, 309–27. New York: Monthly Review Press, 1983.

Katz, Jonathan Ned. *Gay/Lesbian Almanac: A New Documentary.* New York: Harper & Row, 1983.

Keller, Catherine. *From a Broken Web: Separation, Sexism, and Self.* Boston: Beacon Press, 1986.

Kermode, Frank. *The Sense of an Ending: Studies in the Theory of Fiction.* London: Oxford University Press, 1966.

Keyes, Claire. *The Aesthetics of Power: The Poetry of Adrienne Rich.* Athens: The University of Georgia Press, 1986.

Klaich, Dolores. *Woman + Woman: Attitudes toward Lesbianism.* New York: William Morrow, 1974.

Knopp, Sherron E. " 'If I Saw You Would You Kiss Me?': Sapphism and the Subversiveness of Virginia Woolf's *Orlando.*" *PMLA* 103.1 (1988): 24–34.

Koenig, Rhoda. "Books [Review of Winterson's *Written on the Body*]." *New York* 26.4 (January 25, 1993): 61.

Koestenbaum, Wayne. *The Queen's Throat: Opera, Homosexuality, and the Mystery of Desire.* New York: Poseidon Press, 1993.

Kolodny, Annette. "Dancing through the Minefield: Some Observations on the Theory, Practice, and Politics of a Feminist Literary Criticism." In *The New Feminist Criticism: Essays on Women, Literature, and Theory.* Ed. Elaine Showalter, 144–67. New York: Pantheon Books, 1985.

Krafft-Ebing, Richard von. *Psychopathia Sexualis.* Trans. F. J. Rebman. Rev. ed. Chicago: Login, 1929.

Kramer, Heinrich, and James Sprenger. *The "Malleus Maleficarum" of Heinrich Kramer and James Sprenger.* Trans. Rev. Montague Summers. New York: Dover Publications, 1971.

Krieger, Susan. "Lesbian Identity and Community: Recent Social Science Literature." *Signs* 8.1 (1982): 91–108.

Krist, Gary. "Innovation without Tears." *Hudson Review* 43.4 (1991): 690–98.

Kristeva, Julia. *Powers of Horror: An Essay on Abjection.* Trans. Leon S. Roudiez. New York: Columbia University Press, 1982.

———. "Women's Time." Trans. Alice Jardine and Harry Blake. *Signs.* 7.1 (1981): 13–35.

Kroeber, Karl. *Retelling/Rereading: The Fate of Storytelling in Modern Times.* New Brunswick, NJ: Rutgers University Press, 1992.

"Lammys to be announced." *Lavender Network.* Eugene, OR. 98 (April 1994): 19.

Lanser, Susan S. "Toward a Feminist Narratology." *Style* 20.3 (1986): 341–63.

Le Guin, Ursula K. *Always Coming Home.* New York: Harper & Row, 1985.

———. *Dancing at the Edge of the World: Thoughts on Words, Women, Places.* New York: Grove Press, 1989.

———. "She Unnames Them." *New Yorker* 60.49 (January 21, 1985): 27.

Lewis, C. S. *A Preface to Paradise Lost.* New York: Oxford University Press, 1942.

Lewis, Reina. "The Death of the Author and the Resurrection of the Dyke." In *New Lesbian Criticism: Literary and Cultural Readings.* Ed. Sally Munt, 17–32. New York: Columbia University Press, 1992.

Lorde, Audre. *Sister Outsider.* Trumansburg, NY: The Crossing Press, 1984.

———. *Zami: A New Spelling of My Name.* Watertown, MA: Persephone Press, 1982.

Malory, Sir Thomas. *Le Morte D'Arthur,* Vol. 1. Ed. Janet Cowen. New York: Penguin Books, 1969.

Marcus, Jane. "Sapphistory: The Woolf and the Well." In *Lesbian Texts and Contexts: Radical Revisions.* Ed. Karla Jay and Joanne Glasgow, 164–79. New York: New York University Press, 1990.

Marder, Herbert. *Feminism and Art: A Study of Virginia Woolf.* Chicago: University of Chicago Press, 1968.

Marks, Elaine. "Lesbian Intertextuality." In *Homosexualities and French Literature: Cultural Contexts/Critical Texts.* Ed. George Stambolian and Elaine Marks, 353–77. Ithaca, NY: Cornell University Press, 1979.

Martin, Wallace. *Recent Theories of Narrative.* Ithaca, NY: Cornell University Press, 1986.

McClary, Susan. *Feminine Endings: Music, Gender, and Sexuality.* Minneapolis: University of Minnesota Press, 1991.

McDowell, Deborah E. "New Directions for Black Feminist Criticism." In *The New Feminist Criticism: Essays on Women, Literature, and Theory.* Ed. Elaine Showalter, 186–99. New York: Pantheon Books, 1985.

McNaron, Toni A. H. "Mirrors and Likeness: A Lesbian Aesthetic in the Making." In *Sexual Practice, Textual Theory: Lesbian Cultural Criticism.* Ed. Susan J. Wolfe and Julia Penelope, 291–306. Cambridge, MA: Blackwell, 1993.

Meese, Elizabeth A. *Crossing the Double-Cross: The Practice of Feminist Criticism.* Chapel Hill: The University of North Carolina Press, 1986.

———. *(Sem)Erotics: Theorizing Lesbian: Writing.* New York: New York University Press, 1992.

Michel, Frann. "William Faulkner as a Lesbian Author." *Faulkner Journal* 4.1 & 2 (Fall 1988–Spring 1989): 5–19.

Miller, D. A. *Narrative and Its Discontents: Problems of Closure in the Traditional Novel.* Princeton, NJ: Princeton University Press, 1981.

Miller, Isabel. *Patience and Sarah.* New York: Fawcett Crest, 1969.

Miller, Nancy K. "Changing the Subject: Authorship, Writing, and the Reader." In *Feminist Studies/Critical Studies.* Ed. Teresa de Lauretis, 102–20. Bloomington: Indiana University Press, 1986.

Milton, John. *Paradise Lost.* In *John Milton: Complete Poems and Major Prose.* Ed. Merritt Y. Hughes, 173–469. Indianapolis: The Odyssey Press, 1957.

Minh-ha, Trinh T. *Woman, Native, Other: Writing Postcoloniality and Feminism.* Bloomington: Indiana University Press, 1989.

Moi, Toril. *Sexual/Textual Politics: Feminist Literary Theory.* London: Methuen, 1985.

Montefiore, Jan. *Feminism and Poetry: Language, Experience, Identity in Women's Writing.* London: Pandora Press, 1987.

Mulvey, Laura. "Visual Pleasure and Narrative Cinema." *Screen* 16.3 (1975): 6–18.

Munt, Sally. "Introduction." In *New Lesbian Criticism: Literary and Cultural Readings.* Ed. Sally Munt, ix–xxii. New York: Columbia University Press, 1992.

Naylor, Gloria. *The Women of Brewster Place.* New York: Penguin, 1982.

Nestle, Joan. *A Restricted Country.* Ithaca, NY: Firebrand Books, 1987.

Newton, Esther. "The Mythic Mannish Lesbian: Radclyffe Hall and the New Woman." In *Hidden from History: Reclaiming the Gay and Lesbian Past.* Ed. Martin Duberman, Martha Vicinus, and George Chauncey, Jr., 281–93. New York: Meridian, 1989.

Nicolson, Nigel. *Portrait of a Marriage.* New York: Bantam Books, 1973.

O'Brien, Sharon. " 'The Thing Not Named': Willa Cather as a Lesbian Writer." *Signs* 9.4 (1984): 576–99.

Ostriker, Alicia Suskin. *Stealing the Language: The Emergence of Women's Poetry in America.* Boston: Beacon Press, 1986.

Palmer, Paulina. "Contemporary Lesbian Feminist Fiction: Texts for Everywoman." In *Plotting Change: Contemporary Women's Fiction.* Ed. Linda Anderson, 43–62. London: Edward Arnold, 1990.

———. "The Lesbian Feminist Thriller and Detective Novel." In *What Lesbians Do in Books.* Ed. Elaine Hobby and Chris White, 9–27. London: The Women's Press, 1991.

Parker, Alice. "Nicole Brossard: A Differential Equation of Lesbian Love." In *Lesbian Texts and Contexts: Radical Revisions.* Ed. Karla Jay and Joanne Glasgow, 304–29. New York: New York University Press, 1990.

Phelan, Shane. "(Be)Coming Out: Lesbian Identity and Politics." *Signs* 18.4 (1993): 765–90.

Philips, Katherine. "To My Excellent Lucasia, on Our Friendship." In *Poetry of the English Renaissance 1509–1660.* Ed. J. William Hebel and Hoyt H. Hudson, 870. New York: Appleton-Century-Crofts, 1929.

Plato. *Plato: The Collected Dialogues.* Ed. Edith Hamilton and Huntington Cairns. New York: Bollingen Foundation, 1961.

Prince, Gerald. *A Dictionary of Narratology.* Lincoln: University of Nebraska Press, 1987.

Rabine, Leslie W. *Reading the Romantic Heroine: Text, History, Ideology.* Ann Arbor: University of Michigan Press, 1985.

Rabinowitz, Peter J. " 'Reader, I Blew Him Away': Convention and Transgression in Sue Grafton." In *Famous Last Words: Changes in Gender and Narrative Closure.* Ed. Alison Booth, 326–46. Charlottesville: University Press of Virginia, 1993.

Radicalesbians. "The Woman Identified Woman." In *Radical Feminism*. Ed. Anne Koedt, Ellen Levine, and Anita Rapone, 240–45. New York: Quadrangle Books, 1973.

Raiskin, Judith. "Inverts and Hybrids: Lesbian Rewritings of Sexual and Racial Identities." In *The Lesbian Postmodern*. Ed. Laura Doan, 156–72. New York: Columbia University Press, 1994.

Rapi, Nina. "Hide and Seek: The Search for a Lesbian Theatre Aesthetic." *New Theatre Quarterly* 9.34 (1993): 147–58.

Reynolds, Margaret. "Introduction." In *The Penguin Book of Lesbian Short Stories*. Ed. Margaret Reynolds, xiii–xxxiii. New York: Viking, 1993.

Rich, Adrienne. *Blood, Bread, and Poetry: Selected Prose 1979–1985*. New York: W. W. Norton, 1986.

———. "Compulsory Heterosexuality and Lesbian Existence." *Signs* 5.4 (1980): 631–60.

———. *The Dream of a Common Language: Poems 1974–1977*. New York: W. W. Norton, 1978.

———. *Of Woman Born: Motherhood as Experience and Institution*. New York: W. W. Norton, 1976.

———. *On Lies, Secrets, and Silence: Selected Prose 1966–1978*. New York: W. W. Norton, 1979.

———. "Poetry and Experience: Statement at a Poetry Reading (1964)." In *Adrienne Rich's Poetry*. Ed. Barbara Charlesworth Gelpi and Albert Gelpi, 89. New York: W. W. Norton, 1975.

———. "Wholeness Is No Trifling Matter: Some Fiction by Black Women." *New Women's Times Feminist Review* 13 (Dec. 1980–Jan. 1981): 10–13.

———. *A Wild Patience Has Taken Me This Far: Poems 1978–1981*. New York: W. W. Norton, 1981.

———. *The Will to Change: Poems 1968–1970*. New York: W. W. Norton, 1971.

Ricoeur, Paul. *The Rule of Metaphor: Multi-disciplinary Studies of the Creation of Meaning in Language*. Trans. Robert Czerny et al. Toronto and Buffalo: University of Toronto Press, 1977.

Roberts, JR. *Black Lesbians: An Annotated Bibliography*. Tallahassee, FL: Naiad Press, 1981.

Robinson, Sally. *Engendering the Subject: Gender and Self-Representation in Contemporary Women's Fiction*. Albany, NY: State University of New York Press, 1991.

Roof, Judith. *A Lure of Knowledge: Lesbian Sexuality and Theory*. New York: Columbia University Press, 1991.

Rose, Ellen Cronan. "American Feminist Criticism of Contemporary Women's Fiction." *Signs* 18.2 (1993): 346–75.

Rosenman, Ellen Bayuk. "Sexual Identity and *A Room of One's Own*: 'Secret Economies' in Virginia Woolf's Feminist Discourse." *Signs* 14.3 (1989): 634–50.

Ross, Alex. "Grand Seductions." *New Yorker* 69.8 (April 12, 1993): 115–20.

Rule, Jane. *Desert of the Heart*. Tallahassee, FL: Naiad Press, 1985.

———. *Lesbian Images*. New York: Pocket Books, 1976.

Russ, Joanna. "What Can a Heroine Do? Or Why Women Can't Write." In *Images of Women in Fiction: Feminist Perspectives*. Ed. Susan Koppelman Cornillon, 3–20. Bowling Green, OH: Bowling Green University Popular Press, 1972.

Russo, Mary. "Female Grotesques: Carnival and Theory." In *Feminist Studies/Critical Studies*. Ed. Teresa de Lauretis, 213–29. Bloomington: Indiana University Press, 1986.

Scholes, Robert. "Afterthoughts on Narrative II: Language, Narrative, and Anti-Narrative." *Critical Inquiry* 7.1 (1980): 204–11.

Schulman, Sarah. "Guilty with Explanation: Jeanette Winterson's Endearing Book of Love." *Lambda Book Report* 3.9 (1993): 20.

Scoppettone, Sandra. *Everything You Have Is Mine*. Boston: Little, Brown, 1991.

Sedgwick, Eve Kosofsky. *Between Men: English Literature and Male Homosocial Desire*. New York: Columbia University Press, 1985.

———. *Epistemology of the Closet*. Berkeley: University of California Press, 1990.

Sexton, Anne. *Transformations*. Boston: Houghton Mifflin, 1971.

Shakespeare, William. *The Riverside Shakespeare*. Ed. G. Blakemore Evans. Boston: Houghton Mifflin, 1974.

Shaktini, Namascar. "Displacing the Phallic Subject: Wittig's Lesbian Writing." *Signs* 8.1 (1982): 29–44.

Shockley, Ann Allen. "The Black Lesbian in American Literature: An Overview." *Conditions* 5 (1979): 133–42.

Showalter, Elaine. *A Literature of Their Own: British Women Novelists from Brontë to Lessing*. Princeton, NJ: Princeton University Press, 1977.

———. *Sexual Anarchy: Gender and Culture at the Fin de Siècle*. New York: Viking, 1990.

Sidney, Sir Philip. "From *Astrophel and Stella*." In *The Renaissance in England*. Ed. Hyder E. Rollins and Herschel Baker, 323–29. Boston: D. C. Heath, 1954.

Silko, Leslie Marmon. *Ceremony*. New York: New American Library, 1977.

Smith, Barbara. "Toward a Black Feminist Criticism." *Women's Studies International Quarterly* 2.2 (1979): 183–94.

———. "The Truth That Never Hurts: Black Lesbians in Fiction in the 1980s." In *Wild Women in the Whirlwind: Afra-American Culture and the Contemporary Literary Renaissance*. Ed. Joanne M. Braxton and Andrée Nicola McLaughlin, 213–45. New Brunswick, NJ: Rutgers University Press, 1990.

Smith, Barbara Herrnstein. "Afterthoughts on Narrative III: Narrative Versions, Narrative Theories." *Critical Inquiry* 7.1 (1980): 213–36.

Smith, Bruce R. *Homosexual Desire in Shakespeare's England: A Cultural Poetics*. Chicago: The University of Chicago Press, 1991.

Smith, Paul. *Discerning the Subject*. Minneapolis: University of Minnesota Press, 1988.

Smith-Rosenberg, Carroll. "Discourses of Sexuality and Subjectivity: The New

Woman, 1870–1936." In *Hidden from History: Reclaiming the Gay and Lesbian Past.* Ed. Martin Duberman, Martha Vicinus, and George Chauncey, Jr., 264–80. New York: Meridian, 1989.

Spenser, Edmund. "From *Amoretti.*" In *The Renaissance in England.* Ed. Hyder E. Rollins and Herschel Baker, 364–67. Boston: D. C. Heath, 1954.

Spivack, Charlotte. *Merlin's Daughters: Contemporary Women Writers of Fantasy.* New York: Greenwood Press, 1987.

Stacey, Jackie. "Desperately Seeking Difference." In *The Female Gaze: Women as Viewers of Popular Culture.* Ed. Lorraine Gamman and Margaret Marshment, 112–29. Seattle: The Real Comet Press, 1989.

Stallybrass, Peter. "Patriarchal Territories: The Body Enclosed." In *Rewriting the Renaissance: The Discourses of Sexual Difference in Early Modern Europe.* Ed. Margaret W. Ferguson, Maureen Quilligan, and Nancy J. Vickers, 123–42. Chicago: University of Chicago Press, 1986.

Stambolian, George, and Elaine Marks. "Introduction." In *Homosexualities and French Literature: Cultural Contexts/Critical Texts.* Ed. George Stambolian and Elaine Marks, 23–34. Ithaca, NY: Cornell University Press, 1979.

Stanton, Domna C. "Difference on Trial: A Critique of the Maternal Metaphor in Cixous, Irigaray, and Kristeva." In *The Poetics of Gender.* Ed. Nancy K. Miller, 157–82. New York: Columbia University Press, 1986.

Stein, Arlene, ed. *Sisters, Sexperts, Queers: Beyond the Lesbian Nation.* New York: Penguin Books, 1993.

Stimpson, Catharine R. "Afterword: Lesbian Studies in the 1990s." In *Lesbian Texts and Contexts: Radical Revisions.* Ed. Karla Jay and Joanne Glasgow, 377–82. New York: New York University Press, 1990.

———. "The Somagrams of Gertrude Stein." In *The Female Body in Western Culture: Contemporary Perspectives.* Ed. Susan Rubin Suleiman, 30–43. Cambridge, MA: Harvard University Press, 1986.

———. "Zero Degree Deviancy: The Lesbian Novel in English." In *Writing and Sexual Difference.* Ed. Elizabeth Abel, 243–54. Chicago: The University of Chicago Press, 1982.

Suleiman, Susan Rubin. *Subversive Intent: Gender, Politics, and the Avant-Garde.* Cambridge, MA: Harvard University Press, 1990.

Swanson, Diana L. "Subverting Closure: Compulsory Heterosexuality and Compulsory Endings in Middle-Class British Women's Novels." In *Sexual Practice, Textual Theory: Lesbian Cultural Criticism.* Ed. Susan J. Wolfe and Julia Penelope, 150–63. Cambridge, MA: Blackwell, 1993.

Tobin, Lee Ann. "Why Change the Arthur Story? Marion Zimmer Bradley's *The Mists of Avalon.*" *Extrapolation* 34.2 (1993): 147–57.

Tobin, Patricia Drechsel. *Time and the Novel: The Genealogical Imperative.* Princeton, NJ: Princeton University Press, 1978.

Torgovnick, Marianna. *Closure in the Novel.* Princeton, NJ: Princeton University Press, 1981.

Vickers, Nancy J. "Diana Described: Scattered Woman and Scattered Rhyme." In *Writing and Sexual Difference.* Ed. Elizabeth Abel, 95–110. Chicago: University of Chicago Press, 1982.

Wagner, Wieland. "Thoughts on the Mythical Element in Wagner's 'Tristan und Isolde'." Libretto. *Tristan und Isolde.* By Richard Wagner. Deutsche Grammaphon, 1966.

Walker, Alice. *The Color Purple.* New York: Harcourt Brace Jovanovich, 1982.

———. *In Search of Our Mothers' Gardens.* San Diego, New York, London: Harcourt Brace Jovanovich, 1983.

Warhol, Robyn R. "Toward a Theory of the Engaging Narrator: Earnest Interventions in Gaskell, Stowe, and Eliot." *PMLA* 101.5 (1986): 811–18.

Waugh, Patricia. *Feminine Fictions: Revisiting the Postmodern.* London: Routledge, 1989.

Weil, Kari. *Androgyny and the Denial of Difference.* Charlottesville: University Press of Virginia, 1992.

Wenzel, Hélène Vivienne. "The Text as Body/Politics: Appreciations of Monique Wittig's Writings in Context." *Feminist Studies* 7.2 (1981): 264–87.

Whitlock, Gillian. " 'Everything Is Out of Place': Radclyffe Hall and the Lesbian Literary Tradition." *Feminist Studies* 13.3 (1987): 555–82.

Winnett, Susan. "Coming Unstrung: Women, Men, Narrative, and Principles of Pleasure." *PMLA* 105.3 (1990): 505–18.

Winterson, Jeanette. *Oranges Are Not the Only Fruit.* New York: The Atlantic Monthly Press, 1985.

———. "Outrageous Proportions." *Sight and Sound* 2.6 (1992): 26–27.

———. "The Poetics of Sex." In *The Penguin Book of Lesbian Short Stories.* Ed. Margaret Reynolds, 412–22. New York: Viking, 1993.

———. *Sexing the Cherry.* New York: Vintage Books, 1989.

———. *Written on the Body.* New York: Alfred A. Knopf, 1993.

Wittig, Monique. *The Lesbian Body.* Trans. David Le Vay. New York: Avon Books, 1975.

———. *Les Guérillères.* Trans. David Le Vay. New York: Avon Books, 1973.

———. *The Straight Mind and Other Essays.* Boston: Beacon Press, 1992.

———, and Sande Zeig. *Lesbian Peoples: Material for a Dictionary.* New York: Avon Books, 1979.

Wolfe, Susan J., and Julia Penelope. "Sexual Identity/Textual Politics: Lesbian {$\genfrac{}{}{0pt}{}{\text{De}}{\text{com}}$}positions." In *Sexual Practice, Textual Theory: Lesbian Cultural Criticism.* Ed. Susan J. Wolfe and Julia Penelope, 1–24. Cambridge, MA: Blackwell, 1993.

Woolf, Virginia. *The Diary of Virginia Woolf, Vol. 3: 1925–1930.* Ed. Anne Olivier Bell. New York: Harcourt Brace Jovanovich, 1980.

———. *Orlando: A Biography.* New York: Harcourt Brace Jovanovich, 1956.

———. *A Room of One's Own.* New York: Harcourt, Brace & World, 1929.

———. *The Waves.* London: The Hogarth Press, 1976.

Wyatt, Sir Thomas. "Description of the Contrarious Passions in a Lover." In *The Renaissance in England.* Ed. Hyder E. Rollins and Herschel Baker, 198. Boston: D.C. Heath, 1954.

Yaeger, Patricia. *Honey-Mad Women: Emancipatory Strategies in Women's Writing.* New York: Columbia University Press, 1988.

Zimmerman, Bonnie. "Lesbians Like This and That: Some Notes on Lesbian Criticism for the Nineties." In *New Lesbian Criticism: Literary and Cultural Readings.* Ed. Sally Munt, 1–15. New York: Columbia University Press, 1992.

———. *The Safe Sea of Women: Lesbian Fiction 1969–1989.* Boston: Beacon Press, 1990.

———. "What Has Never Been: An Overview of Lesbian Feminist Criticism." *Feminist Studies* 7.3 (1981): 451–76.

Zita, Jacquelyn N. "Gay and Lesbian Studies: Yet Another Unhappy Marriage?" In *Tilting the Tower.* Ed. Linda Garber, 258–76. New York and London: Routledge, 1994.

———. "Lesbian Body Journeys: Desire Making Difference." In *Lesbian Philosophies and Cultures.* Ed. Jeffner Allen, 327–45. Albany, NY: State University of New York Press, 1990.

Index